The Computer Trainer's Personal Training Guide

Bill Brandon, Paul Clothier,
Shirley Copeland, Patty Crowell,
Bernard Dodge, Peggy Maday,
Elliott Masie, Gail Perry,
Garry Slobodian, Carolyn Woodie,
Ron Zemke, and Susan Zemke

The Computer Trainer's Personal Training Guide

International Standard Book Number: 1-57576-253-6

Library of Congress Catalog Card Number: 95-071645

99 98 97 96   4 3 2 1

Interpretation of the printing code: the rightmost double-digit number is the year of the book's printing; the rightmost single-digit, the number of the book's printing. For example, a printing code of 96-1 shows that the first printing of the book occurred in 1996.

Printed in the United States of America

Publisher: David P. Ewing

Associate Publisher: Chris Katsaropoulos

Product Marketing Manager: Susan J. Dollman

Publishing Director
Charles O. Stewart III

Acquisitions Editor
Rob Tidrow

Managing Editor
Jenny Watson

Production Editor
Alice Martina Smith

Technical Reviewer
Michael Stanley

Editorial Assistant
Angela Denny

Book Designer
Gary Adair

Cover Designer
Anne Jones

Production Team
May Ann Abramson
Carol Bowers
Michael Brumitt
Charlotte Clapp
George Hanlin
Mike Henry
Louisa Klucznik
Ayanna Lacey
Paula Lowell
Steph Mineart
Casey Price
Nancy Price
Brian-Kent Proffitt
Andrew Stone
Susan Van Ness

Indexer
Cheryl Dietsch

Composed in *1 Stone Serif* and *MCPdigital* by Que Corporation.

About the Authors

Bill Brandon has managed, developed, and delivered instruction since 1968. His company, Accomplishment Technology Unlimited, provides clients with systematic ways to train, guide, and motivate employees to higher levels of accomplishment. Recent projects include development of computer-based training and multimedia facilities, performance support, documentation, and training materials. Bill has been the System Operator (Sysop) of the Computer Training and Support forum on CompuServe since 1987. Bill is also a past president of the Dallas-Fort Worth Texas chapter of NSPI, the International Society for Performance Improvement (ISPI). He is a frequent speaker at conferences including the Computer Training and Support Conference. He is a co-author of Que's *Building Multimedia Applications with Visual Basic.*

Paul Clothier has been in the training profession for 15 years both in England and the United States. He has been training people how to use computers for more than 12 years. He is president of The Training Edge, a company committed to developing the presentation and communication skills of computer trainers. Paul has presented training-skills seminars and sessions for various companies and organizations in the United States, Canada, and Europe. His articles about computer training have been featured in *The Microcomputer Trainer* and *IT Training* magazine. He is the U.S. correspondent for *IT Training* magazine in England.

Shirley Copeland is a Virginia-based adult educator who designs and develops curriculum in many program areas including complex, specialized computer systems. Shirley designs and develops computer-based training programs and other multimedia training programs. She writes user-friendly documentation and training manuals and helps define user requirements for systems. Shirley also teaches computer classes. She has 12 years of experience in instructional design and training. Shirley has spoken nationally and internationally on training issues. She has a doctorate in Adult and Continuing Education from Virginia Tech. Shirley provides training and consulting services to the public and private sector.

Patty Crowell is the education specialist at the University of Kansas School of Medicine in Wichita. For the past six years, she has been responsible for computer training for staff and faculty on topics ranging from the Internet to Windows applications. She provides technology updates and product demonstrations, and often speaks to computer user groups. Patty received a Bachelor's degree in business education from Fort Hayes State University and is currently working towards a Master's degree in adult education from Kansas State University. She is a member of the ASTD (American Society for Training and Development).

Dr. Bernard J. Dodge has designed award-winning educational games, instructional tools, and expert systems for educators. He is involved in the Pacific Bell Education First initiative as an advisor to the three PacBell/SDSU Fellows who are developing state-of-the-art applications of telecommunications for schools, community colleges, and libraries. Dr. Dodge was a member of the Board of Directors of Computer-Using Educators for four years and chaired CUE's SoftSwap program. He has conducted research for Jostens Learning Corporation, the New Laboratory for Teaching and Learning, and Fujitsu of America; he has delivered workshops on the design of computer-based instruction to trainers at AT&T, Southland Corporation, Digital Equipment Corporation, MediaShare, and Servico Nacional de Aprendizagem Comercial in Sao Paulo, Brazil. He co-directs T²ARP, the Teaching, Technology, and Restructuring Partnership, an innovative teacher-preparation program based at O'Farrell Community School in San Diego. He has a doctorate in Instructional Design and Development from Syracuse University and is a Professor of Educational Technology at San Diego State University, where he has taught since 1980.

Peggy Maday and **Carolyn Woodie** met at a WordPerfect training conference five years ago. Peggy owns Turning Point Training Systems based in Denver, Colorado. Carolyn owns Carolyn Woodie & Associates, a similar training company in the Washington, D.C., area. They offer software training, office automation, conversion, courseware, and consulting services to corporate and government clients in most of the popular PC applications. Because of their similar interests and the heavy demands of this rapidly changing industry, they developed a virtual partnership over CompuServe to share training ideas, problem solve, and collaborate on courseware. They bring together a unique blend of education, computer knowledge, business background, and adult education skills. With over 25 years of combined experience, they have had a lot to share.

Elliott Masie is president of the MASIE Center, an international think-tank focused on the intersection of learning and technology. He is one of the pioneers in the computer training industry, with over 22 years of experience in assisting corporations and government organizations to face the challenge of building workforce skills. Elliott is the founder of The Computer Training and Support Conference and the director of the MASIE Forum, a multimedia resource for computer training professionals.

Gail Perry is a CPA and a computer trainer based in Indianapolis, Indiana. She studied Computer Science at Indiana University at a time when there was only one computer on campus (and 3 A.M. was the best time to find a vacant punch-card machine...). Formerly a tax accountant with Deloitte Haskins and Sells (now Deloitte & Touche) in Chicago, and more recently affiliated with Blue & Co. CPAs, and Geo. S. Oliver & Co. CPAs in Indianapolis, Gail has spent nearly 20 years helping people figure out why they have to pay so much income tax. When April 15 isn't looming on the horizon, she spends her time teaching accountants and other grown-ups how to use their computers. Gail is a computer trainer for the Indiana CPA Society and works with many Indiana businesses designing computer training programs appropriate for their employees. Gail is the author of *The Complete Idiot's Guide to Doing Your Income Taxes, 1996*, and is co-author of *Using Quicken 5 for Windows*, and *WordPerfect for Windows 6 SuperBook*.

Garry Slobodian, a training consultant since 1977, specializes in helping companies implement computer systems by developing custom training programs. He has lectured at the University of Winnipeg and was a featured speaker at five national training conferences. He has won awards for his public speaking and for his computer-based training courseware. He is currently president of the Computer Education Society of Alberta. Recently, Garry developed a 10-hour seminar for computer trainers entitled *Improving Technology Training*. He holds Bachelor's degrees in Science and Education, and a Certificate in Adult Education. He is currently working on a Master's in Continuing Education, specializing in learning in the workplace. Garry lives in Calgary with his wife, Kate (a technical writer), and his children, Matt, Andrew, and Paul. Contact Garry at:

Train Wisely Inc.
285 Lake Lucerne Way SE
Calgary, Alberta
Canada
T2J 3J5
Voice: (403) 278-8030
Fax: (403) 278-7407
E-mail: gslobodian@ccinet.ab.ca

Ron Zemke, author of many training-related books and articles, is senior editor of *TRAINING* magazine and a consultant in Minneapolis.

Susan Zemke is manager of management and professional development for St. Paul Fire and Marine Insurance Co. in St. Paul, MN.

Acknowledgments

The Computer Trainer's Personal Training Guide delivers some of the best thinking about what training visionary Elliott Masie calls "the intersection of learning and technology." As such, this book represents the collaborative efforts of a highly talented, diverse group of training and technology experts. Que Education & Training would like to thank all the contributors to this volume for helping make this book a significant addition to the literature of computer training.

A very special thanks goes to production editor Alice Martina Smith for her good cheer, sensitive editing, and infinite patience. Her editorial savvy and overall moxie helped keep the book on target. Yes, Alice, those bagels and espresso really *are* on the way!

Many thanks also to Rob Tidrow for handling acquisitions, Jenny Watson for coordinating the editing, Mike Stanley for an attentive technical review, and Jim Rock and Gail Perry for many late-night discussion sessions in which the book's direction and content were first articulated. Thanks also to Gary Adair for the internal design of the book, and to Anne Jones for the design of the book's cover.

A final thanks to Dave Ewing for his support of Que Education & Training's efforts to provide computer trainers with the support they need to be successful in the 1990s and beyond.

—Charles O. Stewart III

Forward

by Elliott Masie, President, The MASIE Center

"Why are you a computer trainer?" asked a passenger in the airplane seat next to mine on a recent flight. "What do you get out of teaching people the same thing over and over again?"

It took less than a heartbeat to construct my passionate answer: "It's all about the light bulb!" This person looked a little confused, so I elaborated on my light-bulb metaphor for teaching and learning:

"When learners are working on a new topic, their expressions change. They pass through stages of total confusion, occasional boredom, and even an odd moment of anger. But at the magical moment when it all falls into place, when learning bubbles up to the surface, when they *GET IT*, you can see the light bulbs go off. Several inches above their heads, there are bright glows that an observant trainer will see. And, when those light bulbs go off, it is all worth it! That is what trainers live to see."

This book is dedicated to the millions of light bulbs that will glow brighter because of the hard work of computer trainers. Every day, in organizations and educational institutions throughout the world, trainers ply their trade in pursuit of light-bulb ignition. Whether we are demonstrating a new program from the front of the room, handing a CD-ROM tutorial disk to a fellow employee needing instant knowledge, or answering technology questions as we walk to our car after class, we are all driven by the desire to have our learners' light bulbs glow brighter.

Computer training is an unusual field. Most of us in this industry did not choose it as our career destination during a Career Day in high school. Few of us went to college to pursue a four-year degree in computer training. In fact, most of us got here accidentally. We found ourselves thrown into a situation in which we faced a group of people who needed to master new technology...and we coped. We tried to emulate one of our favorite teachers, we listened to what fellow trainers did in a variety of tough situations, and we ran our own trial-and-error experiments. Computer training is too recent a field to have a deep set of traditions or methodologies. The great computer trainers are on a constant treasure hunt to find new methods, insights, and processes that will improve their craft.

Que Education & Training is providing a much-needed collection of tools, tips, techniques, and perspectives for the computer training industry. This Guide will help every computer training professional in his or her quest to increase the glow in learners' light bulbs. I encourage you to read the chapters with an open heart and mind. Although every person's organizational setting and teaching style are different, we can all learn from each other. The authors of the chapters of this Guide have over a hundred years of experience in this newborn field.

Que Education & Training is on the cutting edge of evolving the computer training industry. Their development work in creating new learning products—from exciting courseware to the BriefingWare series (in conjunction with The MASIE Center), Que is stretching the envelope of the nature of technology learning.

A special note to managers: Although you may not be in the classroom, you are still in the light-bulb business. Your charter is to develop new methods for turning on the learning light bulbs faster, cheaper, and with greater effectiveness. As we move from a dialog about computer training to a discussion about employee technology learning, this Guide can provide valuable insight and perspective. It can help you better support the trainers and learners in your organization.

Elliott Masie
The MASIE Center
P.O. Box 397
Saratoga Springs, NY 12866
1-800-98-MASIE

Contents at a Glance

Table of Contents

3 Adult Learning: What Do We Know for Sure?   39

Part II Before and After the Class   53

4 Training Needs Assessment   55

5 Skills Assessment   77

6 Post-Class Evaluation   95

11   Augmenting Classroom Training with Other Media   193

12 Distance Learning on the World Wide Web   **223**

Introduction

by Gail Perry

This is a very personal book. The trainers who have contributed to this book—and we are trainers first and writers second because it is our passion for training that gives us a subject on which to exercise our writing skills—have shared with you our personal training experiences, real-life incidents that occurred in real classrooms. In some cases, these are heart-warming stories; in other cases, they will make you cringe just as they did us when we lived these moments.

To develop a book about computer training and a guide for recognizing and navigating the potential pitfalls of your chosen career, we have necessarily drawn on our own experiences and learned from them, just as we hope you will. Each of us learns and grows as we teach; each class provides new insights into the world of adult learning.

As you read this book and find yourself reminded of your own classroom experiences, we hope you will choose to share some of your stories with us. We would be honored to make your experiences available to other trainers, both through future editions of this book and currently through online services such as CompuServe and our Internet Web site. Please include your name and (if you like) some general information about the arena in which you teach. Send your tales to one of the following locations, remembering that all information you send becomes the property of Macmillan Computer Publishing and Que Education & Training:

Charles O. Stewart at CompuServe: 73270,2236
CompuServe: GO QUEBOOKS
On the Internet: CSTEWART@QUE.MCP.COM
Also on the Internet: HTTP://WWW.MCP.COM

Macmillan Computer Publishing
Attn: Charles O. Stewart III
201 W. 103rd Street
Indianapolis, IN 46290
Fax: 317-817-7939

This book is a reference we hope you will keep handy for years, studying it, referring back to it, and augmenting it with your own personal experiences. Write in the margins, dog-ear the pages, and most of all, enjoy using *The Computer Trainer's Personal Training Guide*. We wrote it for you.

What You'll Find in this Guide

This book isn't necessarily meant to be read start to finish. Instead, think of it as a general reference, a book you can pick up whenever you have a question about some aspect of computer training for adults. It is a friend in the night as you prepare for the unknown: tomorrow's class.

When you read through the chapters that interest you, you will find a section at the end of each chapter entitled, "From Here." This section is a guide, a treasure map, that points you in the direction of a likely follow-up to the material you have just read.

Here's the rundown of topics you'll find nestled in the pages of this book. Each item is described in an overview with cross-references to the chapters in which the topics can be found.

More than a Guide to Teaching Software

Although *The Computer Trainer's Personal Training Guide* is a book designed and written for computer trainers, it is not so much a book about *computer* training as it is a book about training in general. In other words, you're not going to read detailed information about how to present a particular computer application to a class (please refer to the Que Education & Training Instructor's Manuals for particular applications to meet that need). Instead, you'll find pointers and guidelines for approaching the training of adult learners (Chapter 3), pre-class and post-class (and in-class) evaluation techniques (Chapters 5 and 6), ideas for livening up your classes (Chapter 8 and throughout the book), methods for improving your teaching techniques (Chapter 8), alternatives to traditional classroom training (Chapters 11, 12, and 13), and thoughts about the future of computer training (Chapter 15).

In part, this book is geared toward the new instructor venturing out into the world of computer training. It's a net, if you will, for the instructor who has concerns about working without one. Use the knowledge and skills presented in this book as a silent support system as you walk into your classroom, not quite knowing what to expect. And learn one of the greatest secrets of experienced trainers: no matter how long you've taught, no matter how many times you teach the same class or even teach to the same group of people, *you'll never know what to expect*. Every training experience is a training experience as much for the instructor as it is for the students.

Emphasis is also given to improving skills for the experienced trainer. By studying new techniques and listening to stories of other trainers, you will learn new ways in which to teach subjects that may have become old through repetition. You already know that each new class presents new opportunities for presenting material in different ways and altering your approach to teaching and to the subject matter. This book will open your mind to still more possibilities for change and improvement.

Adapting to Change

One of the biggest challenges facing trainers today is the incredibly fast pace at which the world around us is changing. You know how fast computer hardware and software changes—it sometimes seems that you have barely enough time to install a software program before a new version is available. Then you need faster equipment to keep up with the new software, and then new versions are written to take advantage of the faster equipment, and so on and so on. As an instructor, you must be prepared to adapt to changes and prepare your students for the changes they will face.

The business community is constantly changing, too. There are new approaches to manufacturing, corporate management structures are changing and being reassembled in new forms, expectations of employees are increasing, and (much to our benefit) there is an emphasis on learning and improving new skills. All these changes affect the way you prepare for and approach training. Chapter 1, "The Challenges of Training in the 90s," begins the book with a look at the changing world around us.

How Did You Get that Job?

Most of us, it seems, stumbled into the profession of computer training by having some skills in computers and adult training and by being in the right place at the right time. Not exactly the kind of credentials you might imagine would be held by people who are considered experts in their field.

But this is a new profession, and when you stop to consider, every profession began in the same way. Until a need is recognized and defined, a structured program of education and preparation cannot exist. College courses are now being designed to prepare people for the profession of computer training, and certification programs exist to recognize and endorse particular training skills. Chapter 2, "Becoming a Computer Trainer," addresses the peculiar state of new profession/established profession limbo in which we find ourselves. You'll also get a chance to read how each of us got to where we are today with the "how I got this job" biographies of each author.

The Adult Learner

We spend our entire childhood and young adulthood exposed to *teachers*—people who impart knowledge to those younger and less experienced than themselves. From these encounters, we form our impressions of teachers. We must consider that we may not have the same relationship with those whom we teach as our teachers did with their students. In fact, we may be:

- Younger
- Less intelligent
- Less experienced (not in the subject matter but in the profession of the students)
- Lower in the corporate structure

And this is just the tip of the proverbial adult-learner iceberg.

As you stand before a classroom of computer students, you may find yourself confronted with corporate executives, entry-level clerical employees, people who fall somewhere in between, or a mix of all types in the same classroom.

And status does not denote ability to learn at any particular pace or in any particular style. The president of a Fortune 500 corporation may have never laid his hands on a keyboard before and may spend the entire class asking why the spacebar is so big and why is it easier to type brackets than parentheses. An entry-level employee may have a computer or two at home, may do spare-time programming, and may be a whiz at keyboard skills and figuring out how computer software works.

You should expect no sympathy from the class participants if you are not prepared to teach to the level of every student in the classroom simultaneously and to respect every student equally.

Providing excellent teaching to the adult learner is perhaps the one skill that most troubles instructors, keeping them up at night, providing them with endless stories to share with other trainers and from which to learn.

Examine Chapter 3, "Adult Learning: What Do We Know for Sure?," carefully to discover techniques for training the adult learner. These tips have been compiled from years of research and the experiences of real-life classroom adventures.

Sizing Up Your Class

It's imperative that instructors know whom they are teaching and the skills and needs of that group. Not having this core information is like teaching through a one-way glass: you can't see your class but they can see you. If you can't gauge the responses of your students, you can't know whether they are learning. When you are denied the opportunity to gear your teaching to the needs of the learners, you are severely handicapped.

Chapter 5, "Skills Assessment," deals with assessing the skills of your class. Skills assessment is advance screening to help you discover information about who will be in your training session, why those people will be there, and what kind of computer background they have. Sometimes, you can obtain this information well in advance of the class; other times, you won't know until you get to class and start asking questions. One way or another, however, you must obtain this information.

You must also stay on top of the progress of your students during the class. Chapter 5 also discusses ways in which you can assess as you go, making sure that you and your students are on the same wavelength.

Evaluative Feedback

Are you any good at this job? You may never know if you don't allow yourself and your class to be evaluated. The benefits of evaluations are enormous. Your classes and your training skills evolve as a result of the responses of your students and those who hire you to teach. New instructors are often wary of evaluations—as are people new to any type of performance that is being judged. Chapter 6, "Post-Class Evaluation," provides you with the rationale for evaluation as well as a cornucopia of evaluation styles and approaches you can use to monitor your own progress.

Designing Your Course

Before there was the class, there was the class material. You can't just go into a classroom cold without a game plan. Putting together the right material to teach the subject is just as important as knowing how to teach and knowing who your students are.

Chapter 7, "Course Development," discusses the advance preparation needed for successful training. Not only does this chapter have information about selecting material and customizing it to meet the needs of your students, it also contains a section on getting yourself prepared to teach: mastering your subject and honing your technical skills.

Methodology

So you know what you're going to teach and who your audience is. What's the best way to teach a particular set of information to a particular set of people? And is there more than one "best" way?

Turn to Chapter 8, "Training Techniques," to discover innovative ways to present material. Keep in mind that no matter how much you know about your subject and your audience, you can't predict all the questions that will arise nor can you guarantee the direction in which the class material will flow. You must be prepared to alter material and examples "on the fly" to meet the needs of the particular individuals in your classroom. Chapter 8 addresses techniques for meeting surprises head-on.

Consider also the discussion in Chapter 11, "Augmenting Classroom Training with Other Media," regarding alternative delivery methods to enhance classroom training. Beyond the classroom, there are many ways in which computer techniques can be acquired. Chapter 11 describes a wide selection of media and formats available for teaching individuals and groups.

Growing up in the Chicago area, I remember that we could tune in to *TV College* on Channel 11 (the public broadcasting station) for some of the most boring television around. Now the computer age has brought training outside the classroom into the 90s in colorful, fun, technologically fantastic style. Chapter 12, "Distance Learning on the World Wide Web," covers the topic of self-directed training as an alternative to classroom training. Self-directed training can take many shapes: video training, interactive computer-based training, teleconferencing, and the use of the World Wide Web on the Internet for disseminating course materials and for creating active learning experiences.

Housekeeping

You can't forget your responsibility to introduce your students to the surrounding area. Just as schoolchildren need to know where to stash their mittens and boots, your students have to know where to put the things they brought with them, what behavior is expected of them in the classroom, and the ins and outs of the surrounding area.

Taking care of this business ensures the comfort of your students and helps them feel more at home in your classroom. Chapter 9, "Housekeeping," provides you with an understanding of what types of housekeeping information you need to impart to the learners, why they need to know this information, and how to present the housekeeping rules.

It's Showtime

The door closes behind you and you turn to face a room full of expectant students. What's next? If your reply is, "Panic and run!" you haven't read Chapter 10, "The Flow of the Class." Learn how to put together everything you've read in the rest of the book and create a meaningful and useful class. Included in this chapter are pointers on how to deal with the first five minutes of the class, that awkward time when you and the students are first feeling each other out. You should realize how much of the flow of the rest of the class depends on the information you glean from your students in the introductory minutes. Consider also the wrap-up—the last five minutes of class when you need to establish closure and make sure that your students leave the room satisfied that their needs have been met. Chapter 10 is filled with wonderful anecdotes that provide you with insights into what goes on in computer classes during the rest of the day—between those first and last five minutes.

Sample Forms

We don't just give you ideas, we give you the means for executing these ideas! In the Appendix, you'll find samples of questionnaires and forms that can help you assess the needs of your students or of the company for which they work. You'll also find forms that you, your students, and their supervisors can use to evaluate the effectiveness of your training.

Use these forms as is, or use them as a guide for developing your own forms. We've tried to provide probing questions to help garner *real* feedback from your students instead of canned responses from tired, end-of-day class participants who are in a hurry to hit the road.

How To Make this Manual Your Own

This is your book, and you are a trainer. From this day forward, think of yourself as a member of the team of trainers and writers who put together this book.

Look at this book as more than a training reference book. Think of it as a personal training journal, your own log of experiences intertwined with ours, a memory book of good classes, embarrassing moments, students who caught you off guard; a scrapbook of favorite students, situations you want to repeat, situations you would rather forget, innovative ways to present your material, and techniques for getting your students to open up. Make it a compendium of all the experiences that make you the trainer you are and a handbook that will grow with you as you become even more skilled.

We've intentionally left wide margins in the book so that you can annotate the material with your own experiences, classroom memories, and thoughts about the content of the chapter. Scribble notes in the book, and learn as you go, enhancing our text with your own ideas.

Your Personal Training Journal

In addition to this book and the notes with which you augment it, we recommend you begin your own training journal. This can be a three-ring binder, a file folder, or a pocket folder—something you'll be comfortable using, adding to, and referring to over the years. Keep your journal near this book (or stick it inside the back cover) and add notes and information pertinent to your training and learning experiences.

Feed Me!

As a computer trainer, you will find you are constantly learning new techniques and growing with your profession—and it's important to have room to grow. In your personal training journal, continue to add articles, notes, and other information. To get your juices flowing, here are some sample items you can consider adding to your journal:

- Newspaper and magazine articles about training

- Specific information about the corporate climate in which you teach

- Information about potential contacts and new clients (for the independent trainer)

- A class log containing information about the classes you teach: dates, location, list of attendees, subject taught, evaluation comments

- General information about the specific topics in which you train

- Personal insights into training

- Your own, customized, evaluation forms and questionnaires you like to use in your classes

- Certification information

Don't hesitate to insert material into your journal. You can always change your mind and remove something you decide you no longer need.

Anecdotes

Develop a method for recording class events that can help you in future classes. Whether you use the margins in the printed pages of this manual or add your own journal pages, these real-life stories are perhaps the most important part of growing as a trainer. As you add your own experiences to the pages of this book, you'll begin to cherish those moments when you thumb through the pages, recalling both your highs and lows from classroom events. Record not only the events of your classes, but what *you did* to make the classes successful (or what you might have done to make the classes work better).

For example, if you encounter a student who causes a problem in one of your classes, go to Chapter 3, "Adult Learning: What Do We Know for Sure?" In addition to noting your own experience in the margins on the appropriate page, read what our trainers have to say about similar types of learners. The next time you are faced with a difficult situation with a student, you will have a personal experience to which you can refer.

If a class of yours just didn't seem to get off the ground, take a minute to turn to Chapter 10, "The Flow of the Class," note the problems you had right there in the margins, and read up on how to improve the flow of your classes.

Using What You Added

You've worked hard to customize this book and your journal: you've added significant articles, you've logged your classroom appearances, you've written anecdotes about classroom events, you've noted comments that students write about you. So what good is all that work if the book remains on your shelf?

You're a trainer; it's your profession. This book is *your* resource book and is only as effective as you let it be.

So pull *your* book and *your* journal off the bookshelf, review appropriate sections before heading into a new class, remind yourself of past experiences, seek information about the types of adult learners you'll be facing and how to impart knowledge to them, review techniques for getting the class in gear and keeping it moving, make copies of forms and questionnaires that can be useful to you in your class, and remind yourself of mid-point evaluative techniques for assessing how well your class is learning before the day is over and it's too late to change the presentation.

Why You Want To Make this Manual Your Own

This book is an excellent training resource and we're certain you will be satisfied with the information presented in these pages. But it doesn't have to stop there. By personalizing this book with your own ideas and experiences, you make it a unique resource: you make it better than we could ever have done ourselves.

Tales from the Front

Why is it important to record events from your classes? For one thing, you can learn from past experiences. By compelling yourself to write down your experiences, you can assess what things went well and what made them go well; you can identify problems and what caused those problems. Furthermore, somewhere down the line, you may have a need to re-create episodes from a particular class for your supervisor or the supervisor of those who attended.

A Living History

Computer classes, like good wine and poor complexions, improve with age. The more you teach a class, the more comfortable you are with the topic, the more likely you are to anticipate questions, and the more relaxed you are in front of the learners. All this comes with experience—and you can track this experience in your *Personal Training Guide*.

As you reach certain plateaus of comfort, note in your guide what makes the class easier to teach. Learn from those notes as you prepare to teach new classes in the future. By studying what worked in the past, you can skip some of the getting-acclimated steps that naturally occur at the beginning of a new class.

A Friend in Front of the Classroom

Carry your training guide with you when you teach. Either have it physically present with you in the classroom or keep it mentally at hand. Feel confident in your performance as an instructor, knowing you've studied the tools presented in this guide and added to them with your own experiences.

Reading this book provides you with the knowledge of many trainers and gives you insights into their teaching experiences. When you walk into a classroom, it will be as if you are taking this entire cadre of trainers with you, as if you had a joint force supporting you in your teaching engagement.

Working Together

As you become more and more experienced as a trainer, you will find yourself in the role of leader to newer, less-experienced trainers. Show them your training guide! Your commentary in addition to the examples and information we've placed in this guide can serve as an aid to those who follow in your footsteps. In particular, for instructors who will be teaching the same topics to the same types of people, your comments and experiences will be priceless.

Learning from each other is one of the most valuable forms of guidance and support we have. Computer training is a relatively new profession; for the most part, trainers are self-taught and often find themselves in the role of computer trainer by chance (because they happened to know more about computers than those around them or because they exhibited some training skills). It's kind of a haphazard way to find yourself in a profession.

Few computer trainers today went to college hoping to learn to teach others how to use computer applications. But now that we're here, we can learn from those with experience and improve our own skills.

Your Role as a Trainer of Adults

One of the first things a computer trainer learns is that teaching adults is different from teaching children. Even if you have no previous teaching experience, every one of us remembers teachers from our childhood and the roles they played in our lives as mentors, psychologists, disciplinarians, surrogate parents, friends, and, sometimes, enemies. Perhaps more important than any of those roles, however, was the role of leader, of being in charge of the classroom and in control of the presentation.

The roles of the instructor are not so clear cut when you are dealing with adult learners. All the roles just mentioned are still present and are required of the instructor, but generally appear as more subtle roles, exercised in moderation and even behind the scenes.

The computer trainer has to know how to approach students of varying educational backgrounds and with vastly different experiences, making them feel comfortable and accessible to learning. In addition, the computer trainer must be able to recognize different learning styles and present training appropriate to those styles, often changing gears in the middle of a presentation in response to feedback from the students.

As you embark on your personal journey through this book, treating it like your own training scrapbook and augmenting it with notes and feedback from your personal training excursions, keep in mind your role as a trainer of adults. Rather than shaping the minds of today's youth and tomorrow's leaders, you are right there on the front line, shaping the direction of corporate America today.

Part I

Training Basics

Chapter 1

The Challenges of Training in the 90s

by Paul Clothier

Paul Clothier, president of The Training Edge, has been training people how to use computers for more than 12 years. He has presented training-skills seminars and sessions for various companies and organizations in the United States, Canada, and Europe.

Computer training is a wonderful profession. The computer trainer is forever a learner, the work is rewarding, the feedback is immediate, you see new faces every day, you get to play with new and exciting software, demonstrate your expertise, and be an entertainer. What more could you want? I know many trainers who would not consider doing anything else. As one of them put it, "You'll never get me sitting in one of those gray cubicles every day!" Computer training can be exciting, varied, demanding, and stimulating; it is always challenging. Part of the excitement and the challenge comes from the fact that computer training is never static, it's always changing.

Teaching people how to use computers isn't what it used to be...and it shouldn't be. There have been enormous changes in technology and business since the first PCs hit the desktops; we can no longer use the same model of computer training we did then. In five years, we'll probably need another model. Technological advances and social changes have pushed us forward and have been a driving force behind the re-evaluation of our training model. The model *should* be changed—but whether or not we *are* changing it or are *ready* to change it are other questions. It's human nature to be attached to the old and the familiar because it's comfortable. The new and different takes a bit of getting used to.

Adapt and Change

Perhaps the biggest challenge for us all, whether you train or not, is adapting to change. The amount and the speed of change in our lives is increasing daily. Nothing seems solid, long-term, or stable. Businesses are downsized, re-engineered, and reskilled; software and hardware change monthly, the knowledge and skills we had yesterday are out of date to-day. The word that describes the 90s is *change*. Our response to it must be to adapt.

Gone are the days when we could spend six months planning, imple-menting, and evaluating our training. Nowadays, the software is out of date in six months. Gone are the days when the omniscient teacher stands before the class, directs the training, and offers pearls of wisdom to passive learners. Good training demands responsiveness, timeliness, and a high degree of interactivity. New business processes, technological innovations, and societal changes require new training methods and ap-proaches. We need to change, we need to adapt, and we need to do it yesterday.

Changing the Training Paradigm

A *paradigm* is something that serves as an example or model of how things should be done. The old (or existing) paradigm of computer train-ing has served us for a while but is fast becoming outdated. Just as the old hierarchical model of running a business is being replaced by a broader, flatter, more responsive structure, so should our model of train-ing change, adapt, and become more responsive.

Let's look at this old model of computer training and contrast it with what a new training paradigm might look like. Consider these three areas:

- **The learning model**—the model we use to understand how people learn.

- **The training model**—the model we use to determine and direct the trainer's function.

- **The training delivery model**—the model we use to determine how the training is ultimately delivered.

For each of these areas, we will look at the older model and suggest a pos-sible new and more effective model.

The Learning Model

Our old model and the possible new learning model for computer training have different assumptions and practices for teaching people to learn computer skills. Some of the old assumptions need to be reevaluated.

Old: Learning keystrokes and procedures

New: Learning concepts

One of the old assumptions was that people learned software skills by repetition and remembering keystrokes. The more you used and repeated the same keystrokes, the more you would retain and remember. In some cases, this worked well and was necessary because the logic of the software was unclear and "unfriendly." Applications had no consistency between them as GUI software does today.

Remembering the keystrokes or mouse clicks necessary to use a particular program is ultimately of limited use. The pervasive use of computers in businesses and in the home requires a deeper understanding of computer concepts and processes. To adapt to new software and apply computer skills to solve new problems, we need a fuller understanding of computer concepts. Only with a broader conceptual knowledge can we more easily adapt to the accelerating change of technology.

Once we understand a concept, it serves as a foundation for further learning and acquisition of knowledge. The ability to learn and adapt quickly is the key to succeeding and surviving tomorrow. Developing necessary skills is possible only if we concentrate on learning by understanding *concepts* rather than learning by memorizing procedures. Our computer training should embrace this truth. Memorizing procedural steps is of short-term use—understanding concepts has more enduring benefits.

Old: Training from software features

New: Training from the learners' needs

When we train, we tend to mirror the way the software is organized. We first look at the different features and functions of a program and use this information to determine what to teach. We teach the features and then hope our learners can integrate these features into a method of solving real-life problems. In other words, we look to the software to decide what to teach.

A more valuable way of training is to look at the tasks the learner carries out at work and teach techniques with which these tasks can be achieved. The emphasis for our new model should be on the *task* to be carried out rather than the *features* of the software. When we teach about features, we have to integrate the features and then apply them to a particular task. When we teach by focusing on the task, the features become tools we use to complete the task. The methods and procedures are more readily assimilated and remembered because they relate to a real scenario. They make sense. If they are independent and unconnected features, the level of retention and understanding is lower. We need to train by looking at the learner's needs, at real-life processes, and at what is going on in the workplace rather than teaching based on the features and functions of the program.

> **Old:**   Learning is linear
>
> **New:** Learning is nonlinear

Because we tend to organize our lives in some sort of orderly fashion, we have assumed that learning should be a linear process. Our current presentations, explanations, and documentation have all been developed based on the premise that learning has to be a linear process: First, we cover the screen layout, the different types of cursors, how to enter data, and how to select text; later in the afternoon, we get to macros and mail-merge. The presentation is all structured, linear, and logical with the "easy" stuff first and the "harder" stuff later.

The truth is, learning is about as linear as the Internet and as logical as the weather. When we learn to drive a car, we do not study the gas pedal for a day, move on to the other pedals, and then take a closer look at the steering wheel. No, we learn "incrementally." We learn a little about everything; over a period of time, we expand and fine-tune our knowledge and skills. Teaching in straight lines often hinders learning rather than promotes it.

The human brain works by recognizing meaningful patterns—and these patterns are by no means linear. Our skill acquisitions are nonlinear: think of riding a bike or learning to ski. The way we learn concepts and understand ideas is nonlinear. Learning and understanding result from being exposed to ideas, concepts, and procedures—not in a linear, logical sequence but in an incidental, inferential, and holistic manner. Computer training needs to reflect and embrace this truth.

The question is, how do we implement this nonlinear approach in computer training? The logical, linear, and sequenced model is attractive to trainers because it is easier to plan and easier to implement. The nonlinear model is a little different. We must let go of the idea that we have to teach a class in a particular order with the basics at the beginning and the harder topics toward the end. We must realize that learners can understand and use something like mail-merge before they know all the different cursor movements. They can understand and use macros before learning how to set margins. In fact, we can teach topics in a different order. We can teach some of the more "advanced" work first and fill in some of the basics later. Although this may sound unconventional and frightening to most trainers, you'll be amazed at how well this approach can work.

We must structure computer training and training technologies so that they more closely reflect the incremental, nonlinear way we learn. We must mirror learning processes a little more and software processes a little less.

The Training Model

The role of the computer trainer has to shift. Delivering information to passive learners is no longer appropriate. Learners must play an active and responsible part in their acquisition of new skills. Trainers must become catalysts for learning and they must communicate technology in a language that is not threatening to the learner.

Old: The trainer provides information

New: The trainer facilitates and coaches

The default model of training, which goes back many centuries, is that of a wise and knowledgeable teacher standing in front of us delivering wisdom and insights. The communication flow is from the teacher to those "being taught." The model is one of lecture and demonstration. The trainer does most of the talking and the learners are directed. This model doesn't work too well for computer training.

Effective computer training requires the trainer to be a facilitator and a coach. Rather than the trainer presenting the information, he or she should be a catalyst in the learning process. The trainer helps set up an environment in which learning is possible and encourages *independence* in the learner. The trainer acts as a coach by encouraging, prompting, motivating, and inspiring. The goal is for the learner to become more independent and self-directed. The more successful we are as trainers, the less we are needed.

How the Trainer Can Help Create a New Training Model

- **Use questioning.** Whenever possible, the trainer should use questioning techniques to encourage independent thinking skills. Not single-word-answer questions but "open" questions that require understanding. Trainers should *ask* more questions and talk less.

- **Encourage self-assessment.** When a learner asks, "Is this right?" the trainer should avoid giving a yes/no answer. Instead, turn the question back to the participant: "What are you trying to accomplish?" Have the learner evaluate his or her own work—don't do it for them.

- **Provide challenges.** People often learn best when confronted with a challenge or a problem. This also reflects a typical working environment. Blend some more challenges into your training. Don't spoon-feed them, stretch them.

(continues)

(continued)

- **Teach less.** Spend less time "instructing" and more time with hands-on activities. Try to cut the amount of lecturing in your training. Keep your explanations simple, concise, and visual and then let the learners get on with it. It works better.

- **Teach them how to use resources.** One way of encouraging learners to become independent is to teach them how to use help resources and documentation. When they ask you a question, make sure that they first use the resources available to them. Don't answer every question you are asked.

- **Encourage thinking *not* memorization.** When you ask questions, provide exercises, or choose courseware, make sure that they all focus on thinking and understanding and not on memorization. Too many instructor questions and courseware exercises concentrate on remembering procedures and not on understanding concepts.

Old: The trainer directs training

New: Learners help direct the training

The existing model of computer training has the trainer in the role of the director. The trainer decides the direction of the class, what to teach, and how to teach it. The learners arrive, have information delivered to them, and we hope that some of it will be useful to them. The trainer controls the delivery and content of the training. Although this approach enables learning of sorts, the trainer makes the decisions about what is relevant and what is appropriate for the learners. However, the trainer doesn't always know what is relevant and appropriate...only the learners do.

Learners must become more involved in determining the content and delivery of their learning. Rather than passively receiving instruction, they must be involved in designing and directing their own computer training. The learners know what the training has to deliver if they are to do their job more effectively. Rather than shower the learners with information and hope that some of it is useful, our training must be designed with the learners' input and with their specific needs in mind.

Whether it is through needs assessments, surveys, meetings, or on-the-spot customization, we must design our training so that it directly addresses the learners' needs. When we design computer training, we must make sure that it includes input and direction from the learner. This input should not be limited to comments and suggestions made before the training begins but should be interactive and ongoing throughout the training. Only then can our training meet the real needs of the learners.

Old: Synchronous classroom training

New: Adaptive classroom training

Training models that suit the trainer often don't suit the learner. The "synchronous" type of training that is often used is great for trainers and lousy for learners: "OK, everyone click File...everybody got that...yes?...OK, now click Print...everybody with me?..." and so on. The group presses keys and clicks in unison and the trainer is happy: "They are all following me nicely!" The problem is that the students are being taught to press keys and follow steps and to do it at the pace of the slowest person in the room. Training structured like this limits the amount of learning that can take place. The level of learning during such a class compared to what learning is *possible* in the same time period should be cause for concern. For this reason, certain fast, intuitive, self-motivated computer users never get to our training rooms—they know that the typical class doesn't serve their needs.

Because of not serving the needs of these self-directed users and the increasing need for computer training to be cost effective and productive, the synchronous model has to be replaced by a more effective one. Learning must take into account the characteristics, abilities, and learning styles of the learners to be efficient. The training must be designed so that even though it is delivered in the classroom, it provides individualized, customized solutions for different participants. The training should adapt to the learner—not the learner to the training. The training should be flexible, interactive, and should satisfy the immediate needs of the learner. When we achieve this, we have computer training that truly serves the individual learner and is more efficient, effective, and engaging.

Old: "Techie" trainers

New: Trainers that seem like real human beings

One in four people feels intimidated by computers and technology. Many of the first computer trainers were individuals who had mastered the esoteric world of bits, bytes, and hexadecimal and who spent a large portion their days exploring the virtual universe. As a result, computer training was originally delivered by "techies," "whizzes," and "propeller heads." Although the user friendliness of software has improved dramatically over the last 10 years, many perceive that learning to use computers is still complicated, difficult, and "technical." We must alter this perception. One way of doing this is to have more computer trainers with good communication skills, good presentation skills, and good people skills. Trainers who can pass for real human beings. Trainers to whom the average person can relate.

Currently, this is not necessarily the case. Computer trainers in businesses and organizations are often chosen primarily because of their computer expertise and knowledge. Frequently, the qualities and characteristics needed to become an expert in various software packages are not the qualities needed to become a good computer trainer. A good trainer has a feel and an understanding for what it is like to be confused, overwhelmed, or intimidated. A good trainer is someone to whom the audience can relate. "Well, if he can do it...I'm sure I can!" The best teachers are often the ones who have had the same fears and concerns as the students and who have surmounted them.

Some of today's fear of computer technology has inadvertently been promoted by well-meaning trainers or peers who overwhelm the user with information, jargon, and impatience. This type of trainer knows the product inside out and backwards and "tells" learners what they have to press. This type of trainer fixes problems for learners rather than gives them the tools to fix it themselves. This type of trainer proves to the learner that to understand computers you have to be a certain type of "whiz."

We must change this perception and start hiring (and evaluating) computer trainers based on their ability to communicate and present information effectively. Of course, trainers need a thorough knowledge of the applications they teach but the emphasis should be on trainers with communication and people skills. We need people to teach technology who can make it seem simple, easy, unthreatening, fun, and exciting. We need trainers who have an understanding and appreciation for what it is like to sit in a class and be confused. We need trainers who can speak to an audience using a vocabulary and terms that are easily understood.

To include everyone in the "information age," we must demystify information technology and make it accessible to the average user. One way of achieving this is for trainers to take on the challenge of communicating information technology in a more understandable and less "technical" manner. When we achieve this, we can demote the computer to what it should be: simply a useful tool to get the job done.

The Training Delivery Model

What models do we use to deliver our training to the end user? Are they effective? Do we need to re-evaluate them in light of our experience, new technology, and feedback from our clients? Let's take a look at what changes we may have to make in our delivery of computer training if we are to survive in the future.

1

Old: Instructor-led training

New: "Multimedia" training

Computer training has traditionally been instructor-led classroom training (ILT). The learner receives information in one or two modes. The standard approach has been lecture, demonstration, and "watch what I do and follow me." This works well in some cases but does not provide the learner with many choices in the method and style of learning. People learn in many different ways and have different preferred modes of learning. Some people learn much faster when they listen to information, others learn when they see it, and still others learn when they start using it.

Effective computer training should always include alternative ways of learning so that the learner can choose a medium appropriate to his or her needs. The traditional classroom environment doesn't allow for choice. Computer training in the future must address the different preferred ways of learning. Quite often, a learner in a computer training class finds that only about 10 percent of the material covered is immediately useful to the work he or she is doing. The other 90 percent of the time is spent learning functions or features because they are part of the course outline. Think what people could learn if, in addition to the instructor, they had access to resources like books, audio tapes, computer-based training (CBT), videos, and multimedia with which they could follow their interests or inclinations.

Instructor-led training works and can be effective but it must become a little more flexible. The learner must be given more choice. Other learning media should be made available inside and outside the class to complement traditional training. A learner may find macros very useful in the morning session and decide that he or she would like to learn more about them in the afternoon instead of covering mail-merge. It should be possible for people to learn this way. Those that choose to learn this way can have books, audio tapes, video, CBT, multimedia, and online training made available to them. These resources can be set up in a separate learning lab or can be integrated within the classroom. Either way, it is a great advantage for learners to be given a choice about the learning method they use. Providing such a choice will be an essential ingredient to computer training in the years to come.

An Aside

By suggesting that learners be given a choice about the way they learn, I am not suggesting that learners wander around the training room picking and choosing their lessons and media. I am not suggesting that everyone go off and do their own thing.

(continues)

(continued)

What I *am* suggesting is that, in a computer training class, we must make sure that the learning needs of individuals are met.

The majority of a class will probably move along with the instructor—but there may be a slower learner or a more advanced user who has different requirements. It should be possible for these learners to be able to access some type of CBT or resource that addresses their needs. They can do this in the class if the computers are set up for an appropriate CBT or multimedia resource.

In some classes, I have put a slower learner (whom I may have lost during the standard presentation) on a CBT tutorial while the others are working on a more advanced feature. In other classes, I have hardly taught the faster learners: I simply provided them with additional information sheets, showed them all the online CBT that was available, and answered questions when necessary.

Although this planning takes a little organization, it is worth it.

Instructor-led training shouldn't be replaced by other learning resources; it should be *complemented* by them. The role of the computer instructor, however, may gradually become more of a coach and guide to learning resources rather than an information provider. Proactive organizations that accommodate choice for users in this way will provide learners with a lot more value and will receive a much greater return on their training investment.

> **Old:** Training as scheduled

> **New:** Training when you need it

The time between deciding there is a need for training and actually delivering the training can be anything from a few weeks to a few months. Because of the speed at which business and industry operate and the rate at which they must respond to customer demands, a delay of a month before training is becoming unacceptable. Computer training is needed to help users do their work, and the work usually needs to be done yesterday.

One of the challenges of computer trainers and training organizations is to provide training when needed. Waiting for the next scheduled class is not acceptable. Training must be on demand. If a client has to learn HTML to set up an Internet Web page, a month's delay may mean losing a month's worth of business. If a company has to produce an annual report in two weeks, they have to learn the spreadsheet software this week. Sound unreasonable? Get used to it. Trainers and training organizations must design ways of providing training when and where it is needed.

Those that can will thrive; those that can't will become extinct. It is a considerable challenge but it must be overcome if trainers and training organizations are to survive in the next 10 years.

Old: Training as an event

New: Learning as a process

The rate at which new information was generated a few decades ago was much slower than it is today. Information and skills that were learned were good for a comparatively long time because things didn't change too rapidly. When something new came along, we went off to get some more training. Working and learning were seen as separate activities. Training was an event—you did the training and then you got back to work.

With the rapid growth of information technologies at the workplace and in the home, learning has taken on a new character. Work and learning are no longer separate entities. Increasingly, work equals learning. It can be seen, even now, that most organizations are in the business of collecting, managing, and providing information. Because of the accelerating change in information systems and software, learning is becoming an essential part of the work we do. The distinction between learning and work is becoming less defined. No longer is learning something we do at intervals to update our knowledge; learning is becoming a daily necessity.

The implications are that we must provide computer training that complements and is an integral part of the learning processes at work. Learning should not be a disconnected event but part of a broader program that includes the organization's *and* the individual's learning needs. Those responsible for computer training will have to align it more closely with the learning goals of the organization and the individual. Trainers will have to provide an ongoing process for learning rather than a succession of training "events."

How To Survive the 90s and Beyond

If you are someone who dislikes change or disruption, enjoys the familiar and the predictable, and wants any easy life, don't stay in the computer training field. If, on the other hand, you enjoy people, you enjoy the new and unfamiliar, and you love taking on the challenges that life throws at you, computer training is for you. The next decade will see many changes to the computer training industry. Adapting won't necessarily be a matter of choice but a matter of survival. People will demand new, easier, and innovative ways of learning and we must respond. Those of us who want to ride the wave of change and stay ahead of the game should be prepared to make some changes. Here's a short list for trainers and the "learning" organizations:

- Offer "opportunities to learn" as opposed to "training classes"

- Align training with learner needs and organizational goals

- Allow learners to customize their own instruction

- Help teach people how to learn

- Help overcome "technology fear"

- Provide training when it is needed and where it is needed

- Provide alternative methods of learning in and out of the classroom

- Expect organizations to start looking for trainer certifications

- Never stop being a learner yourself

The role of the computer trainer will necessarily change in the future and the expertise required will include "high-touch" communication skills as well as high-tech knowledge skills. The trainer will become much more of a resource broker and a guide. Trainers will become more like learners; the model of the omniscient teacher conveying facts from the front of the room will disappear.

It won't be easy and it will take a lot of adapting, learning, listening, and innovating. But as the author Samuel Butler once said, "Life is like playing a violin solo in public and learning the instrument as one goes on." He must have been talking about computer training.

Chapter 2

Becoming a Computer Trainer

by Gail Perry

Gail Perry started training 10 years ago when computers weren't personal and software only came on 5 1/4-inch disks. In 1991, she became a WordPerfect Certified Instructor after passing all sorts of tests and being taped and critiqued by WordPerfect Corporation. Initially, she trained at the CPA firm for which she worked, both for their employees and for their clients—and developed her own training manuals and methods of evaluation.

This chapter examines various methods involved in becoming a trainer of computer software. Because this is a relatively new profession, formalized programs designed to train someone to become a computer software trainer are only now beginning to surface. Meanwhile, there is a pressing need for people to fill this niche. How does one go about becoming a computer trainer? Let's start with the desire to train and go from there.

I Want To Be a Computer Trainer When I Grow Up

Actually, very few people plan on becoming computer trainers when they choose a career path. Many of us grew up at a time when a single computer filled an entire climate-controlled room; the concept of individuals using computers at their desks and in their homes was reserved for scenes in science fiction stories.

Because computer usage is so widespread today, and because computers are used in such a variety of situations, the computer trainer must be able to provide training in a large variety of applications to people of widely divergent skill levels.

The best computer trainers not only have many different technical areas of expertise, they also have a knack for teaching and communicating with adult learners. This is a rather uncommon combination.

Education Requirements

Although the computer trainer doesn't have to be a degreed computer scientist, he or she should have a well-rounded background in major computer applications. Expertise in only one or two applications can severely limit the instructor's ability to communicate with students because many students come to the classroom with experience in other computer programs. The knowledge of how those other programs work can give the instructor an edge in drawing on the students' previous experiences to learn new concepts.

Even though it seems to be a rare computer trainer who actually has a background in computers *and* education, higher education of some sort is an excellent prerequisite. As a trainer, you are facing off against a great spectrum of educated and not-so-educated computer users; your ability to communicate to all of them on their own levels is imperative. In general, the better educated you are, the better chance you have of being accepted as a source for knowledge.

You should also have a fundamental background in training the adult learner. Teaching adults is psychologically different than teaching any other group and you must be prepared for the obstacles that can occur in this setting. Look at Chapter 3, "Adult Learning: What Do We Know for Sure?," and also consider additional reading or training in this important area.

Your education doesn't stop when you teach your first class. Instead, it continues in two ways. First, you must seek out the latest information about the topics you teach and stay abreast of changes in the software and hardware capabilities. It's your responsibility to be aware of the newest version of the programs you teach and how they run on various models of computer equipment.

In addition, you will find that you learn as you teach. Students in your classes will bring fresh ideas and innovative techniques from which you can learn and which you can recycle into future classes.

Developing Classroom Skills

No matter how strong a technical background you may have, if you can't impart that knowledge to those in your classes, you lose effectiveness as an instructor. If you have a background in education and were trained in the field, you have an advantage. If you're completely new to the field of education (from the standpoint of being in front of the room as opposed to sitting opposite the teacher), your skills will develop as you teach.

Watch others teach: see what they do to draw out class participants and how they share their knowledge. Question instructors about their techniques and talk to students about what they feel makes a good instructor. Imagine yourself as the instructor as you watch other instructors and think about how you would present the material. Imagine yourself as the student and try to gauge your response to the instructor's presentation. Perform role-playing exercises: don't just *think* about teaching, *act it out* in front of a pretend class. Attend a class in how to teach adults if you can locate one.

More than anything else, practice. Practice while you're driving the car, practice while you're painting the house, practice wherever and whenever you can. Try to practice before every class. The more you practice, the more comfortable you will become, the more comfortable you will appear to your students, and the better your presentation will be.

Finding a Place that Will Let You Teach

If you are an independent trainer, your paycheck depends on a steady flow of work—which you have to find. You can take several approaches to make yourself and your training skills known:

- **Advertise.** Don't be hesitant to promote yourself through brochures, display advertisements (particularly in trade journals), and mailings.

- **Write articles about the topics you teach.** Many business and trade journals publish articles for which your payment is the right to include a brief biography describing yourself as a free-lance trainer.

- **Speak.** Offer yourself as a speaker at business luncheons and trade organizations.

- **Participate in trade shows.** Seek out business-related and computer-related trade shows and set up a booth for yourself. Take along plenty of advertising material to give out.

- **Word of mouth.** When you train, ask your students to mention your name to others. If you're good enough, they'll do it without your having to ask.

- **Ask for recommendations and referrals.** It may be a bit tacky to ask your students to sign testimonials as they're leaving the classroom, but it's not inappropriate to use comments from your evaluation forms in your advertising. If people come up after class to compliment you, ask them if they know of other organizations that might benefit from your training. You can also ask for letters of recommendation.

- **Read the classified ads.** Companies in need of trainers frequently advertise in the newspaper.

- **Watch for opportunities.** Be observant; opportunities can occur without your going after them.

- **Read the newspaper.** Interpret the articles you read from the standpoint of how they affect you. If you see an article about a company undergoing a major computer software upgrade, chances are they are going to need training. Write letters! Make calls!

- **Read trade journals.** Trends in business are frequently described in trade journals. Just as with newspaper articles, if you sense an opportunity, make yourself known.

- **Get certified.** Companies that certify trainers on various software programs often recommend those trainers to people who purchase the software.

In addition, companies that sell computer hardware and software often provide training. They often contract with free-lance trainers to provide this service. Check with dealers in your community to see what opportunities exist for free-lance training.

This is just a start. Use your imagination to think of new and innovative ways in which to find training situations. You will find that the more you train, the more training you will be asked to do.

Certification Programs

Several software companies offer certification to trainers. Once certified, you can refer to yourself as a *certified trainer*—a title that carries some level of credibility. You can also use the name and logo of the software company in your advertising and promotional materials. You can take training classes from various software companies to become a certified trainer in those products. The following sections describe some of the more popular certification programs currently available.

Certified Lotus Professional

Lotus Development Corporation certifies trainers who take a certification exam. Sample exam questions are available from Lotus Development Corporation, which has offices in major cities across the country.

You're on your own when it comes to preparing for the exam (you can choose self-study or attend classes offered by computer training companies). Trainers are certified on a particular version of Lotus software. Drake Authorized Testing Centers administer the exams. Drake testing centers are located in various spots around the country. For the location of a testing center near you, call 800-755-3926 (800-755-EXAM if you like telephone acronyms). Drake centers aren't affiliated with Lotus. As you read on in this chapter, you'll see that Drake offers tests in all the major software programs.

Once certified by Lotus, you can use their name and logo in your promotional material. You receive a plastic card, like a credit card, that indicates you have been certified.

Because you are certified on a particular version of the program, your certification lasts somewhat indefinitely. However, as new versions come out, you must be retested if you want certification on the new version.

Certified Novell Instructor

Novell, Inc. offers an intensive certification program for its networking instructors. Instructors can specialize in one (or more) of several areas including, but not limited to, administration, installation, and configuration. All instructors must attend Novell-sanctioned classes and pass a series of exams; the exams are determined by the track chosen by the potential instructor. Class time includes some sessions in which the instructor-trainee performs some of the training and is judged on his or her performance.

Once certified, you can use Novell's name and logo in your advertising material. You can also teach at Novell's authorized training centers.

Novell offers a recertification program for certified instructors when new versions of the software are created.

Microsoft Certified Trainer

Before you begin thinking about becoming a Microsoft Certified Trainer, you should know that the certification is only available to trainers who intend to deliver Microsoft official curriculum through Microsoft-authorized education sites. Start by finding a Microsoft-authorized education site (they are in the Yellow Pages of your phone book under *Computer Training*; you can get names of authorized sites by calling Microsoft at 800-426-9400).

You are required to attend any course you expect to teach at the authorized site and pass a certification exam (sometimes there is more than one exam for certification in a particular course) offered through Drake

Prometric. You must purchase a Microsoft Certified Trainer Information Kit from Microsoft (call the number in the preceding paragraph for more information). You are also expected to demonstrate your training skills at the authorized training site before receiving certification. Exam preparation guides are available through Drake as well as from Microsoft.

Certified Technical Trainer

The Certified Technical Trainer (CTT) program provides a credential recognized worldwide to designate proficient technical trainers. Educational Testing Service (ETS) is developing this cross-industry program, available in November 1995. The software industry sponsors and supports CTT. To be certified, you must take a knowledge test and a performance test.

Needs of the Independent Trainer

Unlike the staff trainer at a company, the independent trainer has special needs that include keeping skills honed, finding students to teach, having a place to teach, having up-to-date computers and software on which to teach, and acquiring training materials. The independent trainer also has marketing and promotional needs. No one is going to take care of these needs for you: As you progress in the field of computer training, these needs become your responsibilities.

Skills

The independent trainer is responsible for maintaining a current skill level. When students come to your class, they have the right to make the assumption that you will teach from the latest version of the software and that you will have skills of an advanced level—even if you're teaching an introductory level course.

Students should feel comfortable asking questions at a level beyond the course material and should feel confident that you are capable of answering those questions.

Maintain your skills by reading books and articles about the program(s) you teach, by studying and experimenting with the software, by using the software you teach, and by taking courses yourself.

Experience

The more you train, the more you learn about training as well as about the subject matter you teach. You'll find your expertise increasing with each class you teach because every class is different. Classes are made up of different people with different backgrounds, different levels of education, and different needs.

As you listen to the questions asked by your students and notice how well they absorb the material you teach, you will mold your presentation to fit the needs of your students.

Classroom Facility

As an independent trainer, you may be faced with having to find a venue for your training. If you don't have your own training site, you may be able to rent a room from a variety of sources.

You can find rooms equipped for training at the following locations:

- Computer stores
- Corporations
- State licensing agencies
- Temporary agencies
- Computer training centers

If you don't need a room with computers but instead need just an overhead display and a place to plug in your own computer, you can be much more flexible in choosing a site. Hotel conference rooms, meeting halls, public buildings, auditoriums, and many other locations become available for you.

You should always make arrangements well in advance of your training so that you can lock in a date.

Equipment

Finding a training room with computers already in place may be easier than finding an empty training room and filling the room with computers, but it's possible to overcome obstacles like computerless training rooms. Search through the Yellow Pages for used-computer dealers and computer-equipment rental companies. Contact computer manufacturers to find out whether they would be willing to equip a training room for you, perhaps in exchange for some publicity. Consider purchasing equipment if your budget permits.

In addition to hardware, you have to acquire the latest versions of the software on which you are training. Don't skimp in this area. It's much more appropriate to teach from the latest version of the software, pointing out the features that have changed since earlier versions, than it is to teach from an old version and attempt to explain the new features that would be available if the new version was loaded on the machines.

Even if your students have an older version of the software at their jobs, it's generally safe to assume that their company will upgrade to the newer version in the future. The exception is a situation in which you have had a specific request to teach from an older version of the software.

Our Stories

Everyone who becomes a computer trainer, it seems, has a story to share. Those of us who wrote this book didn't start out with this profession in mind. Instead, our professions *evolved* and grew from other careers, just as your place in this profession is growing now. Following are some of our stories.

Paul Clothier

My first introduction to computer training came 12 years ago when an instructor at a local college said, "Paul, can you teach a DOS class next month?" I was an ex-high school teacher from England, living in Tahoe, who needed an extra $100 for new skis. "Yes, sure I can—no problem!"

I spent the next week studying the manual. The first thing I wanted to do was to figure out what a DOS was. After I had worked that out, I set about trying to find someone who had a computer and where I could get some hands-on experience. Three weeks later, after immersing myself in DOS till 2 A.M. every night, I faced a class with my new-found knowledge. Many of the students struggled to understand my DOS fundamentals, even though I repeated my "explanations" several times. I assumed they had given me one of the "slower" classes.

The next day, the director of education called me into her office and handed me a stack of evaluations from my DOS class. I read them solemnly. Tactfully, she explained that they were the worst evaluations she had seen in a long time. "We need to do something about these," she said. I think she used the word *we* to soften the blow. Not being one to take defeat easily, I spent the next week rereading the comments on my evaluations and trying to figure out what went wrong. I began to realize that computer training was more than just "explaining things." There were *people* out there.

Not long after, I bought my first PC clone with a huge 20M hard drive and headed down the road to nerd-dom. Still numb from my first evaluations, I became committed to two things: learning more about software and improving my training. Twelve years later, I find my commitments haven't changed much. Fortunately, the evaluations have.

Bill Brandon

My experience as an "end user" of computers started in 1964 with an IBM 1620-IID and Fortran. Although I continued to use computers in part of my work, by 1968, I was also teaching occupational skills to firefighting crews, welders, mechanics, and equipment operators. Over the next 10 years, this scope shifted to emphasize management and supervision skills. During this same period, I supplemented my Bachelor's in History with post-graduate work in Human Behavior. These experiences—successes and failures alike—helped me understand how to create and deliver instruction for adults in the workplace.

Computers became increasingly common in the workplace in the early 80s. It seemed to me that teaching employees to actually use their PCs was a very low priority in most companies. It was as difficult to find experienced instructors who knew anything about computers as it was to find power computer users who could teach. To help fill the gap, I began teaching people to use MS-DOS, dBASE, VisiCalc, WordStar, and DisplayWrite in 1984 or 1985. There was nothing special about this decision—it was simply an extension of what I had been doing for the previous 17 years. By 1987, I had started my own company, Accomplishment Technology Unlimited; I developed courseware, taught classes, spoke at conferences, did consulting, and wrote custom computer programs. About the same time, Elliott Masie asked me to become the System Operator for the Computer Training forum on CompuServe, where you can still find me every day.

There seems to be plenty of work to do in the computer training field for the foreseeable future, to say the least. I especially enjoy helping trainers discover and apply critical instructional technology. It is my hope that readers of this book will enjoy long and prosperous careers teaching people to use computers!

Carolyn Woodie

More than 16 years ago, before the advent of the PC, I first used a dedicated word processor and it was love at first keystroke! I was thrilled to be able to type, make corrections on the screen, save my work to edit later, and even print multiple copies. I jokingly told my husband that I wanted one of those $10,000 units for home. Little did I imagine that a few short years later, PCs would be available and I would have my word processor and much, much more. Because of my interest, I was often called on to train new employees or troubleshoot people's problems.

After PCs became available, I began a consulting business, helping small businesses select their software, shop for their hardware, and then train the staff. Back then, there were few good computer software training courses available and even less available on computer training methods. I received much of my classroom training experience

(continues)

(continued)

teaching advanced word processing courses to corporations through five different local community colleges. My computer knowledge has been gleaned through hours of working through the manuals and books. Over the years, I have taken computer training methodology courses through the WordPerfect Corporation and Computer Training and Support Conferences. Computer training has changed a great deal over the years. In the early years, people required a lot of "hand-holding" because they were almost fearful of the new technology. Today, so many people have home computers that we are teaching much more in a shorter period of time. It is still an exciting, fast-paced field and I continue to enjoy helping people discover new things they can do with their computers and software.

Peggy Maday

I don't think anyone really says, "I think I will be a computer software trainer when I grow up," but somehow many of us have ended up doing just that. I started my professional career as an accountant working in a large, computerized accounting department back in Dakota City, Nebraska. When I moved to Denver in 1974, I found it very easy to find a job primarily because of my experience in computerized accounting systems.

I spent seven years in the oil and gas accounting world before the decline in the industry forced me into several layoffs. My resume showed four different jobs over a two-year period. On the positive side, I had a wealth of experience and had been involved in setting up and creating several accounting systems. I had even played a major role in the design of a manual for a computer accounting system. I decided to take this show on the road and began consulting as an oil and gas accountant. I spent two or three years working as an accounting consultant.

This happened to be the same time that the IBM PC came on the market. I taught myself to use the PC and used the first version of Lotus 1-2-3 as a tool in my consulting business. Before I knew it, several clients were asking how I created my various reports and documents. They were impressed with the level of detail I was providing and wanted to be able to do the same. I was spending more time showing them how I created a report in Lotus than I was in providing accounting services. From there, I began teaching my clients basic PC skills, Lotus 1-2-3, and WordStar.

To refine my skills, I took a job with a small firm as a trainer for their custom oil and gas accounting package. I taught our small clients how to use a PC, basic word processing, and spreadsheets; I also taught them how to set up and operate their accounting package. After two years as an employee, I left and started my own software training company. That was in 1985—I have been a computer software trainer ever since.

Garry Slobodian

While in university during the 1970s, I studied both mathematics and computer science. My aim was to teach high school mathematics. I liked computing, but it wasn't my first love. After I completed my Science degree, I began work on my Education degree, taking as many computer science teaching courses as possible.

I taught junior high mathematics and science for four years. They were fun years, and I enjoyed them immensely. In 1979, our school got a grant to purchase one personal computer for our handicapped students. Because I was the only teacher with any computing background, I became the technical resource for the project. I spent my lunch hours and prep periods typing lines of BASIC code into the machine and storing the programs on its cassette-tape recorder storage device.

I was one of the first to learn that the magnetic field from the monitor erased the tapes if the recorder was placed on the right side of the machine!

In 1980, a university friend called me about a computer training job opening up at his company. They were looking for someone with teaching experience and a computer background to train new mainframe programmers and end users. Although I regretted leaving the school system, I took the job.

Hundreds of computer users haven't been the same since!

Shirley Copeland

Many years ago, I took a respite from a regular job and worked as a temporary. It seemed that each time I took a new assignment, I had to learn a new word processing program or spreadsheet program. These assignments afforded me numerous opportunities to improve my knowledge of computers and their capabilities. I also learned about computers when I had to decipher programming codes and error messages when writing documentation for mainframe systems. I've never taken a formal computer class—instead, I've relied on the computer manuals (*ugh!*) and trial and error.

Eventually, more of my assignments involved technical writing and training. I began teaching computer classes at a community college and contracted courses for the federal government. I also taught classes individually to executives and others who preferred to learn in the privacy of their offices or homes. After I had written numerous documentation and training manuals and trained many computer users, I decided to take formal courses in instructional design and development, which culminated in a doctoral degree in Adult and Continuing Education. Currently, I provide training and consulting services in curriculum design and development. I develop computer training courses, primarily for complex, specialized systems; write user-friendly documentation and training manuals; and help define user requirements for systems.

Gail Perry

I took some computer courses in college (back in the dark ages of punch-cards), and even tutored in a Computer Logic course, so I had some interest in computers and some related skills when I came out of college as an accountant in the early 1970s. At my jobs during the '70s and '80s, whenever there was a computer around, I would futz with it in my spare time and figure out ways to use it in my work. People quickly realized that I could figure things out about these strange machines and started coming to me with questions.

In the mid-1980s, this all came together when my boss at the CPA firm where I worked asked me if I would be willing to put together some brown-bag lunch seminars, demonstrating computer techniques to others in the office. We tried it, and it seemed to work. A couple of years and many brown bags later, I was teaching full-day classes to the other accountants in the firm. Pretty soon, a need for training for our clients was recognized and I started putting together classes and promoting them to our clients with a newsletter and a formal training calendar. Now I train for the Indiana CPA Society and customize classes for a number of Indiana corporations.

From Here...

Once you've made a commitment to embark on this new profession and are convinced you're ready to unleash your training skills on unsuspecting students, you're ready to dive into some chapters that cover the nuts and bolts of the actual training:

- Before the class starts, you must have the class material. Take a look at Chapter 7, "Course Development," for pointers on acquisition and preparation of class material.

- Open the classroom door and in you go—but not before picking up crucial information about how to train adult learners in Chapter 3, "Adult Learning: What Do We Know for Sure?"

- Who will you encounter in your classroom? Get prepared to meet your students ahead of time with the "Skills Assessment" methods presented in Chapter 5.

- How are you going to teach this class? Take a look at some innovative "Training Techniques" in Chapter 8.

- And don't forget to read Chapter 10, "The Flow of the Class," to give you some insights on how you can control the direction in which your class moves.

Chapter 3

Adult Learning: What Do We Know for Sure?

by Ron & Susan Zemke

Ron Zemke, *author of many training-related books and articles, is senior editor of* TRAINING *magazine and a consultant in Minneapolis.*

Susan Zemke *is manager of management and professional development for St. Paul Fire and Marine Insurance Co. in St. Paul, MN.*

However you care to define it, learning is as natural to human beings as breathing, eating, sleeping, playing, or procreating. And as far as anyone can tell, we maintain that natural capacity as long as any of the others. For the last century and a half or so, educators and psychologists have tried to develop ways to deliver instruction, practice, and experience that enhance this innate capacity to learn.

For the last 20 to 75 years, depending on who's doing the counting, an evolving school of thought has defined adult learners (as opposed to children, adolescents, college sophomores, and lab rats) as a unique subgroup in need of specialized study, theory, and educational practices.

Adult-learning theory emerged from the academic backwaters in 1973 with the publication of Malcolm Knowles' highly readable book, *The Adult Learner: A Neglected Species*. Knowles, then a Boston University professor, scored an instant hit with adult educators and trainers. In *The*

Adult Learner, he dusted off the word *andragogy*, a term popular in German education circles in the early 1800s, and used it to label his attempt to create a unified theory of adult learning. Knowles' contentions were based on four assumptions:

- As they mature, adults tend to prefer self-direction.

- Adults' experiences are a rich resource for learning. Adults learn more effectively through experiential techniques such as discussion or problem-solving than they do through, say, passive listening.

- Adults are aware of specific learning needs generated by real-life events such as marriage, divorce, taking a new job, losing a job, and so on.

- Adults are *competency-based learners*, meaning that they want to learn a skill or acquire knowledge that they can apply pragmatically to their immediate circumstances.

The concept of andragogy generated a flurry of debate and study. Today, andragogy is considered something less than the all-encompassing explanation of adult learning Knowles had hoped it would be. Knowles himself later acknowledged that pedagogy and andragogy probably represent the ends of a spectrum that ranges from teacher-directed to student-directed learning. Both approaches, he and others now suggest, are appropriate with children *and* adults, depending on the situation.

Sharan B. Merriam, a professor of adult education at the University of Georgia, summarizes the current state of adult-learning theory this way:

It is doubtful that a phenomenon as complex as adult learning will ever be explained by a single theory, model, or set of principles. Instead, we have a case of the proverbial elephant being described differently depending on who is talking and on which part of the animal is examined. In the first half of this century, psychologists took the lead in explaining learning behavior; from the 1960s onward, adult educators began formulating their own ideas about adult learning and, in particular, about how it might differ from learning in childhood. Both of these approaches are still operative. Where we are headed, it seems, is toward a multifaceted understanding of adult learning, reflecting the inherent richness and complexity of the phenomenon.

Fourteen years ago, in the June 1981 issue of *TRAINING*, we published a review of adult-learning theory and research entitled, "20 Things We Know for Sure about Adult Learning." We recently revisited the information pile from which we culled that article. We then added more than 300 new references to the stack and asked ourselves, "Has anything changed?"

As far as solid, reliable information goes, most of what the literature has to tell us today is what it told us then. But although we haven't seen the equivalent of the dramatic changes wrought by Knowles and the andragogy movement in the early 1970s, some important differences in nuance and understanding have occurred that add to our knowledge of the training craft.

As in our previous synthesis, we have divided what we garnered from our scan into three basic categories:

1. Things we know about adult learners and their motivation.

2. Things we know about designing curricula for adults.

3. Things we know about working with adults in the classroom.

The same caution applies now as did then: These categories are neither definitive nor exclusive. They overlap more than a little. But they help us understand the implications that current theory and research hold for our day-to-day work in training and development.

3

Motivation To Learn

Adults can be ordered into a classroom and prodded into seats, but they can't be forced to learn. On the other hand, adults who see a need or have a desire to know something new are quite resourceful. Witness the legions of gainfully employed people enrolled in continuing education programs at community colleges, vo-techs, and universities around the world, not to mention the success of proprietary self-development seminars, sports-skills camps, and independent study groups in virtually every industrial and postindustrial country.

When the conditions are right, adults seek out and demand learning experiences. Much of what we know about adult motivation to learn describes those conditions and comes from the work of Allen Tough, Carol Aslanian, Henry Brickell, and others engaged in the study of self-directed learning. The key to using adults' "natural" motivation to learn is tapping into their most *teachable moments*: those points in their lives at which they believe they need to learn something new or different.

For example, several longitudinal studies in corporations have demonstrated that newly promoted supervisors and managers should be trained as quickly as possible. The longer such training is delayed, the less impact it appears to have on job performance.

In short, there is a window of opportunity during which adults are most receptive to learning—and a time after which they cannot be enticed with a chateaubriand or a baseball bat.

The idea of a window of opportunity applies not only to people's motivation to learn, but also to their ability to retain what they *do* learn. If trainees begin to acquire a new skill but then have no opportunity to practice it, the skill quickly fades. Information-technology trainers have been reporting that training on a new software package or upgraded hardware configuration loses its effectiveness unless the equipment or software is installed and ready to use. The longer the group has to wait for the new system, the less impact the training has on effective use. This is a reconfirmation of an old lesson: Use it or lose it.

Adult Learning Is Problem Centered

People do learn for the sake of learning: Hobbyists go to model-train conventions and take archery classes, retirees take golf and tennis lessons, and lots of people join book clubs. None of that is job-related or "problem"-related. But more often than not, adults seek out learning experiences to cope with life-changing events. Marriage, divorce, a new job, a promotion, being fired, retirement, death of a loved one—these sorts of occurrences often create a perceived need to learn.

The more life-changing events adults face, the more likely they are to seek out related learning experiences. In fact, learning may be a coping response to significant life changes for many people: some knit, some drink, some go to school. People who are highly educated are more likely to seek out learning opportunities as opposed to other coping options.

The impulse to go learn something in response to a life-changing event is to some extent generic: The subject the person suddenly desires to learn about won't always pertain directly to the change that sparked the desire. Witness the divorcee who signs up for a course in art history. Predictably, however, adults usually seek out and respond best to learning experiences they perceive as directly addressing the changes that face them. If a change is primarily work-related, a learner will be more motivated if the learning event is primarily work-related.

Adults are generally willing to engage in learning experiences before, after, or even during the life-changing event. Once convinced that the change is a certainty, they will engage in any learning that promises to help them through the transition, including seminars on coping with change.

Adult Learners Are Motivated by Appeals to Personal Growth or Gain

Although immediate utility is most often the motivation behind adults' learning efforts, it's not the only motivation. For instance, some evidence suggests that adults more readily engage in job-skills training if they see it as relevant to the rest of their lives as well. Adult learners also can be motivated by the promise of increasing or maintaining their sense of self-esteem or pleasure. Developing a new skill or expanding current knowledge can do both, depending on the individual's perceptions.

A newer subfield of adult learning, sometimes referred to as *feminist pedagogy*, suggests that emancipation from domination is a strong motivator. Although most of the research in this area is related to feminist issues, the idea may have wider scope. You could argue that line employees who are enthusiastic about team training and participation techniques are motivated, in part, because they anticipate being liberated from management dominance in the workplace.

Motivation To Learn Can Be Increased

3

Although it may be true that "the best motivation is self-motivation," some evidence suggests that adult learners who are with you in body but not in spirit can be led into participating and learning. If you can stimulate curiosity about the subject matter, demonstrate early on that the learning will be immediately useful, and ensure low risk for learners, you can convert some of the uncaring. Sometimes, simply exploring learners' positive and negative expectations can clear the air and increase participation.

Curriculum Design

Knowles cautions that adults confronted with a classroom and 30 chairs facing forward know exactly how to act: like bored 12-year-olds. Twelve to 18 years of pedagogic conditioning can do that to you. But the warning is important for designers of adult-learning experiences. If you think that those 30 forward-facing chairs represent the optimum learning environment, don't be surprised if you end up with bored compliance. The most dramatic alternative is self-directed curriculum design (see the sidebar at the end of this chapter), but adult-learning theory offers clues for corporate curriculum design as well.

The Learning Experience Should Be Problem Centered

Working adults are likely to be less enthralled by survey courses than are full-time, professional students. Adults tend to prefer single-concept, single-theory courses that focus on applying the concept to relevant problems. This tendency increases with age. The learning experience should acknowledge and be relevant to the learner's personal goals for the program.

Preprogram Assessment Is Important

It is almost unconscionable to design a program that doesn't take into account the entry-level knowledge and understanding of participants. To begin a team-building experience or diversity seminar without assessing where individuals stand on critical issues, without ferreting out information on the state of relationships in the company, or without clearly defining management's goals for the training borders on malpractice.

The Learning Design Should Promote Information Integration

To remember and use new information, adults need to be able to integrate it with what they already know. Information that conflicts sharply with what they already hold to be true, and thus forces them to re-evaluate the old material, is integrated more slowly. Information that has little conceptual overlap with what they already know also is acquired more slowly. Fast-paced, complex, or unusual learning exercises interfere with the learning of concepts or data they are intended to teach if the new information is too "foreign" to participants.

Adults tend to want a structure to help them keep track of details and facts in relation to one another. One school of thought suggests that adults have "personal maps of reality" in their heads that they use to organize information and experiences. Instruction should help the learner place new information on that "map."

Information conveyed through storytelling is more than entertaining; evidence suggests that it is more easily integrated with existing knowledge. Well "storied" information has a sort of learning adhesive that makes it stick to previous learning and experience.

To help learners organize and integrate information, present one idea at a time. Summarize frequently to facilitate retention and recall. And pace the training so that learners can master one element before moving on to the next.

Exercises and Cases Should Have Fidelity

Adults are not enthusiastic about far-fetched cases and artificial exercises. They prefer activities that are realistic and involving, that stimulate thinking, and that have some (but not too much) challenge. Adults evaluate exercises and games quickly and decide whether they are entertaining, useful, or just plain silly.

The term *praxis*, a Greek word meaning "exercise or practice of an art, science, or skill," has begun to appear in adult-learning literature to describe exercises and activities. The concept acknowledges that although adults prefer active to passive learning (meaning that they like exercises, cases, games, and simulations), the activity must contain a reflective element if learning (or change) is to occur. The literature enthusiastically endorses interactive computer simulations and games as high-fidelity learning experiences, although it holds little data that evaluate these methods.

Feedback and Recognition Should Be Planned

3

Learners need to know what they are trying to accomplish and how they are doing. The program design should include time to explore participants' goals and expectations, to acknowledge those that will not be met, and to discuss both participants' and trainers' responsibilities during the training.

Adults tend to take errors personally and to let them affect their self-esteem. Therefore, they're liable to stick to tried-and-true solutions and take few risks. Adults will even misinterpret feedback that corrects errors as positive confirmation. If you plan to ask participants to give each other feedback, demonstrate beforehand how to give effective feedback.

Curriculum Design Should Account for Learning-Style Differences

If we've learned anything from all the attention paid to the Myers-Biggs Type Instrument, DISC, and Neurolinguistics Programming in the last decade, it is that adults have learning-style differences and that your design should accommodate them, where possible. (For more on adjusting to learning-style differences, see "Different Strokes: Learning Styles in the Classroom," *TRAINING*, March 1995.)

Do not, by the way, assume that all instruction must take place in a classroom/seminar/workshop. Although most adults learn well when they have an opportunity to share their life experiences and actively contribute to the learning effort, plenty of people also learn well from nonhuman media. Tough and others have found that adults planning self-directed learning projects routinely include books, television, computer-based training, and other solitary media.

Regardless of media and learning style, most adults prefer straight-forward, how-to content. As many as 80 percent of the polled adults in one study cited the need to learn applications and how-to information as their primary motivation for involving themselves in a learning project, self-directed or otherwise.

Design Should Accommodate Adults' Continued Growth and Changing Values

Although it is not as hot a topic in literature as it once was, the idea that adults go through developmental stages just as young children and adolescents do is still with us. Not only do adults' needs and interests continually change, so do their values. A seminar group composed of new college recruits and one composed of 50-year-olds can be quite different. The trainer must take into account the life stages and values of the participants. In an orientation course for new employees, for instance, recent college grads might require not just indoctrination into the company's culture but some background information about the business world in general. With the 50-year-olds, the trainer may more safely assume that they have such background knowledge.

Equally important to curriculum designers is whether concepts are in concert or conflict with the organizational and personal values learners accept as valid. A company attempting to move from, say, a low-profile, reactive market strategy to an aggressive, high-visibility stance will likely encounter significant resistance from employees schooled in the "old way." Changing an organization's values dramatically requires more than new brochures and a few buckets of paint. Changing people's long-held values takes careful, planned intervention. New or radically different ways must be explained repeatedly and in different ways before they will be understood and accepted.

Designing Transfer Strategies

More often than we care to admit, the training was a smash hit with the participants but the performance problem didn't go away. And more often than not, the fault lies in a training design that stops at the classroom door. Adults engage in workplace-learning activities for a productive end. The training is supposed to "transfer" to the real work environment; something is supposed to change back on the job. Failure to design transfer activities into the training breaks the implicit contract between trainer and trainee.

Transfer strategies include pre-training and post-training activities, as well as discussions during training that focus on using the new knowledge or skills back on the job. Proven pre-training strategies such as self-assessments, discussions with supervisors that define expectations, and pre-classwork such as reading or data-gathering set the stage for effective transfer of training. Successful post-instruction strategies include application discussions with supervisors, refresher training, and support group meetings for graduates of the training.

In the Classroom

Before the Knowles era of adult-learning theory, most of the research in adult education focused on teacher behavior. So it is ironic that we still know so little about effective classroom facilitation techniques. Yes, tomes have been written on the subject, but most of what is presented as "proven" is simply a compost of tricks, tips, and theory passed on from master performers to their acolytes.

The problem with that approach to accumulating wisdom is that it usually takes an objective observer to distill the essence of how to become a master performer. As communications guru Marshall McLuhan put it, "We don't know who discovered water, but we can be pretty sure it wasn't a fish."

Still, it is possible to piece together the common threads that run through all this advice and to suggest some useful guidelines.

Create a Safe and Comfortable Environment

If you've ever walked into a dark hotel meeting room the morning after a late-night party and wondered how in the heck you are going to turn this into a learning environment, you know the importance of staging. Both the physical and psychological environment must be managed. Light, sound, heat, cold, supplies, and amenities must be conducive to thought, focus, and serious discourse. Participants need a mix of known and unknown, active and passive, serious and whimsical to keep them involved at an optimum level.

Facilitation Is More Effective than Lecture

Straight lecture is effective when trainees have zero grounding in the subject matter, when rules and regulations have to be passed along, and when matters of finance, fact, or law are the subject of the training. But facilitation tends to work better to engage learners in setting objectives, to tap into learners' experience and opinions to create parts of the content, and to help participants reach consensus.

What constitutes good facilitation? Although there are myriad views, most agree that a good facilitator does the following:

- Establishes goals and clarifies expectations (both the facilitator's and the participants').

- Gives up the need to hold forth and be in control.

- Uses questioning techniques to provoke thinking, stimulate recall, challenge beliefs, confront opinions, draw implications, and promote conclusions.

- Understands that adults have something real to lose in a classroom. Their egos are on the line when they are asked to risk trying a new behavior in front of peers.

- Balances the many factors that make up a learning event: presentation of new material, debate, discussion, and sharing of relevant trainee experiences. And does all this within the allotted time.

- Develops a learning environment that draws on participants' experiences, protects minority opinion, keeps disagreements civil, makes connections among various opinions and ideas, and reminds the group of the variety of possible solutions to the problem.

- Uses descriptive feedback and reinforces participants for their contributions and accomplishments.

Actively Promote Understanding and Retention

In some ways, this is as simple as recognizing that most adults aren't used to sitting passively for long stretches. Without activity, they turn into mushrooms before your eyes. But there is more to it than that. Despite (and frequently because of) the presence of an instructor/authority figure, many participants are reluctant to share ideas, feelings, confusion, and annoyance with the group. Techniques such as breaking participants into small groups increase the chance that the reticent will contribute and collaborate.

The opportunity to exercise new skills in the relative safety of the training room is critical. Frequently, participants are hesitant to try out new and untested skills in front of others. Using small praxis teams that practice, reflect, and try again can overcome the reluctance to risk.

Helping adults acquire new skills and knowledge is an exhilarating, irritating, challenging, and frustrating way to make a living. It takes patience, forbearance, flexibility, humor, and a strong belief that what you're doing matters. If we keep trying and prodding and testing and trying again, we might yet turn this art form into a science of sorts.

Adults Who Do It Their Way

The developing area of self-directed learning offers plenty of evidence that adults are perfectly capable of acquiring skills, knowledge, and self-insight on their own. They don't necessarily need any experts to design or manage the learning process for them. And when they perceive a need to learn something, they don't stand around waiting for such experts to appear.

In the 1970s, Toronto researcher Allen Tough, a faculty member at the Ontario Institute for Studies in Education, found that typical adults spend 500 or more hours a year engaged in five "learning projects" of their own design. That finding greatly surprised most adult-learning experts, and subsequent research disputes Tough's numbers (one highly regarded study put the figures closer to three learning projects and 150 hours a year). Whatever the "true" numbers may be, adults' status as self-directed learners is well established.

A significant amount of research focuses on the way adults organize their self-directed learning projects. Some researchers contend the process is linear and orderly; some suggest it is more a haphazard, trial-and-error affair. Whatever the case, Malcolm Knowles, Tough, and others have worked out a useful heuristic for making the most of a self-directed learning effort.

Step "zero": You become aware that there is indeed something you need to learn. Let's say you bought a new graphics software package and don't have the foggiest idea how to use it.

Step 1: You identify what you want to learn. Do you want to become a high-tech Van Gogh with that new software or just learn to plop prepackaged cartoons into reports?

Step 2: You diagnose the skill or knowledge you need to achieve the end you have in mind. Think of it as a do-it-yourself needs assessment: You load the graphics program, fiddle with the menus, and see what you can make it do without opening the manual. (You *know* you do.)

Step 3: You develop a plan of inquiry and a list of resources. Translation: Browse the manual, call two people who already use the program, and check the local bookstore for a "Graphics for Idiots" guide.

Step 4: You begin proactive learning. You start to read the manual, you try the program, you fit some graphics into an old report. And when you get stumped, you call people on your list to help you get unstuck.

Step 5: You evaluate whether you have met your learning objectives. The next time you have a report, you try using the package for real.

Step 6: You rediagnose your learning needs and repeat the process. Knowles adds one important caveat to his enthusiasm for self-directed learning: Self-direction is only effective when the learner has some basic level of experience with the content. "Pedagogical methods are appropriate in those cases in which the adult is indeed a dependent learner," he told *TRAINING*. "For example, the person may have no experience

(continues)

(continued)

with a personal computer. The andragogical teacher will have to provide didactic instruction up to the point where the learner has acquired enough information and skill to be able to direct his or her own learning."

According to Tough's research, self-directed learners tend to be eclectic in their choices of media and method. Although adults prefer self-direction 7-to-1 over group-learning experiences led by a professional educator, they will attend lectures and short seminars if these seem the shortest route to the desired destination.

Apparently, the self-directed learner is very efficiency minded. Tough suggests that the typical adult asks, "What is the cheapest, easiest, fastest way for me to learn to do that?" and then proceeds along this self-determined route. An obvious implication for corporate trainers: trainees must have a hand in shaping the curriculum of a program.

Tough's research further suggests that an adult's typical learning project is hardly a solitary affair. He finds that the average self-directed learner enlists 10.6 other people in a given project. Adults engaged in regular self-directed learning projects develop learning networks to help themselves acquire the skills and knowledge they need. In return, they act as learning resources for others.

More evidence of the collaborative tendencies of adult learners comes from a five-year study conducted during the mid-1980s by Honeywell Corp. in Minneapolis. The company found that on-the-job experiences, relationships with others, and formal training accounted for 50 percent, 30 percent, and 20 percent, respectively, of a manager's ability to manage effectively on new assignments. In other words, managers learned more about succeeding in a new position through trial and error and by getting a little help from their friends than from formal training.

People familiar with successful self-directed work teams suggest that acquiring and using learning resources is an important part of a team's discipline. The idea of a group of like-minded adults coming together (unfacilitated) to meet mutual learning goals has a long history. In 1727, Benjamin Franklin created a group he called the *Junto*. It was composed of fellow entrepreneurs who shared the belief that "individuals associated can do more for society, and themselves, than they can in isolation." Franklin's Junto was, in turn, founded on an earlier form, the Friendly Societies, developed in England by writer Daniel Defoe.

In the 1990s, encouraged by the recent "learning organization" rhetoric, several corporations have experimented with the idea of making space and resources available for groups of employees to design and conduct their own ongoing learning without the intervention of a trainer or manager.

From Here...

The themes and issues of adult learning are woven throughout this book—and apply to trainers and learners alike. Trainers are learners, too. To continue your exploration about adult learners, refer to these chapters:

- Chapter 8, "Training Techniques," explains how you can adjust your method of training to appeal to adults.

- Chapter 10, "The Flow of the Class," provides pointers you can use or adapt to help make your training sessions smoother—even when you have an adult version of a troublesome student.

- Chapter 12, "Distance Learning on the World Wide Web," helps you set up a long-distance connection between your students and yourself. The tips you find here are especially appropriate for self-motivated adult learners.

3

Part II

Before and After the Class

Chapter 4

Training Needs Assessment

by Garry Slobodian

*Garry Slobodian, a training professional since 1977, develops custom
training programs to help companies implement computer systems. He holds
Bachelor's degrees in Science and Education, and a Certificate in Adult Education. Garry currently is working on a Master's in Continuing Education,
specializing in learning in the workplace.*

Too many training projects begin without a clear understanding of the
need for the program. Trainers often don't understand who needs the
training and what those people need to learn. Instead of finding out, we
make some assumptions and plunge right in to create the program.
When the program fails and we are beat up for the poor results, we wonder why everyone is against us.

I like to think of a training needs assessment as the creation of a fence
around the training need. The assessment defines what training is to be
included in the project and what is to be excluded. The assessment also
answers some of the basic questions about the project, such as who needs
training, what those people need to learn, when they need to learn it,
and what methods are best for providing the training.

Identify the Business Problem

A training needs assessment investigates the business need for the training program. It identifies what the business problem is and why training
is the best solution. Often, several other possible solutions should be considered before a training project commences.

Here are some sample business problems you may be asked to assess because they have a potential training need:

- Your organization will acquire a new computer system that is unfamiliar to the staff. The system will run new hardware on a different platform. It will use new software to run new business application packages.

- The productivity of your sales force is declining. Management decides to give the salespeople portable computers to improve their prospecting of customers, to enable them to create sales illustrations in the field, and to expedite the collection of order data.

- Increasing business volumes are putting pressure on your existing warehouse inventory system. The computers in your retail outlets will be linked with a new expert system to control inventory stock and place orders with your suppliers.

- The volume of telephone inquiries to your organization has skyrocketed, and customer service measures are plummeting. A hypertext-based customer inquiry support system will replace the printed service manuals now being used.

- Your company has acquired a smaller competitor. Its computer operations will be taken over by your operations, so the staff in the smaller company must learn how to use your systems.

Examine Alternative Solutions to the Business Problem

Sometimes, training isn't the solution to the business problem. Teaching people to use antiquated equipment and outdated software does not improve a productivity problem.

In these situations, I try to disprove the need for training. I play the role of devil's advocate and argue with the program sponsor that training is not needed. Of course, the sponsor attempts to prove that training *is* the best solution. Often, this means we carefully consider all the alternative solutions to the problem and develop a solid business case for training.

Following are some of the possible solutions to business problems, other than training:

- **Change the supervisory approach.** Performance problems may exist because people don't understand what is expected of them. The solution may be to set clear standards, make them known throughout the organization, and reward people who meet the standards.

- **Change the computing environment.** People may become more productive if the organization changes the operating software, improves the software interface, and replaces the hardware. Training them to use the existing computing environment may not improve their productivity.

- **Provide documentation, online help, electronic demos, wizards, and electronic performance support.** Sometimes, a computer system is so complex that no one can be trained to operate it well. Some features are used so infrequently that it is impossible to maintain skill in them. A better solution is to provide reference materials that users can consult when needed.

- **Provide job aids.** Some computer operations require more procedures than can be reasonably remembered. Rather than training people to remember all the details, supplying job aids that list the key steps is cheaper and more effective.

- **Provide a support network from departmental experts.** A network of user support people throughout the departments permits people to get help locally for their software questions. This arrangement relieves the need to train everyone about every potentiality.

- **Provide appropriate help desk support.** Similarly, user support that is a telephone call away is more effective than training everyone. The help desk can develop people's skills in advanced techniques like sophisticated spreadsheet macros better than sending users to training that is too basic. A 15-minute help desk session can teach a skill needed *now* more effectively than going to an 8-hour course next week that teaches a dozen other unneeded techniques.

- **Provide time to learn independently.** Many veteran computer users do not need training to learn new software. They understand what they want to do with the software and are familiar with the general principles under which the software operates. They are also motivated to solve their own difficulties and to operate independently. Strong self-learners do better if they are allowed time to read the manual and experiment with the new software.

Of course, sometimes the solution to the business problem is that you must train people. The rest of this chapter assumes that training is needed to solve the business problem.

Define the Goals for the Training Project

At its most basic, needs assessment answers these six *W* questions:

- Why is training needed?

- Who must be trained?

- What do they need to learn?

- What's the best way to teach them?

- When do they need to learn it?

- Where do they need to learn it?

If you can get answers to these questions, you have a good overall understanding of the training required. You also have a clear strategy for the development and delivery of the training program.

Identify the Training Gap

One of the six *W* questions is, "What do people need to learn?" This is a key area of investigation in needs assessment (and the main area of investigation for skills assessment, a topic presented in Chapter 5, "Skills Assessment").

To identify what people need to learn, you must understand each part of this equation:

$$\text{Desired knowledge and skill} - \text{Current knowledge and skill} = \text{What must be learned}$$

You must identify what knowledge and skill people must have to do their jobs and solve the business problem facing them. State these requirements in broad terms. Here are some examples:

- The programmers must use Visual Basic to create graphical user interfaces from the designs given to them by the analysts.

- The secretarial staff must be able to use the mail-merge feature to produce form letters.

- System administrators must be able to restore the network from backups when the network fails.

Notice that these statements do not describe all the procedures and all the concepts needed to perform these tasks. That information comes in the skills assessment phase.

You must also identify what people already know about the tasks they are to learn. For example, do the programmers know how to create a GUI with other tools? Do they know what a radio button is?

It is often helpful to record your findings in a table. Tables are an easy way to see the differences between the two columns and to identify what skills and concepts the group being studied requires. Here's a sample table:

What They Need To Know	What They Already Know	What They Must Learn
Create a GUI with Visual Basic	What a GUI is	How to use Visual Basic to create the component
	What the components of a GUI are	
	How the components operate	

Why Trainers Must Conduct Needs Assessments

When I was a boy, my dad would take me and my brother, Doug, out on the Canadian prairie to learn how to shoot a rifle. Dad was no outdoorsman. In fact, his idea of being in the outdoors was to mow the lawn around our house in Winnipeg. Instead, he believed that learning how to shoot was just another important thing a youngster should know, like how to rotate your tires, how to play an instrument, and how to balance your checkbook.

I was never much of a threat to the gophers at my uncle's farm in central Manitoba, because I never got to be much of a sharpshooter. But I did learn two important lessons: I learned how to handle a firearm safely and I learned that "ready, fire, aim" is a foolish approach for target shooting.

Thirty years later, Dad's advice still applies to my work in training people to use computers. The "ready, teach, plan" approach is just as foolish as "ready, shoot, aim." Yet, we often rush into that trap. We get an assignment to teach some group something, and we rush out to teach them. We don't take the time to find out what the group needs and plan how best to teach them.

We must assess the training needs before we proceed to the development stage of training.

Get the Entire Picture about the Business Problem

For any business problem, training is never the complete solution. Other tactics—in addition to training—may be needed to solve the problem.

You may produce the greatest training program the world has ever seen. It will fail if you do not couple it with other approaches to ensure that the students can and *do* use their new skills on the job.

In addition to training, consider using some of the alternative solutions to the business problems mentioned earlier in this chapter. To make the training really stick, you may be wise to provide a job aid or arrange a support network, too.

You must understand all the factors causing the business problem before you can establish a strategy for the training effort. Simply developing the world's greatest training program will not solve the problem.

Produce a Strategy for the Training Effort

Delivering a training program is just one part of a complete strategy for solving the business problem. Your strategy must also consider several other factors, such as these:

- **When will the training occur?** Determine what lead time is required for orientation, education, training, and practice.

- **How will it be announced?** If the change in technology is a major initiative, plan a commensurate advertising campaign for the training program. Be sure to build sufficient awareness of the need.

- **What resources will be required to conduct the training?** Estimate the capital needed to acquire equipment, facilities, and training materials.

- **What preparations must occur before the training is given?** Determine whether orientation and education must take place to ready the students for training. Describe how the work environment needs to change. Indicate what stage the systems implementation must reach before training can be given.

- **How will supervisors support the training back on the job?** Recommend how much time will be needed by students after the course to practice new skills and to adapt them to their work. Suggest what allowance supervisors should make for reduced productivity immediately after training.

■ **What follow-up will be used to reinforce what is learned in the course?** Recognizing that students will not absorb everything they need to learn during their training, arrange for post-training study groups, follow-up seminars, or FAQ (frequently asked questions) newsletters. Recommend how supervisors might look for changes in job performance and reinforce these changes.

You collect this information during your needs assessment investigations to produce an orchestrated plan for providing the training.

Build Motivation in Students by Inviting Them To Participate in the Assessment

To increase the likelihood that people will share responsibility for the outcome of decisions, we invite them to participate in making the decisions. This principle also applies to assessing training needs.

Harvesting input from those to be trained demonstrates the seriousness of the business problem and the company's determination to solve it. When asked what they need to learn, the staff will realize that the training is being done for their benefit.

Collecting input from those to be trained ensures that you view the business problem *and* the training solution from all perspectives. Although management may believe that training alone can solve the problem, the staff may realize that new job aids are also needed to ensure that the new skills can be easily performed back at the job.

Establish Commitment from Management

Management is more likely to accept your strategy if you carefully examine all sides of the business problem. Looking at all possible solutions and developing a strategy to ensure that the training sticks will raise management's confidence in your solution. Management will understand what the training will solve and what must solved by other means. When you present your training strategy, you should negotiate for the level of management's participation and endorsement before any further work begins. If the training development becomes difficult or if results are not apparent immediately, management will be prepared to weather the difficulties because you took the time to establish their commitment to the plan.

Establish Credibility for Training

Too many computer trainers know lots about computers but know little (and little care to know) about business's problems. The trainers are just other specialists offering something of need at this particular time.

If, instead, you take time to examine all the factors behind the business problem and carefully prepare a strategy for blending the training with other solutions, you show you are interested in the best overall solution for the company. You show you care about solving this business problem and that you are not just providing your particular service.

You become an equal partner in advancing the company's goals. Training becomes a credible and valued company resource. It ceases to be just another piece of overhead.

Questions Trainers Must Answer in a Needs Assessment

Earlier in this chapter, I mentioned that a needs assessment answers six *W* questions. Actually, there are a few more than six questions...but they are all based on these six.

With answers to the following questions, you will have a good understanding of both the business problem and the training required to solve the problem. These questions help you build a fence around the training need so that you can identify what will be included in the scope of the project and what will be excluded.

Who Needs Training?

I always begin by identifying who requires training. I'm a people person, and it helps me to visualize the folks for whom I am doing all this work.

You don't need names or other details yet. You need to know the following generalities about the people for whom the training will be given:

- Job titles and classifications

- Characterization (such as age, education level, experience with technology, and years of company service)

- Attitudes about the new technology being introduced, including willingness to change

When Is Training Needed?

You must clarify when the training is needed. Even if this is a genuine emergency, when—exactly—are you expected to respond to it? Find out what will happen if you can't provide training before the deadline. Determine whether the implementation can be delayed until training is ready to be done right.

Caution

Do not plan to provide training either too soon or too late. Although inventory-control people want you to believe that the abbreviation J.I.T. refers just to keeping things in a warehouse, to me it means Just In Time Training. Training not given just-in-time has limited effect. If provided too soon, people forget what they've learned or they confuse the new procedures with the current ones. If provided too late, people do not have adequate time to practice back at the job before the system goes live and they must operate it for real.

You should allow time for more than one training experience. Sending everyone to one class and hoping that they absorb everything they need is like betting the mortgage on Dragon Fly in the fifth race. It may pay off, but the odds are definitely against you. Instead, plan on attacking the training need a couple of times, using different approaches.

Of course, all this takes time. How much time do you really have?

What Must Students Know To Do Their Jobs?

To identify what students need to know to do their jobs, you perform a high-level task analysis. You identify all the tasks the students will perform with the new technology and you also identify, at a high level, what skills and concepts they must know to perform each task.

Warning! At this stage in the training project, don't go into detail. Task analyses can swallow your time like quicksand. In the next step, you analyze the tasks in detail. For now, herd the needed tasks, skills, and concepts into the fence around the training problem.

When you are finding out what people must know to do the job, don't confuse *wants* and *needs*. People *want* to learn lots of things, from why air exists to how the zebra gets its stripes. Interesting, perhaps, but not of any use when the group *needs* to know how to set up a local area network.

Also note carefully the ascribed needs from the perceived needs from the actual needs. *Ascribed needs* are what other people think the group to be trained needs. *Perceived needs* are what the group to be trained thinks it needs. *Actual needs* are what the group truly needs to do their jobs. These three kinds of needs rarely match. You want to teach only the actual needs.

As you determine what people need to learn, recognize which of these needs the students must learn in the training sessions. Rarely can you meet all their needs in the classroom. Frequently, the training sessions are the starting point for learning; the students will require additional practice and time to assimilate the new ideas. You should also recognize the things that people need to learn *away* from the classroom and create tactics for this learning to occur.

How Well Must People Perform after Training?

You must identify the necessary proficiency level people are to reach after training. You also need to know *how* management will determine whether people are performing at that level.

The training program for NASA's shuttle crews is rigorous and comprehensive because the crews must operate at 100 percent accuracy throughout their flights. There are no allowances for poor performance, and there are no refresher classes 200 miles above Earth.

In some situations, you may be asked to examine the skills of students finishing the course and accredit their abilities. The training program you provide in this case would be quite different from a simple concepts course. It must have enough opportunity for students to practice their new skills so that they can reach full proficiency. Your program must also have enough opportunity for you to observe their performance of the new skills so that you can reliably pronounce them fully skilled.

How Must Instruction Be Conducted?

You need to determine how the program sponsor and the participants expect the training to be conducted. Do they expect traditional classroom training sessions, or are you free to consider using self-study methods? Do they expect you to lecture extensively, or can you use case studies and projects?

Find out whether any training approaches are not acceptable. Find out which approaches usually succeed with the audience and which approaches have failed in previous training projects.

I often recommend a three-tiered instructional approach. First comes *orientation*, in which the participants learn the benefits of the new technology and how it will affect them. Second comes *education*, in which the participants learn the background concepts, terminology, and principles surrounding the new technology. Finally comes *training*, in which people learn and practice the skills and procedures they need to use the new technology.

What Resources Exist for Training?

You must determine what training resources already exist. Try to determine whether you must build the training program from the ground up. It is generally better to adapt existing resources to your purposes rather than re-creating every resource.

Look for existing training facilities and equipment. Search for possible media titles you might be able to use. Determine whether commercial vendors sell courses that remotely pertain to this training need. Identify people who are experts about the topic and who can speak about the benefit of using this technology in this particular situation.

Also look for other resources students can use. Although you don't have to include these in your course designs, these resources can serve as good preparatory or follow-up materials. Books, journal articles, television programs, video conferences, vendors, and the Internet are all good sources of additional materials.

What Follow–Up and Support Is Available?

Estimate how much follow-up and support students can have after the training courses are finished. Typical one-day courses do not prepare people completely to use new technology. It is foolish to expect your courses to make everyone ready for the new technology. It is wiser to plan additional learning activities that reinforce and build on the skills learned in the course.

Here are some follow-up activities you can consider:

- At-work practice using real data in real work situations

- Discussions with supervisors about how the content of the courses will be used on the job

- Seminars with peers to share shortcuts they've discovered and to ask questions about problems they've encountered

- Watching video presentations and reading articles about the content of the courses

- Presentations and demonstrations by expert practitioners to show how they apply the skills at your company

Determine what kind of support will be available for the students after the courses are complete. If reference manuals and help desk personnel are not readily available, your courses cannot scrimp. In these cases, students must be trained thoroughly to know everything they will need and to solve all their own problems. You must allow yourself additional course development time so that you can build a course that contains all the required information.

Of course, all these post-course activities require time. Can you have the time to hold these activities, or must students begin using their new skills immediately after the training classes end? If the classes must prepare students completely, you must design the classes with enough practice opportunities so that people leave ready to work.

How To Plan an Assessment

Like any other important business activity, a good plan can guide you to collect the data you need in your needs assessment. You do not require project management software to plan the work. Three pages of notes should cover all you need to plan.

> **Note**
>
> Most needs assessments I do usually take less than 100 hours of effort to complete—often less than 25 hours of effort. I emphasize *of effort* and not *duration*. I've spent more time waiting for people to give me information than I actually spent harvesting the information from them. Be sure to factor both into your plan.

Discuss your plan with the program sponsor and ask for confirmation. Be certain that you agree on the amount of effort to spend on the assessment and on how you will present your findings. You need the sponsor's backing in both of these areas.

Determine How Much Effort To Spend on Your Needs Assessment

With the program sponsor, determine how much time is available to complete the needs assessment. Obviously, your assessment will be cursory if the course must be delivered next week. If the technology is to be implemented six months from now to 1,000 people across the continent, you must devote more time to conduct your assessment.

As a rule of thumb, I expect to spend 10 to 20 percent of the entire course development time on needs assessment. An ounce of up-front preparation is worth a ton of revisions.

Identify Available Sources of Data

Determine which sources of data are available to you. Don't make the mistake of picking just one or two sources. Remember, you want to get a complete understanding of the training need. You can only get this understanding from several perspectives.

Here are some data sources you should consider investigating:

- **Sources internal to the organization:**
    - Company management
    - Staff supervisors
    - Staff who will use the technology
    - Company documents such as performance appraisals, job descriptions, technology plans, customer service records, and help desk logs
- **Sources external to the organization:**
    - Technology and training vendors
    - Training journals
    - Technology journals
    - Colleagues in other organizations
    - Local universities and colleges

You must collect data from the staff who will use the technology. You must also collect data from other sources. I try to investigate at least three internal sources and at least one external source. I investigate additional sources if I think they can provide something new.

I write each data source on a separate sheet of paper. This allows me to record the data I expect to collect and the data collection methods I might use next to each data source.

Identify the Data Your Sources Can Provide

For each data source, write down the data you believe it can provide about the training need. For example, the staff who is to use the technology may be able to help you determine the following:

- Their attitudes about the technology change
- What they perceive to be their needs

- What they already know about the technology

- Their existing knowledge and skills with the new technology

- Their beliefs about the best training approaches

After you list the data you can get from each source, review the list and circle the repetitions. *You want the repetitions!* They allow you to get multiple perspectives on the same issue. Also look for data elements that have no repetition and reconsider how you might collect this data from another source.

Identify the Methods Used To Collect the Data

Go back over the list you are building and look at each data element. Write down all the ways you can collect this data from that source. (You can find a full discussion about data collection methods in "Methods for Conducting a Needs Assessment," later in this chapter.)

Consider which collection methods you *should* use, not just which ones can be used easily. Sometimes, the best insights come only from the more challenging collection methods.

I try to identify more than one method—especially for the data elements I judge to be important. The additional methods help me confirm and cross-reference my findings.

Now I review all the data sheets, looking for gaps. Are there any data elements I want that have no source? Are there data elements that have no collection methods? I reconsider and find ways to plug the gaps.

Next, I review the sheets again. I look for the sources of data that will give me the best understanding of the training need. I also look for the most expedient collection methods. I pull these sources and methods together into my needs assessment plan.

Plan How You Will Analyze the Data

I spend time at this stage planning how I will analyze all the data I collect. I find it rare that a full statistical evaluation of the findings is needed. At this point, I am only trying to identify general trends.

Usually, my analysis is narrative with estimates of quantities and dates.

> **Note**
>
> For one needs assessment I did, my analysis plan was something like this:
>
> - For each of the five groups needing training, write a one-paragraph description of the group's characteristics.
>
> - For each group, create a half-page list of job tasks they must learn to perform.
>
> - For each group, create a one-page list of skills and concepts they must learn.
>
> - For each group, create a table showing the number of people needing training in each month for the coming year.

Plan How You Will Present the Findings

Finally, I need to know how the program sponsor wants to see the findings. Will she make the final decision about the training project or must I present the findings and get acceptance from a management committee representing 10 divisions? I've worked for some sponsors who wanted my gut feel and a one-page description. I've also worked with others who needed a detailed executive summary, a 100-page report, and all the data.

Ask your business contact how you are expected to present the findings of your needs assessment—and to whom you are expected to present the findings. Do you need a slide presentation, a verbal summary given over the phone, or a short typed summary? It can help you adjust the amount of time you spend conducting your needs assessment if you know ahead of time just what your client expects you to deliver.

Methods for Conducting a Needs Assessment

The methods described in the following sections are presented in order from general to specific. The first methods provide general data about the training audience; the later methods provide data specific to individuals.

Document Review

Often, companies already have extensive records about their people, their previous operations, and their plans for the future.

To learn more about the company and the people you will train, review as many of the following documents as you can get your hands on:

- Information technology plans
- Production statistics
- Audits
- Help desk logs
- Network failure records
- Job descriptions
- Performance reviews
- Results of exit interviews

As you review these documents, keep in mind that you may be beginning a paper chase that can consume lots of time without producing any useful data. I like to find someone who is familiar with the documents to separate the wheat from the chaff for me. On the other hand, reviewing documents does not require anyone else's time, so scheduling this activity is easy. The documents often give me useful background before I use other collection methods.

Interviews

In every needs assessment I've ever done, I interviewed people. There is nothing like getting data from the horses' mouths. I try to interview the key stakeholders in the project and I pick at least one representative from each affected area.

You can interview people individually (which allows for some flexibility in scheduling) or in groups (which can be a scheduling nightmare). For group interviews, I bring together six to eight people from the same affected area. For those who are out of town, telephone interviews can yield useful information. Following are some of the people you should consider interviewing:

- Management
- Supervisors
- Staff affected by the technology change
- The project team
- Technology experts

Interviews are a good way to get at real attitudes, beliefs, and expectations. They also establish you as being legitimately interested in the training need. Because selecting a valid sample of people to interview can be challenging, the data you get from interviews may not be representative. Take some pains to prepare and conduct the interviews well; interviews can fail to produce useful data if the interviewer is not particularly skilled or prepared.

> **Tip**
>
> A few pages back, you planned how you would conduct the assessment. You wrote down the available data sources, the data each source can provide, and the methods you might use to collect the data. You can use that plan now to prepare for the interviews and other collection methods. Your plan can help you create the questions you will ask to uncover the data you want. Because you know what kinds of responses you want, you can craft your questions to give you the amount of detail you need.

Observations

A sometimes useful method of gathering data is to watch people using the new technology and then ask them what they needed to learn to use it. This approach works well when a pilot group is being used to test the new technology. Because these people already have a guinea-pig mentality, your hanging around to snoop on them for a few hours won't strike them as unusual.

You can conduct these observations in a formal, structured manner. Assign certain tasks to people and observe whether they can perform them satisfactorily. In some situations, videotaping what you observe may be necessary.

You can also conduct these observations informally, simply by being around when people use the technology or call for help desk support.

The greatest drawback to the observation method of needs assessment is that you must be a highly skilled observer. You must also possess a comprehensive knowledge of the performances you will observe. This is an uncommon combination. Observing can also be time consuming; hours may pass before the subject does anything wrong.

Questionnaires

Some people think they've done a needs assessment because they've sent questionnaires all over the company asking what people need to know. I've seen well-meaning trainers send checklists to managers who mark the checklist with the numbers of their people needing specific skills. The trainers count up the numbers and conclude that 568 people need Windows 95 training. Then they create a three-day course covering every aspect of Windows 95 and announce its availability. When only 37

4

people sign up (and give ho-hum reviews to the classes), the trainers wonder what went wrong.

Their mistake is believing that their findings are valid, reliable, and complete. They failed to ask the managers about the assortment of skills and concepts needed to operate Windows 95. They failed to recognize that they were asking for *perceived* needs. They failed to identify the types of people who needed the skills.

Questionnaires should be targeted to a specific audience about a specific content area. Ask the Windows network administrators whether they need more information about password security, server maintenance, or how to make only certain portions of the server available to the Internet through Telnet. Ask average Windows users whether they need basic instruction in navigation techniques like the mouse and identifying folders and icons or more advanced training in file management, navigating the network, and creating file associations. Cast your nets carefully into small pools of fish.

Create your questionnaires with the utmost care. Along with your wedding vows, your tax returns, and your will, your training needs assessment questionnaire is a document you should write carefully. I have never seen a questionnaire that has been correctly understood by every correspondent.

I use a mixture of open and closed questions. The closed questions are easy to tally, but they narrow the possible responses. Be careful when creating the options. Open questions are great for bringing in an assortment of views (if people take the time to write them out), but they can be difficult to tabulate. Keep this in mind if the program sponsor wants to see lots of numbers.

Analysis of Work Samples

Looking at work samples is like observing people at work except that you look at the product of the work and not the process. This method is useful, for example, when assessing the need for training programmers about programming techniques. You can dissect the programs they write for errors, flaws, and design weaknesses.

Work sample analysis enables you to collect data without the knowledge of the subjects. As a result, they don't change the way they work because they are being studied. This method requires someone who knows the subject well to analyze the work produced. Sometimes, the analysis can be subjective. Unless standards exist describing what is good work and what is not, the subjectivity of the person analyzing the work may make this data useless.

> **Note**
>
> I've known people to accept the work of programmers simply because their programs ran—regardless of the fact that the code was a mess of spaghetti. I've known others who refused to accept elegantly crafted, efficient, bug-free programs simply because the indentation scheme of the source code was not consistent. Get agreement on what is "good" work.

How To Select the Methods To Use

As part of planning for my needs assessments, I consider several factors before choosing which data-collection methods to use. I also spend an hour with the program sponsor to establish which factors are pertinent to this particular business situation.

Here are some of the factors I consider:

- **Cost.** How much of the budget can I spend to collect the data?

- **Time.** Which data-collection methods can be done quickly? Which require time to produce quality, reliable results?

- **Location of target group.** Where are the people I need to contact? Is it possible to bring them all together for focus group meetings?

- **Appropriateness for target group.** Have I chosen methods that the group will find acceptable? Are there any methods unusable for this group? Make sure that the methods are compatible with the literacy level of the group. Ensure that the methods cannot introduce bias. Choose methods that maintain the confidentiality of the individual responses, if that is a concern of the group.

- **What has worked in the past.** I always ask about collection methods that have been used in the past. I also ask why some methods worked and why some methods did not.

- **Competency of the researcher.** For some methods (such as direct observation of people performing their jobs), I am not competent to judge their performance because I am not an expert in that job. In these situations, I need to use someone who is competent to judge the people's performances.

- **Authority.** What methods do I have the authority to use and which methods do I need someone else's authority to use?

- **Manageability.** Some methods generate a huge volume of data. Consider how much data you can manage to process as well as the minimum required to create a complete picture.

■ **Adherence to external agencies.** Determine which methods the sponsor requires to comply with governmental regulations or collective agreements.

■ **Sponsor's needs.** Determine which methods make the program sponsor feel most comfortable. If the sponsor is best convinced by well-analyzed spreadsheet analyses of data, make sure that you collect numbers. If he or she wants only a big picture, collect some anecdotal evidence.

Methods for Conducting a Needs Assessment: Strengths and Weaknesses

There is no one perfect method for collecting the information you need to assess training needs. Each method has its place—and its failings.

The following chart shows these strengths and weaknesses.

Document Review

Pros:	Often readily available; gives a good look at the past; can be done independently; can give a useful background.
Cons:	Can be time consuming without producing much useful data; may not reflect all the facts.

Interviews

Pros:	Direct input from those affected; good for getting at attitudes, beliefs, and expectations.
Cons:	Must interview lots of people to get balanced views; interview must be skilled and well prepared.

Observations

Pros:	Determines retrospectively what people needed to learn to use the new technology.
Cons:	Requires a representative pilot group to test the new technology; requires a highly skilled observer; can be time consuming.

Questionnaires

Pros:	Inexpensive; easy to tally.
Cons:	Often used as the only method for collecting data; if constructed poorly, can be too broad to collect meaningful data; it is difficult to create a questionnaire that is universally understood; low return rate can jeopardize the statistical validity of the findings.

> *Analysis of Work Samples*
>
> **Pros:**   Able to collect data about a group without its knowledge; good for assessing the needs of individuals.
>
> **Cons:**   Requires standards of good performance; subject to the preferences of the work analyst; requires someone who knows the subject well.

How To Analyze the Data

As mentioned earlier in this chapter, the type of analysis you perform depends on the needs of decision makers.

At this stage of the training project, I believe it is best to keep the analysis as simple as possible. Remember that you are trying to build a fence around the training need. Look for trends, patterns, and other consistencies. I like to summarize the anecdotal and nonnumerical data to show the main themes that emerge. I prefer to handle numerical data by displaying it in tables and charts.

Keep the detailed findings for your course development work, which is discussed in Chapter 7, "Course Development." The needs assessment will uncover a gold mine of valuable input to the development process.

How To Report the Findings

The way I report my findings and recommendations depends on the needs of the decision makers. If at all possible, I try to provide about a four-page summary of the six *W* questions.

If the needs assessment work will take a significant amount of time (for example, longer than a month), I try to give the program sponsor informal glimpses at my preliminary findings. One of the first lessons I learned in business is to give bad news to superiors early. If my findings point to a major training effort when a quick seminar was expected, I want to soften up the sponsor so that my recommendations will not shock.

Present your findings to the decision makers in the manner in which they want to hear the information. Send out reports and ask for comments, if that is their style. Make a presentation at a meeting and lead a discussion of their opinions, if they'd rather do it that way.

After the decision makers accept the data and make recommendations, I formalize the agreement in a memo. The memo summarizes the discussion and the agreed-on plans for future work. The memo does not have to be a rigorous contract. It *does* have to be a written form of signoff from decision makers.

Tip

After the decision makers accept the report, I communicate my findings with all the contributors. Because they have given me their time, they deserve to know what I found about their needs and what I recommended be done. If I do something patently stupid to create a potentially intolerable situation, I want the contributors to tell me now. I don't want to find out when they sabotage my perfectly crafted training program.

I also garner the commitment of the contributors to my recommendations. They realize that I am serious about meeting their training need. Remember that people are sometimes reluctant to give their opinions freely because they never see the results of their truthfulness.

From Here...

The next step is **not** to begin to develop the courses for which you identified a need. You are not yet ready. Remember that all you have at this point is a big picture of the need and a strategy for conducting the remainder of the project. You do not know, in detail, all the concepts and skills every group needs to learn.

■ To get this information, you must conduct a detailed skills assessment. Chapter 5, "Skills Assessment," describes how to make this assessment.

For Further Reading

Custer, G.E. (1984). *Planning, Packaging and Presenting Training: A Guide for Subject-Matter Experts.* University Associates.

Kramlinger, T. and R. Zemke. (1982). *Figuring Things Out.* Addison-Wesley.

Laird, D. (1978). *Approaches to Training and Development.* Addison-Wesley.

Ulschak, F.L. (1983). *Human Resources Development: The Theory and Practice of Need Assessment.* Reston.

Chapter 5

Skills Assessment

by Gail Perry

Gail Perry has been teaching people how to use their computers for 10 years. In her earliest classes, assessing skills was easy: nobody had any! She has since discovered that a careful skills assessment before the class begins can completely redirect the flow of material and method of presentation.

More than anything, the way you teach is determined by the skills of the people you teach. Assessing those skills, therefore, is paramount in determining the success of your teaching effort. Questions like these should fill your mind before you even set foot in your classroom:

- Who are these people attending your class?

- Where do they come from?

- What is their background?

- How quickly will they learn?

- What kind of previous computer experience do they have?

- Have they used this computer program before?

- How will they use the skills they learn?

- Why are they taking this training?

Typically it falls on you, the instructor, to determine the skills of the participants in your training sessions. How you do this, and when, are key elements in ensuring that your class is a success.

Preliminary skills assessments are fantastic tools that not only help you prepare for the students before they arrive but can help group the students into the proper level of training.

In-class skills assessments work best in live classes, where the presentation can be fine-tuned as you go to provide the best possible learning experience.

Even a "non-live" class can benefit from the skills assessment techniques discussed in this chapter. Preliminary assessments can be performed with individuals who will be taking the class remotely by video or a CBT process to determine the class level for which they are ready. Assessments at the beginning of class can benefit the students even if no live instructor is present. Students can discuss their goals for the class before the presentation begins. Doing this helps them analyze and evaluate the class material after they have completed the program to determine whether those goals were met. Students in an instructorless classroom can take some time to get to know one another and share goals for the class so that they are more inclined to help each other as the class progresses.

Preliminary Assessment and Screening

The more information you can obtain about the skill levels of your class participants before you ever arrive at the class site, the better prepared you are to address the needs of your students. You will find that you have more control over the flow of your class and the presentation of your material if you are confident before class begins that you are prepared to offer information that will be useful to and understood by the class participants.

Sometimes, preliminary assessment isn't even an option. If you teach classes to the general public and anyone has the right to attend, it may be extremely difficult to obtain any information about the people you will be teaching before class begins. In cases like these, you must rely on techniques for assessing skills in class, as the class progresses. Alternatively, if you teach in a corporate setting, to employees of the same company, there are several methods available for preliminary assessment. In either case, it is in your interest as well as the interests of the students for you to gain as much insight as possible into the background and skills of your students.

Suppose that you have been hired to teach a beginning level spreadsheet class. Your class could be made up of people with any or all of the following skills:

- Familiarity with other spreadsheet programs
- Complete unfamiliarity with computers

- Familiarity with other computer programs but not with spreadsheets

- Analysis and projection skills

- Database skills

- Mathematical skills

- Engineering skills

- Accounting skills

Ideally, your approach to training people with each of the above skill sets will differ. But how can you determine in advance of training just who will be present in your class?

What Do You Want To Find Out?

Before you contemplate *how* to discover information about your potential class participants, you must determine *what* it is you want to know about the participants. To a certain extent, the type of material you have been asked to teach will guide you in defining what you need to know. If you are teaching a word processing program, you will want to know whether the class participants possess basic typing skills; whether they create documents on their own, typically copy from handwritten drafts, or take dictation; and whether they have used other word processing programs.

Analyze the program you are teaching, its capabilities, and the prerequisites you want to see in students for you to best teach the program. Make a list of key skills, placing them in order of importance (typing skills might be fairly high on the list of word processing prerequisites, even if it's not an absolute requirement; an understanding of layout and design techniques may not be as important).

> **Tip**
>
> When contemplating what information about your students will be helpful to you in planning for your class, try to think of many possible scenarios. One day, an instructor-friend of mine found when he arrived at class that one of his students was deaf and was accompanied by an interpreter who knew very little about computers. The pace of the class was altered significantly as the instructor presented information not just to the computer users in the class, but to an interpreter with no basic keyboarding skills. Having information about this particular student before the class began would have been exceptionally useful.

Divide your list into skills that are *important* to the success of the class and skills that will be *useful* for you to know about but that may not affect the presentation of your material. Here is a sample list of potential skills for students in a beginning Windows-based spreadsheet class:

1. Keyboard familiarity

2. Comfort with computer

3. Current use of other computer programs

4. Current use of other spreadsheet programs (beginning level)

5. Current use of other spreadsheet programs (advanced level)

6. Past use of other programs

7. Mouse skills

8. Windows familiarity

9. DOS skills

10. Knowledge of file-management techniques

11. Network familiarity

Rank these skills in order of their importance to you and your class. From the preceding list, the fourth, seventh, and eighth skills are extremely important for determining the pace of the class. Although the other skills are important, they play a smaller part in affecting the overall presentation of material.

You should try to perform this type of analysis before you begin assessing skills. If you know in advance what information will be important to the flow of the class, you can focus on those issues in your assessment. You may even issue prerequisites for your class, requiring students, for example, to take a beginning Windows class before they attend your class.

Determining skills in advance also serves the important function of determining placement. Some people may already have the skills you will present in your class. These people may be motivated to attend your class as a review or may be looking for a way to take a day off work and don't care about the subject matter—but more likely, potential students don't realize a day is about to be wasted learning about skills they already possess. Perhaps these people should attend a higher level class. A pre-class skills assessment can provide you with the information necessary for getting this student into the right level of training.

> **Note**
>
> Even if your assessment is limited to questions asked at the beginning of class, it's not too late to move a student to another class. If a student doesn't belong in your class, either because the class is too advanced or too remedial, unless the student has traveled a great distance and no other class is offered at the same time, you may have the

opportunity to reschedule him or her for another training session and send that person back to work today.

Methods for Preliminary Assessment

Once you determine the skills for which you are searching, you need a means of collecting information about the presence of these skills in your future students. There are several methods available to you:

- Surveys

- Discussions with supervisors

- Tests

- Prerequisite requirements

- Job-skill lists

You can prepare a written *survey* or a simple checklist of skills and distribute it to class participants in advance of the class date. Ask them to check the skills they possess. Alternatively, provide a ranking system with which the students can self-assess their skills, ranking each skill in a 1-to-5 range, from *Very Knowledgeable* to *No Experience in this Area*. (See these sample surveys in the Appendix: "Pre-Class Assessment Checklist" and "Pre-Class Skills Checklist.")

Meet or *talk with the supervisors* of the potential class participants and question them about the students' skills. Conversations with supervisors are particularly useful because at the same time you are finding information about skills of the students, you can quiz the supervisors about their expectations about the skills with which the students will leave class. Prepare a questionnaire for use in conversations with the supervisors so that you'll be sure to remember each skill you want to discuss. (A sample questionnaire is included in the Appendix: "Pre-Class Supervisor Questionnaire.")

You may have an opportunity to issue a basic *skills test* to participants in advance of the class date. You can provide a picture of a typical computer screen for the program being taught and ask the student to point out key elements of the screen. Your test can include questions about which function performs a particular task or about how a formula that executes a particular calculation would read. Tests are probably best used for advanced-level classes in which preliminary skills are more important.

The class you teach may have particular *prerequisite requirements*. Prerequisites give you an opportunity to have certain expectations of your students. Remember, however, that it may be that your expectations are unfounded (adults tend to fudge on prerequisites).

Job-skill lists are lists some corporations publish setting out the skill requirements of particular jobs. Typists may have to be able to type a certain number of words per minute, accountants may have to attend and pass a certain number of accounting courses or have CPA licenses, and some job descriptions may require certain computer skills. If you can look at the job requirement lists for the people who will be participating in your class, you may gain some insight regarding skills that will affect your training.

I've Got the Information, Now What?

There's not much use in taking the time to assess students before class if you don't take advantage of the knowledge you gain. Once you know the skills possessed by your students, you can revise and customize your class material to meet their needs.

Students with less-than-expected skills may need extra explanations and exercises to reinforce basic learning. If you learn the job backgrounds of the people coming into your class, you may be able to augment training material with exercises that relate specifically to the types of jobs the students perform.

Students with solid skills may move quickly through the material. You may have an opportunity to present more advanced examples or go into more depth on existing examples. If you sense students are going to move quickly through your material, you must definitely be prepared to fill the time with additional subject matter.

If you assess a group of students and find that approximately half of them have used other spreadsheet programs in the past and half have never seen a spreadsheet program, you may want to consider breaking the class into two groups. That way, you can present more basic information to the beginning group and plan on moving faster with the more experienced group.

Assessment at the Beginning of Class

If you're not fortunate enough to find out about the skills of your students in advance of the class, one of the first things you should do in class should be a skills assessment exercise. Before you begin teaching, find out as much as you can about the students in your class. Wouldn't it be embarrassing if you began a class by talking about how to use the mouse when all your students have been using Windows programs with a mouse for years?

Before you begin arbitrarily questioning students, have a sense of what kind of information you want to gather. Know what will be useful to you in determining the flow of the class. Know what answers you want to hear before asking questions.

Assessing skills at the beginning of a class is probably the way you most frequently gain information. Even if you had the opportunity to do a preliminary pre-class assessment, you can only gain additional information and improve your entire class presentation by starting with an in-class assessment.

Not only does an assessment at the beginning of class give you an opportunity to zero in on the skills of the people seated in front of you, it serves as an ice breaker, a way in which to establish a give-and-take rapport with your students, a method to get students relaxed with speaking in the classroom, and a chance for you to get to know your students, feel less like a stranger to them, and relax before your teaching presentation begins.

There are several ways in which you can collect information about your students at the beginning of class:

- Oral survey
- Written questionnaire
- Initial exercises

Oral Surveys

Talk about yourself. Open up and relax. If you can't do this yourself, you can't expect it of your students. These are the attitudes you want your students to have as early in the class as possible. The more relaxed and comfortable they feel in your classroom, the more likely they will ask questions during class, share with you their difficulties, and ultimately learn what you are teaching.

If you can get students talking early and get them to accept you as the conduit for conversation and feedback, they are generally more inclined to feel confident that you have something useful to teach them. They will be more open to receiving information from you throughout the class.

Start class with an exercise that gets your students talking. You can ask probing questions about their jobs and skills and give them a chance to answer with in-depth descriptions. You can ask them about their particular skills and experience with the program you plan to teach. Don't just ask if they've used the program before, ask them how they use it, which features they use most often, what they want to be able to do with it, what they like about the program, and what they *don't like* about it.

Caution

You may find yourself on the defensive when you open the door to what students don't like about a program.

Here is a sample questionnaire for a beginning-of-class oral survey (assuming that this is a beginning spreadsheet class). (This questionnaire is available in reproducible form in the Appendix.)

1. Describe your previous computer experience.

2. Describe previous spreadsheet experience (both on computer and on paper).

3. Have you used Windows and a mouse before?

4. (*If yes to #3*) Have you used the File Manager?

5. Why are you here? (Boss, general interest, particular need?)

6. What types of documents and reports will you use this software for?

7. Is there something in particular you want to get out of class?

8. Will you be creating original spreadsheets with this program or will you be editing files already created?

9. Is there a technical resource at your business location?

10. Do you use a network in your office? Do you share printers?

The larger your class, the less time you have for thorough oral questioning of all students. Instead, you may have to resort to some of the other methods for initial assessment. Even with a large class, however, it is important to get everyone speaking initially through introductions and a brief summary of skills or reasons for attending class.

You may think you can't afford the time to question students individually and wait for their introductions and responses. Especially if you are teaching a class that spans less than a full day, you may not want to take the time even for introductions. You will find, however, that any opportunity the students have to speak about themselves, even if it is just to give their names and job descriptions or some other brief information, is time well spent. The students achieve a level of comfort by having the chance to say their names out loud to the rest of the group. The comfort of your students is imperative to the success of your class.

Written Questionnaires

In a large class, you may not have an opportunity to allow every student to provide detailed information about his or her skills. In that case, a written questionnaire can be useful. The beginning-of-class questionnaire must be extremely brief and concise. You are trying to find out *basic information* about the backgrounds of your students; it's too late to redesign an entire course around detailed skill levels of the students. You are after the simple facts:

- Have you used this program before?

- Have you used a similar program before?

- Are there particular skills you hope to learn in class today?

- Are you familiar with basic Windows skills?

- Have you used a mouse before?

Simple, straightforward questions like these can be answered with yes-or-no checkboxes.

Have students fill out a simple questionnaire before class begins. Collect the questionnaires and take a few minutes to look them over at the start of class.

Because you keep the questionnaire simple and concise, you can glance at the forms and see quickly what kinds of basic skills your students possess. You can then refer to the results of the questionnaires in class: "I see that only a few of you have used a mouse before. Therefore, I'm going to take a few minutes to show you how the mouse works."

Even though students don't get to speak about their mouse skills, they recognize that you are concerned about their needs and abilities and are willing to take the time to teach them a skill that can make the rest of the class easier. They will recognize and appreciate immediately that you are on their side.

Other Beginning-of-Class Assessment Methods

Be creative! Think of ways in which you can get your students talking, meeting each other, and feeling comfortable. Remember that the happier they are to be there, the more likely they are to learn and absorb information. You may not have a lot of time to use oral assessment techniques beyond quick introductions and basic skill descriptions, but there are other ways in which you can help students open up. Both you and they can benefit from the time spent learning about each other.

Try issuing 3-by-5 cards to your students and ask them to jot down something they like about the program or something they don't like about it (if the students are real beginners, have them write something they like or dislike about computers in general). Also have them write down something in particular they want to learn in class today. Collect the cards and make a point of referring to the items on them throughout the day. If you ask students to write down things they want to learn, make sure that you address each of those topics. Even if you can only say, "We can't learn about this today, but you'll learn about it in the next level class," you are giving acceptance to the comment and the student who wrote it.

Tip

One thing I like to do in a beginning-level word processing class is to pass out a typed letter that contains several basic skills such as a right-justified return address, an indented paragraph, a bulleted list, some centered text, a change of type size, and so on. I also pass out a 3x5 card to each student and ask the students to imagine that they are sitting at their own computer and they've just been handed this document to type. They are to think about how they would proceed to type the document and write down on the 3x5 card the first question they have—the first place in this letter they would get hung up if they had to type it themselves. Of course, I make sure that I cover all the topics listed on the cards during the class. As a nice wrap-up, at the end of class I have them type the letter and demonstrate to themselves all the skills they have learned in the class.

Have students introduce each other. This works especially well in classes in which the group will be together for more than a day and they are strangers to begin with. Give students a list of interview questions (the same types of questions you might ask if you were surveying the students for their skills and background information) and have each student conduct a five-minute interview with someone else in class. Then students can introduce those whom they interviewed. This technique provides each student with a connection to someone else in the class and opens up opportunities for students to work on projects together or converse and check with each other when they have questions or are working on independent projects.

As you think of methods for learning about your students, keep in mind a few important rules:

- **Don't put your students on the spot.** Don't make them uncomfortable before class even begins. The goals of the pre-class assessment are to give you some feedback regarding your students' skills and to give the students an opportunity to get comfortable in the classroom. Don't ask questions that make your students uneasy. If your pre-class assessment is limited to an in-the-classroom assessment, you don't want the questions in any way to resemble a test or to present a situation in which a student will feel uncomfortable or inferior for not possessing certain skills.

- **Control the amount of time you allow for responses to your questions by the types of questions that you ask.** If you have a large class and can't afford to have every student speak for 10 minutes, ask questions that lend themselves to yes-and-no answers. If there are only five students in your class, you may be able to afford the luxury of asking students to describe their most frightening (fun, confusing, or whatever) experience with a computer. Consider other topics that lend themselves to lengthy answers, responses from other students, and comfortable conversation.

■ **Show interest in the responses you get from students.** Don't just nod and move on to the next student when someone is finished speaking. Respond directly to comments made by your students. Ask additional questions based on statements your students make. Let the students know you're actually interested in their remarks.

Using the Results of Your Assessment

As you interview students, asking for feedback on particular questions and keeping in mind exactly what you are trying to find out from these people, try to develop ways in which to recall the information they provide you. You are gathering information for a reason: to gain insights about the temperaments, interests, and abilities of your class members.

Here are several ways you can keep track of and use the information you collect from your students:

■ **Take notes during the assessment period.** Refer back to those notes during class or at your breaks.

■ **Display the answers to your questions on a board or flipchart that all students can see.** This technique provides you with a lot of opportunities for gaining rapport with and acceptance from your students. It gives reinforcement to the students by demonstrating that their comments and questions have been noted. It affords you an opportunity to check off topics as you discuss them, giving the students the knowledge that you care about the issues they raised. In addition, your recognition of the items on the chart encourages students to add to the list during the class as they think of questions or other topics they want to discuss.

■ **Break the flow of the class occasionally for a reassessment period.** Use this time to specifically refer back to the topics students indicated they wanted you to cover. You can also check with students about whether or not the material you have presented has met their needs. Address the particular issues the students raise and make sure that the students feel they have learned what they need to know about those topics. Not only does this give students another opportunity to participate in the class, it enables them to visualize (especially if you have a chart of topics displayed) just how much they have learned and to understand that you are taking care of their needs.

Assessment During the Class

Just as preliminary assessment is important to getting your class off to the right start, ongoing assessment keeps your class headed in the correct direction. In the preliminary assessment period, students may *think* they know what they want or need to learn, but as they become more familiar with the topics you offer, they may recognize additional learning opportunities that hadn't originally occurred to them. They may also realize that their needs are different than those they originally suggested. Having a chance during the class to reassess their goals gives students a feeling of control over their learning. It also gives you the opportunity to provide the most useful training possible.

Students aren't the only ones who need to reassess the training. As you teach, you can see how well students are absorbing your teaching material and can make decisions "on the fly" about how much material you can cover, how in depth it has to be, and how much review you should do before introducing new topics. Because each class is filled with different individuals and presents different teaching challenges, you must constantly be aware of the specific needs of those sitting in front of you and adjust your presentation accordingly.

Asking for Feedback

You can use several techniques for assessment during class; as you teach, you will develop and perfect the assessment style you prefer. *Verbal assessment* (asking students for responses about how the learning is progressing) can give you feedback based on how students *think* they are learning the material. Use this information in combination with visual feedback (see the following section) to assess for yourself how the rest of the class should be structured.

At a class break, review the topics originally scheduled to be taught, discuss the remaining topics, and request feedback from class members regarding their understanding of the topics already discussed. Also ask about the interest and level of need in the topics still to be covered. Particularly if time is short, you may want to reorganize the remaining material to put the most significant and pertinent topics first and the less important items last.

You can use a question-and-answer format for mid-class assessment. Analyze responses to oral questions for the potential of peer pressure. If you ask the group as a whole whether they feel comfortable with their knowledge of copying formulas in Excel, for example, and the majority of the class nods and comments affirmatively, chances are some quiet or self-conscious members of the group may nod in accordance with the others, even if they don't have a firm grasp on the subject. Or you may have an acquiescent group that, as a whole, is accustomed to agreeing and not asserting itself. Such a group may, en masse, indicate comfort with a topic when actually they are uneasy with the material. Keep in mind that you are dealing with adult learners; the more elementary the material, the more likely they are to say they understand rather than admit they don't understand basic skills.

To avoid the potential of peer pressure and group acquiescence, consider tossing out to the group pointed questions that require specific responses rather than questions that merely require a nod or head shake.

Consider a list of the topics you've already taught. Ask questions of this variety: "Who can tell me how...." Look for specific responses to general questions about the subject matter. Try to avoid letting the same people answer each question by using some of these techniques:

- Look at the people who aren't answering as you ask the question, as if you are asking them specifically.

- Consider calling on people—but only if you feel totally confident they know the answer and will actually appreciate being called on. Many adult learning experts recommend staying away from calling on adults in just about every situation, but if you know your class well, or if you personally know some of the students in your class, this technique may be appropriate.

- Let the "know-it-all" answer yet another question but then follow it up with something like, "Who can add to John's response?" (This question pretty much excludes John from being able to answer.)

- Avoid general questions like, "How do you move text from one cell to another in Excel?" Instead, use specific examples such as, "If I want to move the spreadsheet heading from cell C1 to cell E1, what steps would I take?" Not only does this test a practical application of something you have taught, a less-confident student may be willing to answer a specific question like this (he or she may be less willing to answer a general question that can be interpreted in many ways).

- Try eliciting a positive response to a negative question. Instead of asking, "How many of you understand how to change the number format of cells in Excel?" try asking, "How many of you feel that we need to spend a little more time working with changing the number format of cells?" What you're really asking is how many people don't understand the topic—but students are more likely to give a positive response to an inviting question than they are to say, "I don't get it."

Uninterested or Quiet? There Is a Difference

I remember a spreadsheet class in which I had one extremely reticent student. I couldn't seem to get any response from this student at all, no matter what tricks I tried. In the afternoon, we began experimenting with dressing up spreadsheets, adding headings, shading, borders, and so on. (This is always a part of class I feel uncomfortable with because I'm not at all artistic.) I noticed that this quiet student's screen was suddenly alive with color, designs (she had found the drawing tools on her own), beautifully balanced headings, and shading techniques—she really had a flair for the artistic. I asked her if she would mind if the other students came around her desk to look at her screen; she not only agreed but began demonstrating to them very sophisticated artist techniques for emphasizing important points on the spreadsheets without getting garish or overdone. Once she felt she was on comfortable turf, she opened up and was an active participant in the class.

So what did I learn from this? Quietness doesn't always signify an unwillingness to participate. Sometimes, people just have to find their niche in the class. Of course, the more you can learn about the students, the better you can be at helping them find that niche.

There are many techniques for retrieving information from your students. Keep in mind what you actually want to find out before forming your questions; the questions will flow much more easily.

Watching for Feedback

In addition to asking questions, you can demonstrate to students (and they to you) what they have accomplished so far. You can get visual feedback in many ways without relying on the oral question-and-answer format.

There's the obvious technique of watching student responses as you teach. In hands-on classes, you move around the room, keeping an eye on student screens as they work through the exercises presented in class. Don't watch only the screens. Observe keyboards to determine how students are accomplishing the things you see on their screens. For example, an Excel student may appear to have the proper answer on-screen where a formula is supposed to appear, but if you watch him or her make an entry in the cell, you may notice that he or she typed the answer to the formula instead of constructing the formula itself.

As you present a topic to your class, observe the physical responses of your students. Learn to differentiate between signs of comprehension and confusion in their facial expressions.

Offer a review exercise in the middle of the class that recaps the topics studied from the first half of the material. Students can better conceptualize those topics they have learned so far, and you, by observing how they perform on the exercise, have a better grasp of how well they have learned the topics you have taught. From the results of this exercise, you can modify the remaining material to accommodate the abilities of the group.

Watch for students who constantly refer to the screen next to them. Just as confused students in an academic classroom look over at the paper on the next desk, confused computer students sometimes look to their neighbors for help instead of asking out loud. Occasionally this can be nice—it gives you a chance to take advantage of more advanced students who can help those who have trouble keeping up. Ultimately, however, the training is your responsibility; if a student relies on a fellow student for guidance, that student is not learning in the way you intended. At some point, you should step in and help get the slower student up to speed with the rest of the class.

Also watch for students who jump ahead in the material, experiment with features other than those you are teaching, or wander off to other programs (or spend time playing solitaire). Students who are intentionally not staying with the class may be overskilled and bored. For such students, you can offer specific topics to work with (you may have an advanced exercise you can assign), you can put them to work aiding slower students, or you may be able to pull them back into the mainstream by peppering your presentation with tidbits of knowledge geared toward the advanced user.

Don't give up on either the slow or the fast student. Use your powers of observation to pick out these learners and then use your training powers to get these students back with the class.

5

Fast and Slow

Frequently, I get a student in class who is way ahead of the rest of the students in his or her grasp of the material. I can spot this student because he or she is working ahead, experimenting with other programs, or just acting plain bored. An easy way to get the student involved is to draw him or her into the teaching process. Suppose that you see a student experimenting with the multiple sheets that Excel provides with each spreadsheet file: "Rick, have you tried working with multiple sheets in Excel? Can you think of some practical uses for this feature in your job?" Get the student talking about a feature he or she knows how to use and make the student believe his or her input is important to the class.

At the other end of the spectrum, if you've got a student who is dragging the class down, who can't keep up, and who requires lots of your attention, you have to make some quick decisions on how to structure the class to accommodate everyone. You can't let the slower student get lost. At the same time, it's not fair to the rest of the class to hold everyone up, over and over again, for one person. In one class I taught,

(continues)

(continued)

one student was clearly not capable of learning the same material as the rest of the class. I gave abbreviated exercises to the slower student. I explained a topic in depth and showed the class how to use that particular feature, then gave them an exercise in which they could sample the feature. While they were working, I explained again the very basics of the skill to the slower student and had him perform only a couple of steps of the exercise. It was a very difficult class to teach, but at the end of the class all the students were satisfied that they learned what they came for.

Everyone Clear Your Desk and Take Out a Clean Sheet of Paper and a Pencil...

Yet another method of determining student response is the test. For the most part, you will find that tests are not the best means of getting feedback from students (most adult learners are offended by the testing process). There may be times, however, when you feel a test gives you the best response from students, or when company policy requires testing to monitor skills.

Tip

If you have to give a test, make it fun.

Tests can be written, fill-in-the-blank, or true/false. However, these aren't usually the best means of judging computer skills. If you need a written test, you can often find one at the backs of training books; alternatively, the students' supervisor may provide a test for the students.

A better test of the students' accomplishments is a hands-on exercise that incorporates the skills taught in class. Provide an exercise that requires the students to recall features you have presented but that also allows students to check their handout materials for answers. (Cheat sheets are fine; people use written resources when they are at their desks in an actual business setting or at home using these skills.) Students should be permitted and encouraged to ask questions while taking a test—either of each other or of you. A test is, after all, yet another learning tool. At all times, try to avoid the negative connotation associated with school tests.

Conceptual Assessments

One of the best ways to assess the amount of information your students have absorbed is by simply asking them what they've learned. Actually, this isn't entirely a simple process. You need to tailor your questions to encourage responses and to provide useful feedback. Your questions shouldn't intimidate students, nor should they smack of a test.

First, set the tone. Sit on a desk, stroll around the room, leave your terminal if you use one, do something to create a more relaxed, conversational image. Let the students know this is a time to recap, to consider what they've learned and how they're going to use that knowledge, and to ensure that the skills you have taught them actually make sense on a practical level.

Your goal is to let the students do the talking; motivate them to do so with general, open-ended questions that lend themselves to discussion. Here are some example questions (continuing the assumption that this is a beginning spreadsheet class):

- Describe the first job you're going to have to carry out using this software.

- What types of features did you learn about today that you didn't know the program could accomplish?

- If you were going to return to the next level of training, what types of features would you like to learn?

- If we had an extra hour of class today, which of the skills you learned today would you like to spend more time on?

- If you were describing this class to someone who is considering signing up for a future session, what single topic discussed today would you tell that person is the most useful thing you learned?

Assessment of Disparate Groups

How can you successfully assess the performance of a group when individuals in the group are at vastly different places in the learning spectrum?

As discussed at the beginning of this chapter, you will often find yourself training a group of individuals with varying skills, learning styles, and needs. The more diverse your group, the more difficult it is to perform accurate assessments and to rework your material as you go to fit the results of those assessments.

The skills you use in such a setting come primarily with experience, trial and error, and time. The longer you are a member of this profession, the more opportunities you will have and the more past experiences you will be able to draw on for training different types of learners, and the more readily you will be able to assess how they learn.

Frequently, you will turn to a combination of the ideas presented in this chapter, fine-tune them to fit the class you are teaching, and place heavier emphasis on the techniques that work in the particular class you are assessing. Because your pool of students is ever changing, your assessment tools must also change to fit each class.

Not assessing is not an option. Not taking the time to assess the learning and performance of your students is akin to teaching blindly, without any feedback, and not caring whether your students learn the subject matter.

From Here...

When you use assessment tools to find out who your students are, what they expect to learn, and what they need to learn (not always the same things), you're better prepared to present the right material in the manner in which it can best be received. Also consider these chapters in determining how best to address your subject matter and your students:

- Chapter 3, "Adult Learning: What Do We Know for Sure?," helps you familiarize yourself with adult learners—and how they differ (if they do) from school-age children. More important, you learn what motivates them to learn.

- Chapter 6, "Post-Class Evaluation," can help you determine whether all your pre-class assessment and altering of materials paid off: how well did the students absorb what you presented?

- Chapter 10, "The Flow of the Class," helps you plan the structure of the class and provides hints for how you can best use breaks to assess the way students are accepting the information.

Chapter 6

Post-Class Evaluation

by Gail Perry

Gail Perry has been evaluated by hundreds of students (you get used to it after a while) and has created evaluation forms that actually ask meaningful questions.

How do you know if your training has been a success? Do you read the smiles on people's faces as they leave and hope they're sincere? Do you ask students to fill out a questionnaire while they're still in the classroom? Do you chase down students months after they've left the class to see whether they remember the things you taught? Do you rely on the fact that you get repeat business from the same company?

There are many ways in which you can gain feedback on your performance and the level of comprehension of your students. You can use this feedback for a number of important functions:

- Monitor your own success and performance in the classroom

- Judge how well the students accept you as an instructor

- Determine the usefulness of the topics you teach

- Analyze the quality of your handout materials

- Ascertain the depth of learning among your students

Without information such as this, you really can't judge whether or not your training is useful and worthwhile.

Evaluations by your students can be performed at or near the end of class. If a class lasts for more than a day, interim evaluations can give you feedback you can use as the class progresses. Evaluations of this type—live evaluations created while the class is still paramount in the minds of the students—can tell you how you and your material are being received. But live evaluations can be misleading. If you've been entertaining as an instructor and the students have had a good time in class, they may evaluate the class based on the fun they had without really concentrating on the usefulness of their learning experience. To get a full picture of how worthwhile the training is, consider some form of after-class follow-up evaluation. This way, students have time to apply the training to real-life conditions and can better judge its usefulness.

In this chapter, I discuss both immediate and after-class evaluation techniques and offer suggestions for posing the types of evaluative questions that produce useful feedback. I also discuss methods of evaluation that involve the supervisors of those who attended your class. Using the techniques set out in this chapter, you can develop tools to effectively measure the success of your training.

End-of-Class Evaluation

Perhaps the most standard form of evaluation is the after-class, right-before-students-leave-the-room, on-the-way-out-the-door, one-page-checkbox evaluation. Class is over, students are ready to go, but before leaving they are asked to fill out an evaluation form. They do it quickly and, probably, somewhat mindlessly, because it's been a long day and they're ready to depart.

The standard evaluation of this type has a handful of questions asking students to rate the quality of the training, the instructor's knowledge, the quality of the handout material, and the facility on a scale of one to five. There is room for comments at the end of the form but students usually skip this part and head for the door. This type of evaluation can provide generalized statistics about the class, the instructor, and the environment, but is fairly nonessential when it comes to actually analyzing the usefulness of the material taught. You can see a sample of this type of evaluation form at the end of this chapter (refer to "Basic After-Class Evaluation Form").

The weaknesses of this race-out-the-door standard evaluation include the following:

■ Students are in a hurry to leave and the evaluation separates them from that freedom. Their minds are already fixed on where they are going and what they will next be doing. They will give the evaluation form only the attention it takes to quickly check the boxes and then they will leave the room.

- Students have seen the stock, "How would you rank..." questions before and have been numbed to any thought-provoking messages that may be hidden in these questions. They are not likely to thoroughly consider the meaning of the questions or the useful insights their answers might provide.

- Evaluation forms of this type are often structured so that the checkbox containing the highest grade is first, right after the question. The student's pen is poised in that first position; because it's easier to give a high mark than a low one, the results of these questionnaires may be unnaturally skewed toward high grades.

- Many class participants have a tendency to give high marks when judging another person's performance, thinking of the kind of marks they would like to receive themselves were they in the position of the instructor. They may not consider that some constructive information might be gleaned from an analysis of these grades.

- Most people are nonconfrontational by nature and are less likely to give someone a low score if there is any chance they may be called on to defend the score. Particularly if students are expected to put their names on the evaluation forms, they are less likely to give low marks.

So how do you alleviate these problems?

Don't wait until the last minute to issue evaluation forms. In a full-day class, students have had plenty of time to form opinions by the time the class is three-quarters over. Give the evaluation forms out at an afternoon break. Students don't have to fill them out right away, but they have the opportunity to take care of that paperwork before the last minute when they are ready to run out the door. You can give out evaluation forms at lunch time, or even hand them out at the beginning of class, explaining to students that they will be expected to fill out those forms before leaving for the day. This approach gives students the impression that you want them to take the time to give some thought to the answers and fill out the forms with care.

It's sometimes hard to get away from the checkbox format, especially if you expect to analyze the evaluations statistically. You can, however, get away from the very basic, "How would you rank..." questions and ask more direct and insightful questions that require the students to spend a little more time contemplating their answers. Instead of, "How would you rank the instructor of this course?" (which is ambiguous and too general), consider, "Did the instructor present the material in a way that was easy for you to follow?" This is a specific, direct question that the student will want to respond to on a personal level. Take a look at the sample evaluation at the end of this chapter created by Ron Wolford of

6

The Future Now in Indianapolis, Indiana (see "After-Class Evaluation Form, Developed by The Future Now"). The questions in this form have been carefully worded to evoke meaningful responses from students, even though the format is still a checkbox style.

Even with a checkbox format, all evaluation forms should have a place for written comments. The student may want to evaluate some area that isn't covered by the questions. A student may want to elaborate on one of the questions. Using only questions and no comment area indicates to the student that his ideas are not important to the instructor or to those offering the class. Give the students an opportunity to expound a bit on either the good or bad aspects of the class.

Give students the option of not signing their names to alleviate any pressures students may have to give positive responses to the questions. Some corporations require that students sign their names to confirm that the students were present in the classes.

If students can place their evaluation forms in envelopes or turn them in to someone other than the instructor, they may be more likely to give honest answers to the questions, particularly those pertaining to the instructor. Students realize that the instructor will eventually learn of the responses to the evaluations, but if students think the responses come to the instructor anonymously, or if they can be confident that the instructor won't read the responses while the students are still in the vicinity (and chase after them shouting, "How can you say that about me?"), they may be more comfortable in describing any problems or concerns they may have had about the instructor.

Tip

Don't just hand out the forms and assume that the students will fill them out in the way you hope they will. Give a little guidance with these evaluation forms. Rather than handing out a form and simply requesting that the form be filled out before students leave for the day, tell the students how and *why* they should fill out the evaluation forms. Explain that the information on these forms is used to improve the classes taught at this location, that future classes will benefit from their input, and that the thoughts and suggestions of the students will be seriously considered.

Emphasize to students the importance of the comment area on the evaluation form. This is their forum, their place to air grievances and to offer constructive criticism as well as compliments. Ask students to take a minute to write a few comments and give them some general suggestions for this part of the form. For example, you can suggest that students describe the part of the class that was most meaningful to them, or ask them what they would like to see changed if they were taking the class again. Remind them that others will be taking this class and that their comments will help future students. Don't be afraid to request comments—they can only be useful to you in future classes.

Closure

It may seem hard to believe, but some students just don't want to leave your classroom. They've had a good time, they've learned new and useful skills, and they've been away from work for a day. They may feel that if they stay and tinker on the machines a while longer, they'll gain more information from you. They may not consider the fact that you've been on your feet all day and are probably ready to go home. They may just be the sort of people who don't know when it's time to get up and go.

Evaluations provide a good stopping point for the class. Even if you handed the forms out well in advance, when class is over, it is time to turn in the forms. This provides a nice transition for ending the class. Announce that class is over, thank the students for attending, and tell them what to do with their evaluation forms—whether it is bringing them to the front of the room, dropping them on a table as they leave, taking them to their supervisors, or leaving them at a drop point outside the room. Receiving an instruction gives the students motivation to get up, take care of the evaluation forms, and continue out the door.

What Do You Want To Know and How Do You Get that Information?

Evaluation forms are for the use of you and the developer(s) of your course (who may be you, also). Present questions and ask for comments that will produce the feedback you will find most useful to the future development of your methods and your course. Remember that it is the nature of computer classes that they are constantly in a state of development.

You certainly want to ask questions about the quality of instruction—you have to know how you come across to your students. Questions like these can give you insight into your own teaching ability:

- Is the instructor easy to understand?

- Is the instruction useful?

- Is the instructor knowledgeable about the topic?

- Did the instructor communicate well with the class as a whole?

- Did the instructor maintain a comfortable pace?

- Would you take another course from this instructor?

- Did the instructor address all the questions raised in class?

- Did the instructor speak at your level?

- Were the instructions easy to follow?

- Did the instructor give you plenty of opportunities to ask questions?

- Was the instructor effective at teaching this program?

You also need feedback about the course itself, the materials, the topics covered, and the depth of the coverage. Questions like these can provide responses about the course:

- Do you think you will use the handout materials after class is over?

- Were the handout materials useful to your learning of the program?

- Was the class material presented in a logical manner?

- Do you think you'll be able to apply the skills you learned today outside of this class?

- Were the goals of the class clearly defined and were those goals met?

- Were prerequisites (if any) set out clearly before class and were those prerequisites appropriate for this class?

- Do you know more about the program now than you did before class today?

- Did you learn the things you needed from this class?

- Do you expect to take higher-level training on this program in the future?

Finally, you will also want to get some general feedback about the facility and the training equipment. Include some general questions about the premises in your questionnaire:

- Were the facilities appropriate for your class?

- Did the equipment operate properly?

- Was the meal service satisfactory (if meal is included)?

- Was the classroom arrangement comfortable and conducive to training?

Try to word your questions in such a way that they provoke thoughtful responses.

Long-Range Follow-Up: After Class Is Finished

Don't be satisfied with the evaluations you receive at the close of your class. Long-range follow-up provides you with an opportunity to find out just how useful your training is once students leave your classroom. It's one thing for students to be able to execute certain computer skills under the watchful eye of the instructor in a safe environment where they know they can't hurt the equipment or precious data. You hope the confidence gained in the classroom will carry students back to their real-life environments where those skills can be put to practical use. But unless you do some follow-up—weeks or even months after the training—you'll never know the true worth of your instruction.

There are a several methods available for follow-up after the class is over. You can take a telephone survey of former students, send a questionnaire in the mail, contact supervisors, casually quiz students who return to your classroom for advanced training, or even make follow-up visits to the workplace of those you trained.

The Telephone Survey

Before you contact former students by telephone, develop a survey, a list of questions you want to ask of them. This survey will differ from the class evaluation because a number of the factors will no longer be pertinent. You are now concerned, not with how they enjoyed their day with you, but with how well the skills they learned in the classroom have transferred to the workplace.

Make sure that students you call have the time to respond. Ask whether you can have five or ten minutes of their time; if they are busy, arrange for a time when you can return the call. You may find that you get a better response from this survey if someone other than you makes the call.

Here's a list of the kinds of topics about which you want to question the former students:

- Did the class meet your expectations?

- Have you had an opportunity to use the program since you attended class?

- *If the preceding question is answered negatively:* Do you expect to be able to use the program soon? (Follow this query with a line of questioning geared toward the user who hasn't yet used the program.)

- *If the second question is answered positively:* Have you had an opportunity to use the specific skills taught in class since you attended class?

- Do you feel you learned enough about these skills in class to apply them to your job?

- Have you noticed any skills you need that you didn't learn in class? (If the student answers *yes,* have him or her elaborate.)

- Do you plan to attend the next level of training in this program?

- Will you return to this location for further training?

6

In addition to yes/no questions, ask some questions that generate more detailed answers, such as any of the following:

■ What skills did you learn in class that have been most useful to you on your job?

■ What skills have you noticed since class that you wish you had learned?

■ Can you offer any comments on the competence and presentation skills of the instructor?

A sample telephone survey is included at the end of the chapter (see "Sample Telephone Survey Questionnaire").

The Mail-in Questionnaire

Questions similar to those you ask in a telephone survey can be included with a mail-in questionnaire. Your response rate may not be as great with a mail-in questionnaire as it is with a telephone survey because you are relying on the former students to take their own time to fill out the form, writing the answers to questions. Send a stamped envelope with the questionnaire to help encourage a prompt response.

Contact Supervisors

You may be able to conduct a phone survey with the supervisors of your former students if you have their names. In fact, you may have the opportunity to arrange in advance of the training to meet with the supervisors, find out what their expectations are, and then meet or talk with them again some time after the class to determine whether those expectations have been met.

If you spoke with supervisors before class, your follow-up questions will flow from the expectations set out at that original meeting. If the first time you speak with supervisors is after class, your questions will be more general, along the lines of these:

■ Have you had a chance to discuss the training with your staff?

■ Is it your impression that your staff members are generally pleased with the training?

■ Have your staff members indicated satisfaction with the training they received?

■ Have you had an opportunity to observe the results of your staff's training?

- Are you personally pleased with the skills demonstrated by your staff members since their training session?

Not only will a question session with the supervisor give you insights regarding the success of your training, it will demonstrate to the supervisor your care and concern regarding your training and your desire to provide a continued high level of training (refer to the "Sample Questionnaire for Follow-Up with Supervisors," at the end of this chapter).

On-Site Follow-Up Observation

If you are fortunate enough to have an opportunity to visit the work site of your students at some point after class, you can gain important insights regarding their use of the program they learned from you.

I have participated in training programs in which a group of students from the same company attended a series of my classes. Then I spent a day at their offices, going from desk to desk, meeting individually with each student. The students were advised in advance of the day on which I would arrive and prepared questions for me. Each student demonstrated to me how he or she uses the software learned in my classes and had an opportunity to ask me questions relating to particular tasks.

This program is enormously popular with the students because they get some guaranteed one-on-one time with an instructor and can ask questions without the worry of taking up time that belongs to other students. In addition, the knowledge I gain from seeing the students in action—watching them take the general skills I present in class and apply them in innovative ways to actual situations—is priceless in terms of developing my own training skills.

I look for particular things in an on-site visit. These questions can elicit information that can help me improve my training skills:

- What particular skills taught in class have stuck with my former students?

- How have skills learned in class been applied to job requirements?

- What kinds of questions still linger now that class is over and the students have had a chance to use the new skills?

- Now that the students have mastered the skills they learned in class, can I show them some shortcuts that will help them in their jobs?

- Have the students been using the written training materials as a reference?

Sample Evaluation Forms

Included in this section are some ideas for forms you might be able to incorporate into your own training program. Pick the parts that seem appropriate to you; mold the forms to meet your style and to provide the feedback you feel you need to make your training a success. If you want to reproduce these forms for your own use, you will find them in a handy format in the Appendix of this book.

Basic After-Class Evaluation Form

Rate the following topics on a scale from 1 to 5, with 5 as the high score:

1. Rate the technical education received

            5   4   3   2   1

2. Rate the practical value of the training received

            5   4   3   2   1

3. Rate the thoroughness of coverage of the designated topic

            5   4   3   2   1

4. Rate the appropriateness of reading material

            5   4   3   2   1

5. Rate the exercises performed in class

            5   4   3   2   1

6. Rate the allocation of time to subjects

            5   4   3   2   1

7. Rate the instructor's knowledge of the subject

            5   4   3   2   1

8. Rate the instructor's ability to motivate participants

            5   4   3   2   1

9. Rate the instructor's preparedness for the training

            5   4   3   2   1

10. Rate the instructor's ability to get ideas across

            5   4   3   2   1

11. Rate the instructor's ability to keep the seminar moving

            5   4   3   2   1

12. Rate the classroom

5   4   3   2   1

13. Overall evaluation

5   4   3   2   1

After-Class Evaluation Form, Developed by The Future Now

The Future Now Computer Education Center

Thank You

COURSE EVALUATION

Thank you for attending a seminar at The Future Now Computer Education Center. Because your opinion is valuable to us, we ask that you please take a few moments to answer the following questions.

Your responses to these questions are an important part of our efforts to maintain the best computer training in Indiana. Please complete all questions, writing comments where appropriate. Your comments are particularly important to us. We appreciate your responses.

Please circle the appropriate response, where "5" is the highest response, "3" is average, and "1" is the lowest.

1   2   3   4   5   A. The lessons were presented in an effective way that helped me learn.

1   2   3   4   5   B. This class aided my understanding.

1   2   3   4   5   C. I feel more confident using the program I learned in class.

1   2   3   4   5   D. Class content was appropriate to my needs.

1   2   3   4   5   E. The class was generally appropriate to the needs of the group.

1   2   3   4   5   F. Generally, the teacher taught at my level of understanding.

1   2   3   4   5   G. Generally, the teacher taught at the group's level of understanding.

1   2   3   4   5   H. The instructor presented the material in a way that was easy for me to follow.

1   2   3   4   5   I. Questions were thoroughly and clearly answered.

1   2   3   4   5   J. I feel confident that I will be able to apply what I have learned in this class.

1   2   3   4   5   K. I found the written material to be easy to follow and understand.

1   2   3   4   5   L. The instructor was knowledgeable of the program taught.

1   2   3   4   5   M. The instructor was effective at teaching this program.

1   2   3   4   5   N. The facilities were satisfactory.

1   2   3   4   5   O. The equipment was satisfactory.

6

The Future Now Computer Education Center

Course Evaluation

1 2 3 4 5   P. What is your overall evaluation of this course?

Y   N   Q. Was it your choice to attend this course?

How did you hear about this class?

_____

_____

Thank you for your responses to the previous items. Please provide us specific feedback by writing comments below.

_____

_____

_____

_____

_____

_____

_____

_____

_____

_____

How soon do you think you would be interested in taking the intermediate or advanced class?

_____

If you would like us to send you a monthly class schedule, the instructor will provide you with a card to complete so that we may add you to The Future Now mailing list.

Course _____ **Instructor** _____

Date _____ **Location** _____

Optional information

Name _____ **Company** _____

The Future Now Computer Education Center

Sample Telephone Survey Questionnaire

1. Did the class meet your expectations?

2. Have you had an opportunity to use the program since you attended class?

If Question #2 is answered negatively:

3. Do you expect to be able to use the program soon? (Follow this query with a line of questioning geared toward the user who hasn't yet used the program.)

If Question #2 is answered positively:

4. Have you had an opportunity to use the specific skills taught in class since you attended class?

5. Do you feel you learned enough about these skills in class to apply them to your job?

6. Have you encountered problems with the software since you took the class?

7. Have you noticed any skills you need that you didn't learn in class? (If the answer is *yes*, ask him or her to elaborate.)

8. Do you plan to attend the next level of training in this program?

9. Will you return to this location for further training?

10. What skills did you learn in class that have been most useful to you on your job?

11. What skills have you noticed since class that you wish you had learned in class?

12. Are there functions we covered in class on which you feel we should have spent less time?

13. Can you offer any comments on the competence and presentation skills of the instructor?

Sample Questionnaire for Follow-Up with Supervisors

1. Have you had a chance to discuss the training with your staff?

2. Is it your impression that your staff members are generally pleased with the training?

3. Have your staff members indicated satisfaction with the training they received?

4. Have you had an opportunity to observe the results of your staff's training?

5. Are you personally pleased with the skills demonstrated by your staff members since their training session?

From Here...

Now that you have a feel for the variety of evaluative techniques available to you, think about how you can use what you've learned in future training situations.

- Chapter 7, "Course Development," takes you on a tour of preparing materials for your classes. Consider the information you get from evaluations when you design your course materials.

- Use in-class methods of evaluation as part of your end-of-the-class wrap-up with students. Chapter 10, "The Flow of the Class," contemplates the last five minutes of your class, a time that can be crucial to evaluations.

- Use the knowledge you gain from evaluations to consider other forms of training for beyond the classroom. Chapter 11, "Augmenting Classroom Training with Other Media," offers innovative ideas for training beyond the traditional classroom model.

Part III

In the Classroom

Chapter 7

Course Development

by Shirley Copeland

Shirley Copeland is a Virginia-based adult educator and consultant who designs and develops curriculum in many program areas. She received her doctorate in Adult and Continuing Education from Virginia Tech. Shirley has 12 years of experience in instructional design and training.

Once you have identified a need for training, you can move on to the next step: course development. Many factors contribute to the development of an instructionally sound course. This chapter provides some insight into these factors; however, it does not provide a foundation in instructional design theory. It simply provides some guidance in using the instructional design process to develop a course. This chapter also highlights the issues you should consider when customizing a course and addresses registration and record keeping.

Before you can begin developing course materials, you must be knowledgeable about the subject matter. Seldom do you have the luxury of employing or contracting with subject-matter experts to provide the content material for your course. It's important to keep abreast of changes in technology and to keep up to date on the subject matter. Much of your learning will be self-directed and motivated by a desire to keep current and a step ahead of your learners. The first section of this chapter outlines a few ways you can maintain technical mastery in the areas for which you develop instruction.

Technical Mastery of Subject Matter

To facilitate your learning, read at least one personal computer magazine a month, attend computer expositions and trade shows, and "drop in" on the computer user groups discussions online. Join at least one computer-related organization or regional data training group. Network with other trainers in the field; discuss problems encountered in the classroom and share ideas about activities and experiences. It's also a good idea to subscribe to specific software-oriented magazines related to your training area. Finally, study the mail advertisements for ideas on unique software capabilities; also study the training-related brochures for ideas on course content and structuring.

Continue to learn more about the software you are teaching, especially the advanced features and functions. If you're new to teaching, practice delivering your course material before you conduct your first class. Be a student at least once a year and use that occasion to reflect on your learning experience as a student. The knowledge and awareness you gain from such an experience can help you design courses suitable for adult learners. Finally, make sure that you're physically fit and mentally alert; both are necessary for attaining optimal learning.

When you're comfortable with the subject matter, you can begin focusing on developing the course material. Course design and development is a challenging job; it is usually done on a low-budget, fast turnaround basis. It requires creativity and talent to pull together discrete pieces of information into a logical, coherent fashion. You're really an artist designing a product—in this situation, a computer course. Your finished product is a course that delivers the type of training a learner requires to build skills in a particular program or area.

Have you ever taken a course that was disjointed, disconnected, and irrelevant to your training needs? If you have experienced such a course, you've been exposed to poorly designed instruction. If you haven't, you've benefited from the results of an instructionally sound course designed for your learning needs. The next section provides an overview of the instructional design process.

A Primer on Instructional Design

A successful course design follows a structured, although not necessarily sequential or linear, process. The instructional design process helps you to design and develop course materials that meet the learner's needs and that are instructionally sound. Good instructional design results in positive learning outcomes and a transfer of learning to the workplace or home environment where the newly learned skills will be performed.

What Is Instructional Design?

Instructional design is a systematic approach to course development that ensures that specific learning goals are accomplished. It is an iterative process that requires ongoing evaluation and feedback.

Numerous instructional design theories and models provide guidance in this arena. Yet, only a few of them have been empirically validated against actual designs—that is, have been tested in a classroom environment to substantiate the soundness of the proposed model. However, do not view the lack of validation as a shortcoming, because the learning process is unpredictable and subject to numerous extraneous variables.

Many instructional design models are based on a behaviorist foundation where the focus is on such things as learning objectives and operant conditioning through reinforcement of the desired behavior. These models fall in the area of *reductionism*, which is defined as the decomposition of each component of an instructional system into parts: the learner, the objective, the content, and the instructional strategy. The instructional system's design models support this view, which is based on a sequential process that begins with the definition of objectives and ends with the development of components of instruction to achieve each objective.

More progressive models fall under the rubric of *constructivism*, which posits the belief that individuals learn best from personally relevant and autonomous experiences. These models tend to be more fluid and less constrained to a sequential process of course design. They also tend to incorporate more collaborative learning activities and place less emphasis on the teacher's role.

Despite the proliferation of instructional design models, several elements are common to most of them. These common elements are defining objectives, determining content (and the sequence and structure of the content), determining the instructional strategies and methods for presenting the material, and developing the curriculum. Most models include evaluation and feedback at some stage in the process. The major discrepancy in the numerous models is in the method or approach to design.

Although most models presented in the literature are linear, much debate has been generated regarding the linearity of the models. The learning process is not as predictable; it hardly ever follows a linear, sequential progression. Keep in mind that any approach you use should be flexible, should reflect the reality of the learning environment, and should attend to the practical process of instructional design (that is, it should be appropriate for the classroom environment and not for hypothetical model-testing purposes).

The fast-paced, time-intensive process of instructional design doesn't always allow you to follow a systematic, step-by-step process. Many of

7

the steps occur concurrently or, in some cases, not at all. Although a model can be helpful in focusing your design efforts, it shouldn't circumvent the reality of your particular training situation. Instead, adapt the model to fit your needs—start with a model that allows you to develop a course within your time and budget constraints. Successful training is not judged by the explicitness of your instructional design model but according to the extent to which your learners acquired skills and were able to transfer them to their workplace or home environment.

Figure 7.1 shows a model to help you visualize and conceptualize how the various components of instructional design link together. This model is used in the ongoing discussion about the primary elements of instructional design. The model presented in the figure is more flexible and circular in nature; it reflects the reality of the learning environment and the practical process of instructional design. When you develop courses, you continuously assess your decisions and how they impact the next phase; you also revise your decisions when necessary. The following sections examine how these elements come together in designing a course.

Fig. 7.1
The six-chain links model of instructional design. © Copeland, 1995

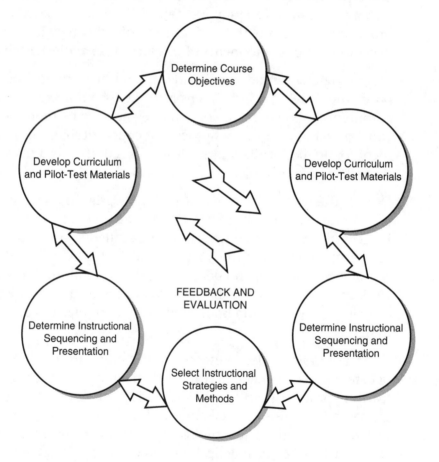

Determine Course Objectives

As you read in Chapter 4, "Training Needs Assessment," the needs assessment determines the training requirements and analyzes the target audience. It provides the foundation for the course development process and is intricately linked to the definition of course objectives. The needs assessment should not be neglected or discounted because you do not want to waste your time and expend valuable resources developing a course that is inappropriate for a particular learner's needs. Before you begin defining course objectives, you must clarify the course requester's expectations.

Clarifying Expectations

You can clarify expectations by asking the following questions:

- What is the overall goal you want to achieve from this training?

- In your view, how will you judge whether the training has met your requirements?

- Is there a specific problem that has precipitated a need for training?

The purpose of this preliminary assessment is to ensure that you're not being tasked with developing a training course for a nontraining performance or productivity problem. For example, if a manager mentions that he or she wants this training to increase the auditors' ability to complete more reports on a daily basis, you should question his or her motives further. In this situation, you can teach auditors how to use the word processing and spreadsheet software programs and perhaps introduce them to some shortcut and time-saving features such as macros, styles, and templates.

However, if the auditors' speed in producing reports is related to their inability to obtain information to prepare the report or poor time-management skills, your training program won't fix the problem. To avoid such a situation, clarify the manager's expectations and enlighten him or her on what computer skills training can accomplish. Once you clarify expectations, you should make sure that you have some knowledge about the audience for the course.

Defining the Audience

In your needs assessment, you analyze your training audience. If you didn't do this, ask the person requesting the training the following questions before proceeding:

7

- What is the makeup of the training audience (age, occupation, reading level, familiarity with the computer, amount of time on the computer per day, and so on)?

- What specific computer experiences do the learners have?

- What kind of tasks do they perform?

Once you clarify expectations and define the audience, you're ready to define the course objectives.

Define Course Objectives

Objectives help you focus on relevant content and develop exercises that enable the learner to achieve the desired outcome. An *objective* specifies what you want the learner to be able to do. In more formal course designs, objectives also specify the level of performance expected and under what conditions it will be achieved. However, when preparing a generic computer skills training course, your objectives are probably more general. Two examples of general objectives are "be able to create a two-column newsletter" and "be able to use the formatting keys to enhance the text on a page." An example of a specific objective is "be able to type a one-page letter in five minutes with no more than two errors."

When you have defined the course objectives, you can move on to determining the content.

Determining Content

Determining content is a task-oriented process that involves compiling a list of topics you want to cover. A content outline is helpful in performing this task.

Developing a Content Outline

The *content outline* lists the material to be covered. Developing the content outline is the easiest task you will perform. The content outline is a beginning stage, so don't worry about having it perfect. You can always adjust it and add to it as you proceed. As you're developing your outline, you can attempt to categorize the information.

Your goal in developing the content outline is to include only topics related to the accomplishment of the objectives. You don't want to overload the learner with unnecessary, or "nice to know," information. When you have completed your first draft of the outline, review it and eliminate all irrelevant topics. Don't expect the first draft to be your final draft; most likely, you'll make numerous drafts of the outline before you feel comfortable with it.

Once you have developed the content outline, spend some time thinking about how this information should be grouped to achieve the desired learning outcomes.

Determining Modules

When you developed your content outline, you listed the topics to be covered. The next step is to put the topics in some kind of logical order and estimate how much time you want to spend on each topic. This process is part of a high-level design effort; it's your first attempt at bringing some order to the course. You aren't "boxed in" based on the decisions you make here, so don't let the enormity of the task stifle your progress.

Determining Course Length

The course design depends, in part, on how much time is allocated to the training session. Time and resources are the primary determinants of whether classes are conducted as full-day or half-day sessions. Full training days can be tiring for the user and require frequent breaks. Brown-bag and breakfast training sessions are more informal and most likely require a different focus. These types of sessions are usually conducted more for an informational purpose (to convey the features of the system or to highlight some work-saving tips, for example).

In some situations, in which learners are not free for any of the preceding schedules, you may be asked to design a mini-lesson tailored around a particular user's needs. For example, a manager may require training in sorting a database for specific informational requirements: a personnel manager may need a listing of all employees hired after 1994 or a list of all employees with a salary greater than $50,000. In either situation, you must design instruction to meet one identified need within a specified time frame.

7

In other situations, you will have full autonomy in structuring the course and determining its length. In such situations, you have to map out a projected time frame for the course and choose a sequence for the modules.

Using a Course Map To Sequence Instruction

A course map and a lesson plan can help you plan a logical, cohesive instructional design. The *course map* provides a visual depiction of the overall course design; it serves as a road map to show where you are headed. The course map is conceived at a higher level of abstraction and gradually reaches a lower level of detail (that is, at the unit and topic levels). Figure 7.2 shows a course map.

Fig. 7.2
A sample course
map.

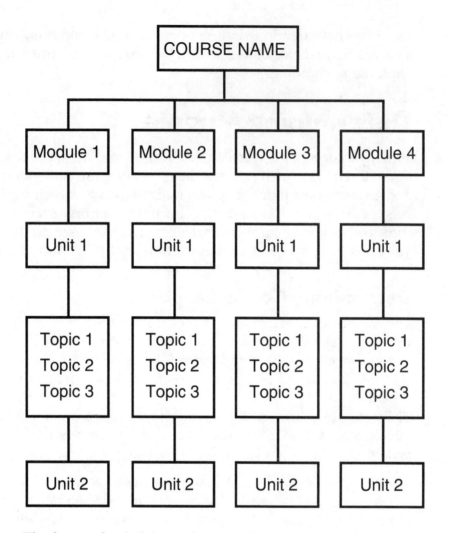

The *lesson plan* helps you keep track of your decisions as you progressively define the course requirements. More information about lesson plans is presented later in this chapter. By using these tools, you can avoid presenting a hodgepodge of lessons that fail to build on previous areas or that do not show any continuity.

Before you create your course map, determine how you want to present the material. Will your design follow a functional approach or an application approach? For example, if you are going to design a database course using a functional approach, you develop the course around key functions such as Indent, Align, Sort, Data Queries, and Setting Column Ranges. Most likely, this approach involves detailed procedural explanations for using these functions and follows a sequential order of the keys and functions involved. The major accomplishment, goal, or objective is a module title, with each function being presented at the unit or topic level, depending on the complexity of a particular topic.

In contrast, a course designed around a work application covers functions and processes as they relate to a specific area such as creating a slide show, inserting graphics in a newsletter, or performing a cost-benefit analysis. In this case, these areas become the module titles; the units and topics flow from each module's major focus.

Both choices are appropriate in certain situations. However, most decisions are based on personal preference. The deciding factor should be which approach best helps the learners develop a skill in the required area. In most cases, the application approach is far more effective, especially for those who have acquired a basic understanding of the program being taught. Learners can immediately make the link about how the program can work for them on the job, rather than having to assimilate information about numerous keys and functions without getting a chance to integrate the information in the context of a work situation.

Once you categorize the content (that is, once you sequentially order the topics and group them within major headings), you can begin developing the lesson plan. The lesson plan becomes your guidepost as you move to a greater level of detail. A design matrix is a useful tool in developing the lesson plan (see fig. 7.3). You can use information from the course map and content outline to begin entering data in the design matrix. From the course map, you can obtain the module, unit, and topic titles. The topics can be generated from the content outline.

Fig. 7.3
A sample design matrix.

MODULE 1: TITLE			
UNIT TITLE			
Time	Topic and Content	Strategies & Methods	Training Aids and Handouts

The length of a particular module depends on the complexity of the topic or the number of topics grouped together. Begin with estimates for each module and then revise the estimates as you proceed. Your final estimates will not be determined until much later—when you conduct a pilot-test of the course materials.

When you have completed the first two columns of the design matrix, you can begin selecting instructional strategies and methods.

Selecting Instructional Strategies and Methods

An *instructional strategy* is the approach you use to teach the material. Your goal is to select a strategy that most effectively conveys the concepts you are teaching. For example, you would not use a role play to teach computer skills. Instead, the more effective approaches for computer skills training are cooperative learning techniques, demonstrations, guided practice, and exercises.

Cooperative learning techniques involve activities structured around team learning. Learners engage in interactions with others and are encouraged to collaborate with others to figure things out. The instructor provides guidance to the learners as they attempt to complete various exercises with their partners. However, this doesn't mean that the learners proceed directly to an exercise; the instructor has to provide some discussion or demonstration about a particular concept or process.

Demonstrations are helpful in relaying information about computers. It is so much easier to *show* learners what you mean as you talk about a feature. You can highlight specific areas on the screen as you talk about them so that the learner can actually see the demonstration. This process helps the learner begin forming *mental models* (conceptual representations of how the system or a feature works). Mental models aid memory retention and learning transfer.

Guided-practice activities give the learners a chance to practice a newly learned skill in a safe, nonthreatening environment. Guided-practice activities afford learners an opportunity to immediately apply what they have learned and help them diagnose the areas that need clarification or that were misunderstood.

Exercises help reinforce learning and give the learners opportunities to practice their newly learned skills.

> **Tip**
>
> Avoid lectures; instead, give learners opportunities to use the system as you are talking about it. Some training situations, however, are geared toward familiarizing people with a particular application or system and do not include hands-on training. In such cases, you may have to use some lecture-based training, although you should emphasize the demonstration of the systems' capabilities.

There are no strict rules to follow regarding the selection of instructional strategies. Before selecting your strategies, consider the content, the makeup of your audience, the amount of time you have to cover a particular topic, and the nature of the material (for example, is it concrete or abstract). By paying attention to these elements, you are more apt to select an appropriate strategy.

When you have determined the instructional strategies, you can enter them in the appropriate sections on the design matrix. By now, you should have a fairly complete picture of what the overall course design will look like. If you are comfortable with the design so far, you can move on to refine the design further. In the next stage, you determine how you will present the material—that is, you sequence the material for effective learning.

Determine Instructional Sequencing and Presentation

Don't confuse *instructional sequencing* with *content sequencing*. Instructional sequencing involves making decisions about how the course material is structured. Many of your decisions about sequencing the material will be based on your thoughts about learning.

Principles of Learning

Computer skills are taught along two dimensions of knowledge: declarative and procedural. At the "getting acquainted with the features of the system" stage, learning means acquiring *declarative knowledge* (that is, the learner is "learning about" concepts and processes). At this stage, the learner is not involved in doing anything. When the learner starts using the computer to perform functions and to do the tasks you are teaching, he or she is acquiring *procedural knowledge* (that is, he or she is learning "how to do it").

In either situation, learners encounter *cognitive overload* when they receive more information than can be processed within a certain time period. Cognitive psychologists have researched this topic extensively and have determined that the most pieces of information an individual can retain in short-term memory is between 5 to 7 informational or idea units.

Another term for *short-term memory* is *working memory*. Working memory is transitional; it simply mediates the exchange of information between what is currently happening and prior knowledge that helps to integrate what is retained in long-term memory (see fig. 7.4). Learning takes place when information is coded and transferred to *long-term memory*, also called *permanent memory*.

7

Fig. 7.4
How working
memory works.

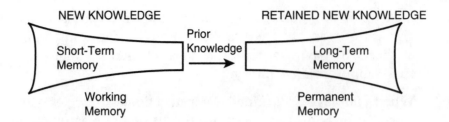

Your goal is to design instruction that strengthens the potential for long-term storage of information. Material should be presented to help the learner *select* appropriate information, *organize* the information, and then *integrate* the information.

"Chunking" of information is a proven, successful strategy for increasing the likelihood of long-term storage. Chunking refers to our ability to store and process information in working memory. When learning new computer systems and programs, novices have to attend to more pieces of information because they cannot link the information to some other function, concept, or process. You can help these learners retain more information by presenting the information in small pieces—that is, at a very detailed, procedural level—and then progressively increase the level of abstraction. As learners become increasingly familiar with the computer, they will have integrated larger chunks of information about the computer and will be able to absorb more complex concepts in a more rapid manner.

Tip

Whenever possible, introduce a concept, key, function, or feature in the context of performing a specific task or accomplishing a goal. This approach helps learners associate what you are teaching with some event or process that has occurred previously or that will occur as a result of performing a particular task. Analogies also help learners to integrate the information.

Your goal should be to structure the course so as to avoid cognitive overload for the learner. Cognitive overload occurs when too much information is presented at a rapid pace without giving the learner a chance to assimilate and integrate the information. This is where the sequencing of instruction can help.

Sequencing of Instruction

There is no magic formula to follow for the sequencing of instruction. In most cases, you select a particular approach based on the complexity of the material being presented. The following are representative of instructional approaches commonly used in computer skills training:

- **General to specific.** If the concept you are teaching can best be understood at the task-accomplishment level, structure the presentation so that you begin with the big picture and work down to the details.

- **Specific to general.** In other situations, you may begin with a specific task and proceed to a broader outcome. If the material is complex, it may be easier for the learner to begin working at a step-by-step level: mastering each step and then moving on to the next step.

These are just two approaches to sequencing material. For more robust learning, use a variety of sequencing approaches—but only if they are appropriate to the material being taught. Other ways you can improve the transfer of learning are listed in the following sidebar.

Ways To Improve Transfer of Learning

- Build numerous guided practice sessions into the course.

- Continuously provide linkages between new information being presented and previously learned information.

- Divide lessons into small chunks and build on previously learned concepts.

- Include elements of instruction that are related to the job tasks of the individuals. For example, instead of having students look for all occurrences of the word *Alison* to change it to *Mary*, provide a problem situation that requires the use of the search-and-replace feature. Consider presenting this scenario: it's 4:45 and Federal Express will pick up a document in 15 minutes. You've just discovered that the dollar amount of $50,000 should really be $500,000. What feature can you use to quickly make these changes that will also allow you to verify each occurrence before the change?

- Use summaries to help focus learners on what has occurred and to help them relate what they have learned to existing knowledge.

- Use learning checks in the form of questions and short exercises to help learners diagnose where they have failed to grasp a concept and to determine where they require more practice.

After you have determined the sequencing of the instructional material, you're ready to begin developing the curriculum.

Develop Curriculum and Pilot-Test Materials

The completed design matrix can be used as the basis for structuring and developing the course materials. Remember, however, that the design matrix is only a guide. Adapt it as necessary to achieve a smoother flow or a better presentation of a particular idea. Once you develop the course materials, you are ready to pilot-test the materials.

If possible, conduct a trial run of the course; note the time breakdowns and solicit constructive feedback about the course. Make sure that the exercises are appropriate, that the instructions are clear, and that the learners can accomplish the course objectives.

Other purposes of the trial-run are to verify the accuracy of the course materials; determine whether the materials conform to sound instructional design practices; determine whether the course achieves the specified objectives, and assess the extent to which the instructional strategies work in the classroom environment.

Use the feedback you receive to assess the materials, make the necessary changes, and finalize the course. At this stage, you've come full circle: you've completed the course development process.

Course development doesn't follow a cookbook approach; you'll find that each course is a little different and requires a varying mix of activities and instructional strategies to achieve the desired outcome. The tips in the following sidebar can help your ongoing design efforts.

Tips for Designing Effective Instruction

Here are some tips for designing effective instruction. Consider them in the context of the course you are developing and adapt those that fit your particular situation.

- Design courses for immediate practical application. Avoid focusing solely on describing keys and functions.

- Present information in the context of a specific situation and in such a way that learners can start using the information immediately to perform a task.

- Focus on material, examples, exercises, and activities relevant to the learner.

- Design exercises that build on previously learned functions and keys.

- Integrate learner errors as part of the learning process. Include design flexibility to incorporate discussions on "what went wrong and how can I fix it."

- Include some opportunities for *discovery learning* (that is, unguided exploration of the content being taught).

- Provide some challenges and include some intrinsically motivational features.

Other aspects of successful course design, such as attention to learning styles and individual learner characteristics, are covered elsewhere in this book. However, these elements are also critical to the design process and the delivery of the material.

Customization

You'll find that the quality of instruction presented in off-the-shelf materials varies. In most cases, you must customize the materials to meet your training requirements.

Off-the-Shelf Material: Is It Right for You?

Off-the-shelf material can offer some savings in the time and effort you devote to course development. If you're offering a basic introductory course that teaches concepts and specific functions, a customized course may be the most cost-effective approach. However, if you're offering courses that must be tailored to a specific client's needs and requirements, you must weigh the costs of revising an existing course against the time and effort required to develop the course. In some situations, where time is critical, customizing an existing course may be the only feasible solution.

As the following chart shows, the disadvantages of customizing existing courses appear to outweigh the advantages. However, don't automatically exclude customization as an option; consider each training need separately.

Advantages	Disadvantages
Reduces course development time	Module formats and time lengths are pre-determined
Materials already tested	Course content is predetermined
Frees up resources for other course development projects	Examples may be inappropriate for your audience
	Design could be inflexible (difficult to change units, content, and emphasis)
	Level of instruction could be inappropriate (too advanced or too basic)
	May have to pay a royalty or licensing fee

Will Customized Software Meet Your Needs?

The decision to customize is an individual decision that varies with each trainer's requirements. However, you can make a better decision by considering the questions in the following sidebar.

Should You Customize?

Consider these questions before deciding to customize an off-the-shelf training course:

■ Is the material designed to meet your training audience's needs (age, background, and reading level)?

■ Does the material meet the goals and objectives of your course?

■ Can the modules be easily resequenced?

■ How many of the existing exercises require revision?

■ Can you delete or add sections without disrupting the course flow?

■ Does revising the off-the-shelf course require more time and effort than it would take to develop a course?

■ How cost effective is it to purchase versus develop the program? In other words, what is the estimated per trainee cost of development versus purchase?

How To Customize Training Modules

To customize training modules, follow these basic steps:

1. Review the existing course materials to determine what material is superfluous and what material is missing.

2. Review the exercises to determine which should be customized for your specific audience.

3. After your review, prepare a revised outline/presentation of the course materials.

4. Revise the material to follow the outline. Delete inappropriate sections and add sections where necessary.

5. Revise the exercises. Revisions include changes in examples, names, or companies mentioned, or in reducing or increasing the complexity of the exercises.

   For example, if you're training teachers how to use a spreadsheet program, you may want to use examples related to averaging grades when teaching a particular concept. On the other hand, if you're training executives to use the same program, you may want to emphasize using the spreadsheet program to perform "what if" analyses to determine the effect of an increase or decrease in price on profits.

   Keep in mind that you want to make the material personally relevant and linked to the overall goals of the particular course.

6. Test the revised materials.

Handling Registration and Enrollment

Many of the time-consuming tasks—such as compiling lists of registrants (names, telephone numbers, available dates, and so on), developing training schedules, and sending confirmations—related to registration and enrollment can be automated. You can use something as simple as a table created with a word processing program or you can use a database program customized for your needs. On the other hand, you can purchase sophisticated, state-of-the-art enrollment and tracking software.

Software for Tracking Enrollment and Scheduling

Numerous training administration software packages are available. Two popular programs are *Training Records Plus for Windows* and *Training Administrator*. For large-scale efforts, you can have programs customized or developed to meet your unique requirements.

Before purchasing a training administration package, request a demo disk and evaluate the software. Most companies offer evaluation copies at no cost.

When evaluating the software, you may want to consider the elements listed in the following sidebar.

Checklist for Evaluating Training Administration Software

- Ability to import existing data about the learners (for example, if the learners are employees and you have access to a database of basic information about the employees).

- Ability to sort training activity by participant, department, team, class, course, instructor, or any other field you require.

- Ability to print course rosters, enrollment letters, transcripts, and certificates.

- Ability to view and print monthly, weekly, and daily training schedules.

- Ability to develop customized reports.

- Ability to generate graphs and charts.

- Ability to print a variety of reports such as class rosters, instructor schedules, agendas, data sorts, calendars, reminders, and memos.

- Ability to register students by class, location, and time period.

7

Keeping Training Records

The requirement to keep training records varies with each organization. Follow your organization's rules regarding keeping training records. You may want to use the automated software to keep track of your training records. If you are an independent contractor, the decision about what type of records you want to keep is a personal one. At a minimum, you may want to keep information on the types of courses conducted, the number of people trained, the dates classes were conducted, results of course evaluations, and a contact person's name.

From Here...

You've gone from the request for training to a completed course. It's such a rewarding accomplishment because you can see a product through to its completion. In this chapter, you learned how important it is to clarify expectations about the course and to determine course objectives. These objectives provide a focal point for developing the course and determining the content. You also learned how a course map is helpful in designing the course layout and how a design matrix helps to focus on instructional sequencing and methods. Of course, you want to pilot-test the materials after they're developed. In some situations, you may have to customize an off-the-shelf course; just weigh the advantages of doing so against the disadvantages. You also learned that automation of registration and record keeping reduces the amount of time spent on paperwork and frees you to do what you love to do—design and develop courses!

Now you're ready to consider how you will deliver the training. The following chapters should be helpful:

■ Chapter 8, "Training Techniques," provides helpful hints about how to take your well-designed presentation off the paper and into the classroom.

■ Chapter 9, "Housekeeping Tasks," presents some of the necessary chores you must do to keep your time in the classroom running smoothly.

■ Chapter 10, "The Flow of the Class," outlines how a typical classroom session progresses—and what you can do when things don't go according to plan.

Chapter 8

Training Techniques

by Bill Brandon

Bill Brandon has managed, developed, and delivered instruction since 1968. His company, Accomplishment Technology Unlimited, provides clients with systematic ways to train, guide, and motivate employees to higher levels of accomplishment. Bill has been the Sysop of the Computer Training and Support Forum on CompuServe since 1987.

This chapter presents classroom techniques used by effective trainers to produce successful, happy, and self-reliant computer users. But before you begin strip-mining this mother lode of information, reflect for a moment on the question, *"Why bother?"*

When you come right down to it, the number of people who have learned to do things on their own is amazing. There are millions of successful, happy, self-taught jugglers, three-chord guitar musicians, particle physicists, and brain surgeons. Some people even teach themselves to use computers and application software without the assistance of another person. You yourself may be such an individual.

The ways in which people teach themselves are constantly increasing in number and effectiveness. In the beginning, the rugged individualist who wanted to learn about computers built an Altair from a kit, wrote a bootstrap program to make it run, and created a personal brand of BASIC to use in programming it. That's how Bill Gates got started. Now there are books, audiotapes, videotapes, computer-based training (CBT), and CD-ROMs to teach the curious whatever they want to learn, whenever they want to learn it.

So the question is, why does *anybody* need *you*, Mr. or Ms. Classroom Computer Trainer? Classroom training not only survives but flourishes in the midst of this abundance of self-instructional methods and means. There are four reasons why this is so.

First, self-teaching requires time that busy people don't have. It is true that effective CBT can teach certain skills in half the time required in the classroom. But it is just as true that self-instruction takes far longer. People need about *two to three weeks of steady use* of a piece of software to pick up what they could have learned in about *six to twelve hours in a classroom.* And there are some useful bits of knowledge that most users will never be aware of unless they learn about them from someone else.

Second, people don't know what they don't know about how to use computers well. This means it is hard for a person to figure out where to start and what to learn. It also means it is hard for that person to decide *which* book or CD-ROM to buy to learn what he or she needs to know. To make it worse, there is plenty of bad advice available from friends, computer mavens, and passers-by about what's important to know and about what's trivial. There are even badly designed CBT and CD-ROM products that don't teach or that take longer than good classroom instruction. A novice computer user doesn't know the difference between them and the well-designed products. A credible classroom instructor is a trustworthy guide through unknown territory.

Third, a great many people just don't believe that they can learn to do anything involving a computer. Some trainers make the mistake of labeling such learners *computerphobic.* The plain truth is that these people are not afraid of the computer, they just can't see themselves being successful in using one. They may know why they *should* learn, they just think they *can't* learn. Or they may not see the point in changing the way they've always done a particular task. Think of the secretaries you've heard about who print an executive's e-mail and put it in the executive's in-basket because the boss won't learn to use the computer on the credenza. Expert instructors do what expert magicians do: They get other people to temporarily put aside their lack of belief that something is possible. Experts create a space in which the reluctant or the stubborn willingly learn to do what they had refused to learn before.

Finally, left to their own devices, many people do not manage to learn how to use computers or software correctly. They fail or fall short of their goal of being effective, efficient, and self-reliant. They may learn to do certain tasks but they may also learn to do them wrong. Take word processing software. Workers who were around when every desk had a typewriter will think of and use a computer loaded with Microsoft Word as a glorified Selectric. Neither they nor younger workers know that there is a way to use any word processor to cut the time it takes to produce a finished document by 30 percent or more. You yourself may not know this secret—and you are far more expert than most users who try to teach themselves. If you know the technique, it's because somebody taught it to you.

What does a successful trainer do in the classroom to overcome these four obstacles?

The master trainer has a knowledge base and a set of techniques for dealing with the problems a user may encounter. Although a competent trainer always plans the instruction and uses a lesson guide, there is more to be done in the classroom than using the prepared materials.

In the classroom, a master trainer does certain things that other instructors almost never do. At the end of this chapter, you will also be able to do the following:

- Apply certain basic concepts that facilitate learner progress toward new skills, knowledge, and understanding.

- Tailor the printed course design on the spot to fit the individuals in the classroom.

- Create readiness to learn, promote confidence, and produce self-efficacy.

- Deliver course content, using media and classroom techniques in a way that helps learners acquire productive new skills, relevant knowledge, and applied understanding in less time than they could gain these on their own.

What Every Computer Trainer Should Know

The practitioners in any profession develop and share a body of knowledge for the advancement of that profession. Training is no different, except that, for the most part, computer trainers have not been the recipients of a lot of the common body of knowledge.

Much of the common body of knowledge in our profession has come from the field of educational psychology, especially the part that deals with teaching adults. Other large components have been borrowed from sociology, such as information about dealing with people in groups. Finally, the accumulated experience of trainers provides the practical aspects of that body of knowledge.

What these elements have in common is that they deal with changing the behavior of people. In fact, the way to test whether learning has taken place is to determine whether people can do anything after the training that they couldn't do before. In other words, did their behavior change as a result of the training?

8

The information that follows focuses on a few particulars from these common elements to provide a solid base for your understanding of the techniques presented in the rest of the chapter. Although some of these points are touched on in other chapters, the intent here is to supplement what you read elsewhere, not to duplicate it.

Using What You Know about Adult Learners

In Chapter 3, "Adult Learning: What Do We Know for Sure?," you can read an in-depth analysis of adult learning styles and general tips about how to teach adults. This section contains some tips for specific application of your knowledge about adult learners.

Tip

Adults learn by interacting with other adults, by using their senses, and by applying their experience.

When an adult needs to find out how to do something that he or she has not done before, how many ways to proceed does this person have? There are a great many, but here are some of the more common ones:

- Trial and error
- Seek out and consult with experts
- Seek out and consult with people who have done the task before
- Find a book, a videotape, or an audiotape on the subject
- Look up magazine or newspaper articles on the task
- Attend a class
- Go to a user group, special interest group, or support group meeting
- Listen to a speaker talking about the task
- Watch a television talk show dealing with the subject
- Write a letter to the manufacturer and ask for advice
- Build a model or a simulation and try out different ideas

Tip

Match the technique you use to the kind of result you are trying to achieve.

Adults can and do learn on their own successfully, if haphazardly, from the methods in the previous list. Each of these methods has a parallel that can be used in your classroom. The closer the courses you teach approximate natural learning, the better students learn. The key is to know what results you want to see and to apply techniques that will give you those results.

Basic Techniques for Adult Education

A panel discussion is one of the techniques that can contribute greatly to how much members of a class understand about using software to solve problems. On the other hand, you wouldn't expect a person who *only* heard a panel discussion about FoxPro to be able to go out and build an enterprise-level database application the next day.

Table 8.1 shows the relationship between types of results sought and the most effective techniques to achieve each.

Table 8.1 Techniques and the Type of Educational Results Best Suited to Their Use

Technique	Knowledge	Understanding	Skill	Interest
Lecture	✓			
Demonstration		✓		✓
Interview	✓			✓
Panel	✓	✓		
Reading	✓			
Discussion	✓	✓		✓
Case Study		✓	✓	
Exercises		✓	✓	
Drills			✓	
Coaching		✓	✓	
Group Work	✓	✓	✓	

Tip

For any given outcome, bias your choice of technique toward the one that involves the students as active participants.

8

Some techniques rely on the abilities and experience of the instructor, some on the abilities and experience of outside resources (panels, interviewees), and some on the abilities and experience of the students. In Table 8.1, the techniques toward the top of the list generally do not involve the students as actively as those techniques toward the bottom.

One key to effective classroom courses is to use a variety of resources. As you discover from reading Chapter 3, adults have different learning styles. By using different resources, you deliver important content in ways that match the different learning styles. In addition, some techniques are more versatile than others. Lecture is suited to delivery of knowledge only. But group work can contribute to knowledge, understanding, and skill, depending on how you set it up.

Notice that for some techniques such as demonstrations, interviews, and panel discussions, you have the option to videotape the event or to stage it live in the classroom. Favor the live presentations so that students have the opportunity to ask questions of the panelists or the interviewee.

How To Apply the Basic Techniques

Who can you use for outside resources when you have selected the panel or the interview as your technique? To a certain extent, this depends on the context in which your course is conducted. Take the case of a company rolling out a new Customer Information System for use by customer contact employees in many different departments. A panel discussion at the start of the training program is a good way to generate understanding, interest, and support for the change if the panel includes the following kinds of people:

- The head of the department whose employees are in the class

- The customer service manager or the head of the sales department

- The lead programmer from the development team

- An employee who helped with the beta test

There are several points in most course designs at which it can be appropriate for you to bring in a "guest" to interview. You can interview someone who is a "power user" of the software being taught or an employee who was a "convert" to use of the software. An especially effective interview is one in which the instructor interviews the head of the department whose employees are attending the course. The purpose of this interview is to get the department head to explain what he or she hopes the students will gain by attending and how this education is important to the group.

Generally, case studies, exercises, and drills are included in the course by the course designers. You should add or substitute such techniques where they can contribute to better results. This is especially true in the case of courseware purchased from an outside vendor. See the tips in Chapter 7, "Course Development," in the "Customization" section, for some specific ideas in this area.

With demonstrations, case studies, and exercises, the way you set them up and the way you analyze the results are very important. These techniques can contribute to the students' understanding of the concepts behind the software as well as to their interest and skill in using it. When you begin a demonstration, case study, or exercise, point out to the students the features and key points for which they should look. You may even want to post "What To Look For" on a flipchart or marker board. You can also assign to specific students or groups the responsibility to watch for each point. As part of the summing up, have these "watching teams" report what they observed and how they might apply it to their work.

As you see later in this chapter, the effective use of groups of learners in the way you deliver a course is an important and often overlooked technique.

How Training Differs from School and Presentations

Many of us have a model for training based on elementary and secondary education methods used by our teachers. These methods focus on the teacher and make him or her the source of all knowledge, the enforcer of rules, and the arbiter of disagreement. The teacher is there to teach, and the students are there to listen and to learn.

> **Note**
>
> To be fair, education methods for children have changed. Modern teachers are more likely to encourage discovery by students than they are to serve as the main or only resource in the room. This approach is similar to the methods we have been discussing for adults. A consequence of this change is that younger individuals increasingly come to the training room expecting to direct their own learning. These employees may be totally put off or bored to tears by an authoritarian trainer. Older persons, on the other hand, may act in ways consistent with the old rules. They may have to be convinced that they are accountable for their own learning. You can find more about this topic in the section "Creating Readiness To Learn," later in this chapter.

8

The "schoolhouse" model is not appropriate for adult learners because it does not provide what they need: the ability to connect their own experience and skills to new information for the solution of their particular problem. There are two other models whose techniques are sometimes mistakenly applied to teaching adults. These models are borrowed from business presentations and from public speaking. Like the schoolhouse model, these models are uncritically and inappropriately applied by trainers who mean well but don't know, understand, or appreciate the nature of adult learning.

The Center of Attention

The objectives of business presentations and speeches do not include producing skilled, self-reliant users of a product. Typical objectives in presentations and speeches are to inform, enlighten, or persuade the audience. There is usually no active participation by individual listeners. However, the speaker or presenter clearly hopes that the members of the audience will be moved to some kind of action later. A great deal of attention is focused on the presenter and what he or she does to get the attention, interest, and compliance of the audience.

Tip

In your training sessions, remember that the center of attention must always be the learners and the learning, not the trainer and the training.

In computer training, by contrast, the focus is on what the learners are doing. The important outcome is what those learners can do with their computers or with the software after the training is over. Informing, enlightening, or persuading may be necessary parts of the process, but they are not the objectives in and of themselves. The key techniques in training are the ones that obtain the active participation of the learners.

Centering Instructors During Development

If you are responsible for the development of computer trainers, here is a technique to help put the emphasis where it belongs. You may be familiar with "feedback": you videotape the instructor during an actual class and then provide a critique of what the instructor does and the way he or she does it. A better way to develop instructors is to arrange the camera so that it records what the learners are doing. As long as the audio track captures what the instructor says, this videotape can provide valuable feedback. Watch the tape with the instructor and consider together the following questions:

What are the learners actually doing from minute to minute? If, for most minutes, the answer is "watching the instructor" or "listening to the instructor," the focus in the classroom is in the wrong place. For most minutes, the more desirable answers are "using the computer," "working with other class members," and "identifying how to use a given software feature on the job." You should see big movements and hear the students talking. If they look like they are thinking (or staring or nodding off) all the time, they aren't gaining the skills, understanding, and self-efficacy they should be gaining.

Are the learners succeeding most of the time? When they are not, how do they get help? Adults who are going to turn into self-reliant computer users should get more and more of their answers from the software's help feature and from each other as the course progresses. The "Power Techniques" sections, later in this chapter, show you two methods for ensuring that students succeed most—if not all—the time.

Is the character of what the learners are doing changing about every seven minutes? If the course design does not provide frequent changes of pace, adult students tend to feel that the class is too slow. At the same time, the changes should not be mechanically timed—move on when the learners are ready to move on, not by the clock. On a videotape of the students, it is easy to spot the nodding heads and wandering attention that indicate a need for change. It is also easy to spot the confusion and frustration when they are left behind.

Give Learners Control over the Pace

During a class, it is often hard for the instructor to judge whether people are satisfied with the pace of the class. There is no reason why the instructor should feel solely responsible for regulating this flow.

One interesting way to give control of the pace to the learners is to hand out small paper ballots just before a break. On each ballot, students mark whether they feel the class is moving too slowly, too quickly, or about right. Collect these in a small receptacle at the door. Tally them on the marker board or on the newsprint pad so that students can see the results of the vote. Adjust your pace accordingly.

If you are lucky enough to be working in a classroom equipped with *responder units*, you can do the same thing without having to wait for a break. (In fact, you can use the responder units to ask whether students want to take a break.) A responder unit is a small box at the student's station that provides a variety of buttons for responding to true/false and multiple-choice questions. The results of the responses to a question are automatically tallied and displayed to the instructor on a separate monitor. Similar systems are sometimes used in distance-learning classrooms to give feedback to instructors who may be located miles away from their students.

8

Understanding the Value of Enjoyment

At about this point, some readers are objecting, "I'm an educator, not an entertainer." Even though you *are* an educator and not an entertainer, students learn more if you make your class enjoyable. In part, student enjoyment springs from involvement. For the rest, their enjoyment comes from the way you choose to teach.

> **Tip**
>
> An appropriate amount of fun helps people learn without making them consciously aware of the fact that they are learning.

There is a line between being entertaining and being entertainment. You cross that line only when the learners cease to be involved as active participants in the learning process. If you had the video camera running when the line was crossed, you would see students' behavior go from "using the software" to "watching the instructor" and stay there.

So how does an instructor stay entertaining, yet keep the focus and the activity out among the learners?

Do the expected in unexpected ways. For example, if you need to "borrow" somebody from the class for a demonstration or to lead a group, ask for a volunteer. Say only that you need this person to do a very important job. Eventually someone will volunteer. Then tell this person that his or her important job is to pick the actual person who will be involved in the demonstration or lead the group. This is a very safe way to get a big laugh—much better than using a joke. It may also help you manage the person who would like to be the "teacher's pet" (you know—the one who always has his hand up first to answer a question).

Do things in a way that requires people to move around. When you review a step-by-step procedure, use a Koosh ball. Toss the ball to one of the students. This person must give the first step in the procedure and then toss the ball to another student. The second person gives the second step and throws the ball to someone who hasn't given a step yet. If someone misses a step, anyone who knows what comes next calls it out and gets the ball to pass on. This continues until the procedure is complete. Not only does this wake everyone up, it gets the know-it-alls to stop playing solitaire.

Require the last person back in the room from a break or from lunch to sing. You won't have to do it more than once.

Periodically award "fabulous prizes" (coffee mug, mouse pad, imprinted ball-point pen, whatever) for correct responses or performances. You should have a group that is fairly evenly matched if you plan to use this approach fairly.

The key word is *appropriate*. Should your classroom look like a three-ring circus? Absolutely not. Should people be smiling and looking as if they are having a great experience? Absolutely yes!

If you keep thinking along the lines of finding ways to surprise participants and of using things that happen to cause people to smile, you will never run out of ideas. You can also order books of icebreaker exercises from the ASTD (American Society for Training and Development)

Bookstore for those times when you're fresh out of ideas. You can contact the ASTD at the following address:

ASTD
1640 King Street
Box 1443
Alexandria, VA 22313-2043
(703) 683-8100

Another useful resource is Susan Boyd's book, *Accelerate Computer Learning with Analogies*. This volume contains over 500 analogies for computer concepts as well as reproducible illustrations for overhead transparencies. Contact Susan at 215-886-2669 for details on obtaining the book.

Speakers at national conferences on computer training often deliver sessions on the subject of increasing learner involvement and enjoyment. For example, at the 1995 Computer Training and Support Conference, the following were some of the topics and speakers in this area. You can order audiotapes of these sessions from Professional Programs Audio Cassettes at 805-255-7774.

- Franz E. Fauley, Director, National Computer Training Institute (708-438-8271). Session 110: *Deadly, Dull, Boring Computer Training—NOT!* (How to keep learning light and humorous as well as effective.)

- Nelda Bradley and Ed Cohen, Seer Technologies (919-319-2217). Session 111: *Aha! TaDa! Designing Games that Work* (Going beyond typical classroom games into the realm of discovery and insight using a training technique of modeling behavior.)

- Marion Piller, Senior Course Developer, Sybase, Inc. (510-922-4652). Session 210: *Making Students Think—The Art of Questioning* (Options trainers have in the choice, timing, and delivery of questions.)

- Paul Jacobson and Chet Seviola, I/S Resource Group (614-431-0585). Sessions 410 and 510: *Crazy Stuff that Works* (Three proven and fun simulation exercises—StringLAN/PeopleNet, Client/Server House, and PocketProtector/Propeller Hat.)

- Bob Mosher, Logical Operations (716-224-7328). Session 411: *Creating Independent Learners* (A four-step approach to allowing, encouraging, and teaching independent learning.)

8

Planning Course Organization: Discuss, Demonstrate, Do

Learning styles aside, there *is* a way to deliver instruction that helps most adult learners tremendously. Sometimes this is referred to as "the three Ds." Specifically, the three basic steps are Discuss, Demonstrate, Do.

These three steps are applied across the "chunks" taught to learners. The chunks add up to the total performance being learned. Figure 8.1 shows the principle. In the "Power Techniques" sections, later in this chapter, you see that there are several ways to organize the chunks; for now, we are going to look only at the learning sequence.

Fig. 8.1
Each module is delivered with the Discuss, Demonstrate, Do technique.

	Discuss	**Demonstrate**	**Do**
Module 1	Terms and Ideas	Exercises	Practice
Module 2	Terms and Ideas	Exercises	Practice
Module 3	Terms and Ideas	Exercises	Practice

Tip

Be sure that your students understand the concepts behind what you are doing and the language you use to describe what you are doing before you have them actually try it on their own. Then give them plenty of chances to practice with corrective feedback.

Discuss What Is About To Be Learned

The first step is to Discuss what is about to be learned. The purpose of the discussion is to give the learners just enough theory and terminology to allow them to follow the demonstration that will come next. Be sure that you keep the learners involved actively in the discussion.

Suppose that you are going to teach eight people in a class how to format a floppy disk. Table 8.2 shows the terms and concepts related to this procedure.

Table 8.2 Terms and Ideas Students Should Understand about Formatting a Floppy Disk	
Terms	**Ideas**
Teach these terms and ideas first:	
Floppy disk	Rules for handling and storage
5.25-inch floppy disk	Magnetic medium storage
3.5-inch floppy disk	Formatting/unformatting
Disk jacket	Disk capacity and density
Byte(s)	Which drives to format

Terms	Ideas
Teach these terms and ideas when demonstrating:	
Format/Unformat Command	Write protection
Write-protect notch	Disk drive operation
Write-protect tab/switch	
Teach this term later, if at all:	
Volume Serial Number	

During the discussion, learners should acquire the following information:

- An overview of what they are about to learn (for example, how to prepare a new floppy disk for use or how to recycle a used disk).

- An idea of how this relates to what they already know (for example, "you can't keep everything stored on your hard drive all the time, and you may want to send some data to somebody whose computer is not linked to yours").

- The key ideas and terms (in Table 8.2, these are the items under "Teach these terms and ideas first").

- The *task theory* (for example, the steps in the formatting process).

A term that may be new to you is *task theory*. This is a sort of road map of the task about to be taught. It helps to keep the learner oriented as you go through the procedure. In the case of formatting a disk, the task theory is pretty simple:

1. Check the disk to be sure that it is ready to be formatted.

2. Insert the disk properly into the drive.

3. Type or select the FORMAT command.

4. Remove the disk from the drive when formatting is done.

It is a good idea to post the task theory on a piece of newsprint or project it onto an overhead screen while you do the next step, the demonstration. If you prepare your own handout materials, include the task theory steps on a handout so that students don't have to try to copy them, make notes, and watch the demonstration all at the same time.

Demonstrate the Procedure

There are three parts to a demonstration. Part one consists of the instructor showing what to do. Included in this step is the explanation of any additional terms and any new ideas that must be acquired by the students. These are shown in Table 8.2 under "Teach these terms and ideas when demonstrating."

Part two of the demonstration consists of the learners doing the procedure as the instructor tells them what to do. As you go through the procedure, be sure that all the learners have done each step correctly before you go on to the next step. Encourage questions. For very simple procedures, you can sometimes skip this part of the demonstration.

Part three is a review of the procedure. This may be a place to use the Koosh ball mentioned in "Understanding the Value of Enjoyment," earlier in this chapter. When you are satisfied that the group understands the procedure thoroughly, you are ready to go on to the next stage: having the students do it on their own.

Do It

The next step of the teaching process is to give the students the opportunity to do the process on their own and to practice it. You have to exercise a little judgment here.

For many procedures, you can give the students an exercise and release them to complete it. When teaching how to format a disk, for example, you probably don't have to give any additional help before the students can format a disk successfully. Consider having them format two or three blank disks for use later in the course and then move on.

For other procedures, you may want to have the students do the steps as you prompt them. Teaching how to do a query in a database application might be an example of such an occasion. You can also combine the exercise with the review of the steps in the procedure.

In every case, be sure that you allow adequate opportunity to practice the new skill before you move to the next procedure to be taught.

Tailoring the Course Design to the Audience

Perhaps you or a colleague designed the course you are teaching. Perhaps you bought the course from a vendor. In either case, the writer was thinking of a certain audience when he or she developed the objectives and the materials. The writer made some assumptions about this ghost audience, its entry level skills, its attitude about the course content, and so on.

When you arrive in the classroom, you are no longer dealing with a ghost audience. You are dealing with what may be a very different group: The People Who Came to Class Today. If all you do is deliver the course as written, you risk an unhappy, dissatisfied crowd if the course writer's assumptions turn out to be wrong.

Chapters 4, 5, and 7 address part of what you must do to tailor the course to the audience by adjusting content and scheduling. This tailoring, for example, can provide examples and exercises relevant to the group.

In particular, Chapter 7, "Course Development," pointed out the need to customize the courseware by injecting examples taken from the learners' daily work into the course materials. This is an important step overlooked by an amazing number of trainers. If you are conducting public classes, have a variety of different kinds of demonstration and exercise material available for instant use.

However, there is more to be done in this area once the class has started. Some important opportunities for learning can be developed and enhanced with judicious changes in the way the trainer does four things (provided that these changes serve to match the course to the group):

- Identify learner expectations

- Tap into the power of differences

- Help learners transfer skills to the job

- Deal with objections from learners

Identifying Learner Expectations (Why Are They Here?)

Most trainers spend a minute or two explaining the course objectives, as suggested in Chapter 10, "The Flow of the Class." Some trainers also take a minute or two to find out where the learners are in their skill level (as explained in Chapter 5, "Skills Assessment"). It is also a good idea to ask the students what they expect to gain from the course.

8

> **Tip**
>
> It is critically important for you to *ask the learners* what they expect to gain from the course. The easiest, most natural time to do this is at the beginning of the first class session.

When you ask students what they expect to gain, there are several ways to have the students answer:

- Each student calls out his or her expectations and objectives.

- Students take two minutes to list their expectations and objectives individually, then combine lists with their immediate neighbor, and finally combine the list of that pair with the list of another pair of students. A spokesperson for the group then reads the list out loud.

- Each student writes down on a small piece of paper one thing he or she hopes to learn in the class and crumbles it into a small ball. On a signal, each student tosses his or her paper across the room to another student (this can be done several times to get good mixing). After everyone has somebody else's objective, the items are read off the notes one at a time.

The last two methods generate much more activity than the first. They model the level of participation desired and generate a sense of fun and cooperation. The third method has the added benefit of protecting group members who may be shy about saying what they think is important. On the other hand, the first method is good to use when the group is comfortable together or already has a good sense of play and team spirit.

In each case, the instructor (or an assistant selected from the group) should record the expectations on a large piece of newsprint or a flipchart at the front of the room. When the list is complete, tear it off and tape it to the wall so that it remains visible throughout the class.

The instructor should indicate which expectations fall outside the scope of the course. As the course progresses, the instructor should note when one of the learner objectives is being addressed. If necessary and feasible, the instructor can make short excursions from the course plan to address learner objectives at appropriate times. At the end of the course, include the learner objectives in the summary.

Tapping into the Power of Differences

Some groups of people in classrooms are made up of individuals who are all at about the same level of knowledge, skill, or understanding concerning the subject at hand. Other classes are more mixed: some students know very little about the subject, some know a great deal about it, and some are in between these extremes.

> **Tip**
>
> Use the fact that there is a mixture of skill levels in the room to increase the level of participation by learners.

When you do the skills assessment suggested in Chapter 5, "Skills Assessment," you will know what mixture is present in the room. It is much better to use open-ended questions to assess skill levels than to ask, "everybody who knows how to create a pie chart from a spreadsheet, raise your hand." Open-ended questions not only elicit more information, they establish a norm that not only is it okay to talk during the class, it's expected. Another benefit is that it helps you gain rapport with the individuals in the room. From rapport comes trust and confidence, which make later steps in the training process easier to take.

You use the information about skill levels as you teach. Most courseware is created with the assumption that everyone is at the same level. If you learn that this is indeed the case, you can proceed with creating readiness to learn, knowing exactly the point from which all your learners are beginning.

However, it is far more often the case that the group's skill levels are mixed. A strategy that works well is to deliberately place two people at one computer during the exercises that follow demonstration of a procedure. It is neither necessary nor desirable to pair people up according to ability. An effective way to do the pairing is to use a totally arbitrary personal characteristic. For example, individuals can only partner with someone who was born in the same season of the year or on the same day of the week as themselves.

While paired up for an exercise, each partner must complete the exercise, with coaching as necessary from his or her "buddy." Questions may be asked of the instructor, but *both* partners must each raise a hand, indicating that collectively they could not solve the problem. Change partners after each exercise.

Helping Students Transfer New Skills to the Job

One of the major challenges in teaching adults is to get the skills taught in the classroom to *transfer*. This means getting people to do on the job what they learned in class. Sometimes, skills don't transfer because the course design did not include time for the students to plan how they could use their new skills.

> **Tip**
>
> Every course should include a transfer strategy; that strategy should be implemented when the students are still in class.

Chapter 11, "Augmenting Classroom Training with Other Media," suggests some methods for supporting continuing learning back on the job. All these methods work, but they are not enough by themselves. Learners must begin applying everything they learned in class as soon as they get back on the job. Just as there is a "learning curve," there is also a "forgetting curve."

Any skill not used within 24 hours of being learned begins to decay. After three weeks, most of the skill is gone if it has not been used. In most cases, the methods for continuing learning on the job do not reinforce what has already been learned, so it is necessary to take some additional measures.

It is easy to include a transfer strategy as a regular part of your review at the end of each module. Ask the students to identify ways they will use what you just taught them. Try to elicit fairly specific responses.

After a module about setting up workbooks in a spreadsheet, for example, students ought to be able to tell you which of their job duties will be made easier by this feature. Get the learners to write down these applications on a separate sheet of paper. Have them write the date when they will have the first opportunity to use this new skill next to the application.

Ideally, this sheet of paper is not bound into course workbooks; it should be a loose-leaf sheet that can be taped or pinned somewhere near the student's computer back in the office. Figure 8.2 suggests a format for the sheet. You can make up one of these sheets for each course and fill in the "Features" column.

Fig. 8.2
A loose-leaf sheet like this one can help remind your students to use their new skills on the job.

...Remember to use these features in Excel back on the job!

Feature To Use:	Date or Task To Use It On:
1. Autoformat a range of cells	
2. Autostyle an entire worksheet for a report	
3. Autofill a range of cells with names of months	
(etc.)	

If you are teaching courses in the company where you work, you can implement a "follow-up" program. About a week after someone has been in one of your courses, you can give that person a call. During this call, you ask three questions:

1. How has the learner been using what he or she learned in the class?

2. What did you include in the class that actually wasn't important to this person?

3. What did you not include in the class that the learner wishes you had addressed?

Asking these questions gives you more information than you typically get from an end-of-course rating sheet. It also provides an opportunity for the learner to get any clarification needed. And of course, it lets you remind them of that loose-leaf sheet pinned up next to the computer.

Dealing with Objections from Learners

Even in a well-planned, well-run course, everybody won't always be totally satisfied. In some classes, you will have a learner who seems to have some problem with everything you are teaching. In other sessions, all is well until—*bang!* You get blindsided by a protest from a learner.

This happens to every trainer. What's important isn't that you got an objection, it's how you handle it.

> **Tip**
>
> For any objection or question from a learner, you have more than one way to respond so that everybody wins. The choice is yours.

A simple system can help you remember the four basic responses to any objection you get in class from a learner. Figure 8.3 is a visualization of your possible responses.

Meet the Objection. The most basic, and perhaps natural, response is to meet the objection head on. Stick to your story and explain how your idea works. Sometimes this is effective. Sometimes it just starts a fight, makes you look defensive, and alienates class members.

If you decide to use the head-on response, consider using Ben Franklin's method: "It seems to me..." or "In my opinion..." helps to soften the response. It's better if you turn to face the other person squarely when you do this, but don't take a step toward or away from the person. Stepping toward the person can seem aggressive. Stepping back weakens your point.

Fig. 8.3
You can take one of four directions when confronted by an objection from a learner.

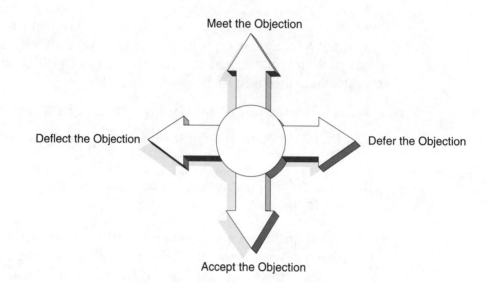

Consider using the word *and* in your reply instead of *but*. For example, saying, "I understand how it might seem that way to you *and* I believe you are overlooking..." keeps the other person listening to you and seems much less harsh than, "I understand what you're saying *but* you haven't considered..." By using *It seems to me...* or substituting *and* for *but*, everybody wins.

Accept the Objection. Another basic response is to back off your point. Let the objector have it his or her way. If you realize that you were wrong, say so. The positive side of this choice is that you can come off looking better in the long run. The down side is that it may invite further attacks or undermine your credibility. Face the person squarely when you back off the point. If the other person is emotional about the objection, take a step back as you say, "You know, you're right." Then drop it and move on. Everybody wins.

Deflect the Objection. A third response is good to use when someone has made an objection you'd either like to check out or to discredit totally. Throw out a related question "overhead" to the group: "Has anyone else had an experience like this?" Take note of the answers and respond accordingly. If the question is discounted by the group, face the objector and say, "I'd like to understand the problem better. Are you willing to meet me on the break about this?" In most cases, this will be the last you'll hear about it, and you have helped the person save face. Everybody wins.

Defer the Objection. The fourth response is reserved for those times when you want to deal with the objection later. Perhaps someone brings up a point that you plan to address in another part of the program. Perhaps someone raises an objection that has an "agenda" attached. Smile, say you think that's a great question but you want to deal with it a little later in the course, *and then write the objection on a piece of newsprint and hang it on the wall.* You have acknowledged the point. You can get back to it when (and if) you want to. You are being fair and the objector has had his or her say. Everybody wins.

Creating Readiness To Learn

If you have read Chapter 3, "Adult Learning: What Do We Know for Sure?," you are aware that adult learners tend to be problem centered in the way they approach learning. Said another way, adults who choose to take a course do so because they have a problem they want to solve. This is one reason why well-designed computer training programs are organized around business problems ("How To Use WordPerfect for Legal Secretaries") rather than subject matter ("Word Processing 101").

However, you will find students in your classroom who didn't choose to be there and don't want to be there. You will also find those who don't mind being there but aren't really quite ready. My favorites in this crowd are the poor souls who have been using WordPerfect 5.1; when the office upgrades to Windows, they have been sent to learn Word 7 without having ever been to a Windows class. Sometimes, you may find people who say they have no idea why they are in your class, but they were told they had to attend. And there are the usual shy ones who think they aren't cut out to use a computer at all.

You may have to find a way to send some of these people back to work until they are ready, willing, and able to learn. Or you may have to find ways to help some of them learn. The concept of *readiness to learn* is the key to figuring out what action to take.

> **Tip**
>
> Adults are ready to learn when they feel a need to learn and when they see that the goals of a learning experience are in line with their own goals and abilities.

The "Teachable Moment"

One way in which adults may come to feel a need to learn is the arrival of a *teachable moment*. Teachable moments happen when an adult becomes frustrated at not being able to do something other people can do, even though this adult is apparently ready in all respects to do it.

For the most part, adults arrive at teachable moments because their role in life, or a significant part of it, has changed or is threatened. Taking away a graphic artist's Macintosh and Freehand software and giving her a Pentium and Painter software certainly qualifies as such a change (or threat). But there are *developmental tasks* and *readiness to learn* that must also be taken into account.

Before the graphic artist can learn to use Painter on the Pentium, she must learn to contend with a very different computing environment. Even considering the evolution of Windows, the Pentium does not work just like the Mac did. The process of learning to work in the new computing environment is a series of developmental tasks. The artist will not be ready to learn Painter until she has completed them.

Along with development, the artist must arrive at a readiness to learn. This mainly means getting answers to some rather serious concerns. Will she be able to make the transition? Will she ever like using the new equipment and software as well as her beloved Mac? How will her job change? Why is this change being forced on her?

By the time an instructor sees this artist in a class on how to use Painter, the previous developmental tasks and some of the readiness questions should have been dealt with. The artist should arrive prepared to deal with the Pentium and Windows. She will probably already have the information about why the change was made and how it will affect her job. Given these conditions, she will be at a teachable moment for learning to use Painter.

What To Do When Development Is Not Complete

Probably the hardest case to deal with is when a student arrives wanting to learn but without having completed the developmental tasks. The person sent to the PerfectOffice course who has never used a computer and who has never had a Windows course is a good example. Your choices are simple: turn this person away and deal with the consequences, or accept him or her in the class and deal with the consequences.

If you are teaching a public course in a training center and you turn the person away, the center should have a policy that supports you. That is, the person (or his or her company) will get either a refund or a credit toward one of the prerequisite courses the person must complete before coming in to learn PerfectOffice.

If you are teaching an in-house course, a policy should also be in place that supports turning the person back to take the prerequisites. Because this can be a hard choice, politically, the policy must be well advertised and fully supported by the management of the company.

In many cases, you cannot turn the person away. Perhaps he or she has flown in from another city, at his or her own expense, to take the course. Perhaps there is no prerequisite policy in place so you have no leg to stand on. For such cases, you need a Plan B ready before you ever start registering people for the course.

Plan B

When a person has not fulfilled course prerequisites and you cannot turn him or her away from the course, your Plan B should provide that person with a minimum set of competencies in a hurry. In situations in which the student has to be able to use an operating system different from the one he or she is used to, the biggest issues you have to deal with are the user interface and the way the system stores and organizes files.

In most cases, operating systems come with a "quick tour" feature that at least teaches the student how to use the pointing device, the file system, and the menu system. Have the student use this quick tour while you get the other students started. It is a good idea to keep the tour loaded and available on one machine in your training room.

Some mainframe systems also have tour features, but you may have to create a set of job aids or cheat sheets to help a user become minimally operational in a hurry.

In some cases, students may have missed the earlier courses on an application (they didn't come to the *Introduction to Access* class but here they are in an advanced course on Query). In this situation, a printed mini-lesson and job aids may be enough to get them through. If the application offers "wizards," help the students use them to perform some of the setting up.

In all cases involving a Plan B, advance preparation and practice by the instructor is a must. You should rehearse your Plan B when you get ready for a class. You never know when you will need it.

Suspension of Disbelief

Suspension of disbelief is a term borrowed from magicians and stage entertainers. When you go to see a play or a magic show, one part of you knows that what you are seeing isn't real. But the rest of your brain ignores that part for a little while. This happens for only one reason: the magician or the actors persuade you to stop *dis*believing.

When someone thinks that he or she can't learn to use a computer or the software you are teaching, it is time for you to do a little magic of your own. Essentially, you must get the person to stop disbelieving in himself or herself for a little while. *Notice that your objective is **not** to get the student to **believe** anything.* Did I mention that you may not know who this student is?

8

The key to this effort is your own belief that the other person *will* be successful. Because you don't know who the person is who needs to have disbelief suspended, you must suspend everyone's disbelief; you do this with your language and the way you have structured the class.

In the case of language, replace one word in your vocabulary with a better word. The word to replace is *try*. Rather than say you are going to *try* to teach something, say that you **will** teach it. Rather than ask learners to *try* to do something, direct them to **do** it.

You have already seen how a class is structured to proceed from an overview to a demonstration to releasing the students to practice their new skill. This procedure, among other things, helps support the learner. Later in this chapter, you learn about the *backward chaining* technique, which goes one step further: it guarantees that learners will be successful at each step because they have already mastered the step that comes next.

Create and Maintain Rapport with Students

Finally, as you teach any class, be very careful to create and maintain *rapport* with the learners. Rapport is the state of mind that results in trust. It is very difficult for people to learn from someone whom they do not trust.

You are probably already very good at developing rapport in situations outside the classroom. The same skills work in the classroom as well—but it takes some extra effort to maintain the level of trust.

One of the key factors is your own technical mastery of the subject matter, as suggested in Chapter 7, "Course Development." Rehearse your class until you are confident of your ability to maintain the flow and continuity. This includes the ability to anticipate and deal with problems you may have with equipment or the software.

Students who are just learning to use a software application may not comprehend its organization, logic, and user interface in the same way you do. Even though their eyes may "see" the same icons, cues, and menu items as yours do, learners often overlook or misinterpret this information. As a trainer, it is important for you to anticipate the elements that are "invisible" to the learners or that are likely to be misunderstood. If you have access to the staff and logs of your company's help desk, it is a good idea to get a list of the common problems users ask about—as well as the standard solutions for these problems—before you teach your class. This will help you see the software and the system "through the eyes of the students."

Finally, be aware of the words you use and the body language you display. These have a powerful impact on whether learners think you are on their wavelength or not. Some of these elements were discussed under "Dealing with Objections": Use *do* instead of *try*, replace *but* with *and*, face learners squarely, and step forward when making a point. Here are some more tips about words and body language:

- When you stand, keep your feet about shoulder-width apart, one foot slightly toward the learners to whom you are speaking.

- Turn your whole head to look at learners as you speak to them, not just your eyes.

- Use your hands to gesture and emphasize points; keep your elbows loose, not tucked into your ribs. Relax your shoulders and make your hand movements large and free.

- Move into the group of learners as much as possible, rather than staying up behind a lectern or your own terminal.

- If you are using overhead slides or projected images, say a few words related to what is on the next image before you display it.

- Choose short words, action verbs, and active voice when you talk.

Delivering the Goods

Everything discussed so far in this chapter has dealt with tailoring instruction to match the needs, styles, and readiness of individual adult learners. This final part of the chapter deals with the structural and presentation matters that affect all the learners in the room in more or less the same way.

The major structure in teaching a room full of adults is what Malcolm Knowles calls the *learning design model*. For a given training program, the model contains a number of *activity units* that get people involved in their own learning. The most numerous and important types of activity units have to do with *small group work*.

When people are not doing small group work in a computer training class, they are often involved in a *general session*. There are two *power techniques* for these general sessions: One is referred to as *backward chaining* and the other can be called *Teach the Easy Things Last*.

Finally, instructors should be comfortable and familiar with the use of a variety of types of *instructional media*. It is also necessary to address what to do when things go wrong with the equipment.

8

The Learning Design Model

Knowles defines a *learning design model* as a plan for a flow of events guided by a conceptual scheme. The result of this flow of events is the accomplishment of the course objectives. Two of his five learning design models are of special interest to computer trainers.

The *operational model* replicates the step-by-step sequence of procedures involved in operating a computer or using a piece of software. For example, an operational model for using word processing software in the most efficient manner (that is, to save up to 30 percent of the time needed to produce a document) can be built around these procedural steps:

1. Entering text without using the backspace, delete, or tab keys.

2. Using the spell-checker and grammar-checker, and proofreading to correct errors in the text.

3. Formatting the text.

4. Printing the document.

The *organic model* is a more basic plan consisting of seven steps. These steps are really the basic plan for giving a group of adults total control over the way a course is designed and conducted, in consultation with an instructor. The organic model is a good plan to use inside a company for teaching executives to use computers. You can also use it to teach any group that has the power and freedom to set its own agenda and pace. The seven steps incorporate the ideas addressed in this chapter:

1. Climate setting (establishing rapport).

2. Establishing a structure for mutual planning (suspension of disbelief).

3. Diagnosing needs and interests (creating the teachable moment).

4. Formulating objectives (establishing readiness to learn).

5. Designing a pattern of activities (course organization).

6. Carrying out the activities (delivering the goods).

7. Evaluating the results and rediagnosing needs and interests (transfer strategy).

Tip

The closer a course comes to the organic model, the more successful and popular it is likely to be with the students.

In the usual course in a corporate setting or in a training center, of course, the operational model is used. Elements similar to the organic model fill out the structure, but learners normally have no participation in steps 1 through 5.

Activity Units within Learning Designs

Six types of activity units can be incorporated into learning designs. Five of these involve the learner individually. Unfortunately, computer trainers tend to focus on only the first of these five types and almost never look at ways to use the sixth kind of activity unit, the small group activity.

Here are the six types of activity units:

- **General sessions** are meetings in which all the learners are present together for a presentation by the instructor and for participation as a class. Nearly all present-day computer training courses use this type of activity unit to the exclusion of all others. This is too bad for the learners.

- **Individual coaching or consultation** (sometimes called *directed study*) makes the services of resource persons (note the plural) available to individual students for help.

- **Reading** (of handout materials or references) can be scheduled between class meetings. The only difficult part of this is getting employees to read "required" materials on their own time, or getting their supervisors to allow time on the job for it.

- **Socialization**, or ice-breaking, is a more important activity in teaching adults to use computers than most trainers believe. It helps establish rapport and comfort in the group and makes it easier for learners to approach each other for help.

- **Preparatory activity to be done by students before the class** should include a consultation with their supervisor so that the student finds out why the class is important, hears what the supervisor expects them to learn, and has a chance to express particular needs for information. It can also involve some "up front" work like reading or analysis of work patterns.

- **Small group work** is the key to effective learning and skill transfer from the classroom to the job. These activities can take place before, during, or after "class time." The design of these small group experiences requires careful consideration and planning.

8

> **Tip**
>
> Building in several of these activity types makes your course more interesting and better meets the learning needs of your students. Build in the small group work first, then add the other types as necessary to achieve the course objectives.

Small Group Work

You can choose from a great variety of small group types based on the functions to which they can be put. These small groups can meet during designated class periods, between sessions, or after the course is over. You may want to have several of each type formed and dissolved during a course. You can also use small groups to create a "curriculum without courses" for an organization. Here are some of the types of small groups most applicable to computer training:

- **Topic discussion group.** The group meets to react to, discuss, and share ideas about information received from reading or from the speakers during the class.

- **Laboratory group.** The group is set up to try out skills taught during the class and to share information about how well these skills worked for them.

- **Special interest group.** The group is organized according to the interests of the participants so that they can share experiences and explore their common concerns.

- **Instructional group.** The group is set up to receive instruction from experts in a specialized area.

- **Skill practice group.** The group is organized to facilitate the practice of certain types of skills.

- **Buzz group.** The group is made up of a random collection of individuals, during a general assembly, for the purpose of pooling ideas, reactions, and problems and reporting them to the whole assembly through a spokesperson.

With this discussion, our consideration of techniques designed to implement the principles of adult learning comes to a close. However, the power techniques and information about techniques for the use of media are critically important to consistent success in teaching adults. These items are addressed next.

Power Technique #1: Backward Chaining

Backward chaining is an exceptional technique most computer trainers have never heard of. Yet backward chaining is a very old and natural approach to teaching and learning. It increases learner motivation, can speed up learning, and helps the instructor deal with some of the problems commonly encountered when a class is made up of people from a wide range of skills and experience.

In some families, when the children learn to bake holiday cookies, the first step they learn is the last step in the process. That is, they begin by icing and decorating the cookies after they have been removed from the oven and have cooled. The next thing the children learn is how to tell when the cookies are ready to take from the oven (and how to keep from getting burned while doing this). They then ice and decorate the cookies when they have cooled. In the next step, the kids get to roll out the cookie dough, cut out the shapes, grease the cookie sheet, and put the shapes on the sheet. They then remove the cookies from the oven when they are done and decorate them. Only in the last two "lessons" do the children actually gather, measure, and mix the ingredients themselves. Note that in both of these lessons, the children also cut out the cookies, bake them, and decorate them. This is backward chaining.

Why Does Backward Chaining Work?

With each lesson, the children complete the task and get to feel (and taste!) the sweetness of success. With each lesson, the children "work into" something they already know how to do.

Adults like the sweet taste of success, too. Think about the last tough job you did around the house. Along with relief that it was over, didn't you feel proud of yourself for managing to get it done? Backward chaining allows you to give that feeling of accomplishment to your learners, too. Furthermore, you get to give it to them early in the course and at the end of each exercise. This is powerful motivation and an excellent antidote to the "I can't do anything with computers" feeling that some students may have.

Another reason backward chaining works is that it keeps learners more focused. They already know *why* they are learning a given step because they know where that step is leading. In addition, by working backwards, you are more likely to keep the advanced users in the group occupied and learning rather than having them play solitaire and "get the teacher." At some point, you will have progressed far enough in the course that the advanced users are getting into things they already know. When this

8

happens, you can dismiss those advanced users. This permits you to continue to work with the less experienced learners, with fewer interruptions and distractions.

Setting Up a Task To Be Taught as a Backward Chain

Backward chaining takes a little effort on your part to set up. For each exercise, you must set up a file that has already been "done" up to the point where the learners are to start. Be aware that not every task is practical as an opportunity to apply backward chaining. But backward chaining can be applied to many, if not most, tasks computer trainers are called on to teach.

In "The Learning Design Model," earlier in this chapter, you learned that there is a way to use word processing software that cuts document preparation time by 30 percent or more. This method was outlined like this:

1. Enter text (without using the backspace, delete, or tab keys).

2. Use the spell-checker and grammar-checker, and proofread the text.

3. Format the text.

4. Print the document.

This entire method can be taught as a backward chain. Figure 8.4 gives a grand overview of the entire course. This figure incorporates a learning design based on the operational model.

A *lesson* includes all the instructions, exercises, and practice needed to achieve a major learning objective. In Figure 8.4, Lesson 1 has the title, "Printing a Document." The learning objective is "Given a formatted document that has been proofread and corrected, the learner will be able print the document in its entirety on the printer connected to LPT1." Because this is such a simple objective, the student can do it immediately following the demonstration. Additional practice is provided in the exercises that follow in the modules of the next lesson.

Lessons are made up of modules. A *module* contains the instruction and exercises necessary for a student to master a "chunk" of a procedure within a major learning objective.

Lesson 2 in Figure 8.4 has the title, "Formatting a Document." This lesson uses several modules, four of which are shown in Figure 8.4. The major learning objective is "Given a document that has been proofread and corrected, the learner will be able to format headers and footers, paragraphs (using styles), fonts, tabs, borders and shading, and bullets and numbering and then print the document." Each of the types of formatting is the subject of a module; each module consists of one or two exercises in addition to a demonstration. As the modules and exercises progress, the learner adds the new skills in the "practice" exercise, always concluding in a finished product.

The chunking of steps shown in Figure 8.4 is fairly simple. It is entirely possible for a module to require several exercises. The module on bullets and numbering, for example, might take up to six exercises. The complete backward-chained course design for word processing would include a Lesson 3, teaching how to proofread and how to use the spelling and grammar checkers. Lesson 4 would be on the subject of entering the text, saving and opening files, and starting the word processor.

Fig. 8.4
This plan teaches how to use a word processing application, using backward chaining.

Lesson	Module	Demonstrate	Exercises	
			Do	**Practice**
1 **Printing a Document**	**1** **Printing to Paper**	Print Document 1 to LPT "as is"	Print Document 1 to LPT1	(No exercise)
2 **Formatting a Document**	**1** **Headers and Footers**	Format headers and footers, Document 1	Print Document 1 to LPT with new headers and footers	(No exercise)
	2 **Paragraph Styles**	Add paragraph styles, Document 2	Format headers and footers, Document 2	Print Document 2 to LPT with new headers and footers
	3 **Changing Font Styles**	Change font styles for selected text, Document 3	Add paragraph styles, Document 3	Format headers and footers, then print Document 3
	4 **Formatting Tabs**	Change tabs in selected text, Document 4	Change font styles for selected text, Document 4	Add paragraph styles, format headers and footers, print Document 4

In some of the lessons—either for variety or for convenience—the instructor may want to teach the procedure in task-order sequence (forward chaining). It is not necessary to teach *every* lesson as a backward chain (although it doesn't hurt to do this, either).

Power Technique #2: Teach the Easy Things Last

This technique is one of those ideas that flies in the face of the commonly accepted views of training. In fact, when you are helping learners master software, it makes a great deal of sense to do the following:

- Teach first the things that are hardest to learn (the course gets easier as you go, not harder).

- Teach together the things most easily confused with each other (because students know fewer "things," they have less trouble sorting them out and keeping track of them).

8

The reason these strategies work is that they deal with the *forgetting curve* (the opposite of the *learning curve*). Students often appear to forget as fast as they learn. What is actually happening is that the learners are getting confused by similarities between words, concepts, and procedures. They may respond to different items in inappropriately similar ways. Or they may make just one wrong choice in a multiple-step procedure.

In the teaching word processing software example outlined in Figure 8.4, the most complicated module is likely to be the one on formatting text. This includes formatting fonts, adding bullets and numbered lists, changing margins, doing headers and footers, setting paragraph indentation and spacing, and many other procedures.

Your first task may well be to figure out which procedures you are *not* going to teach. Then identify which of the remaining procedures will be hardest for your learners. Suppose that it is doing headers and footers that change with new sections of a document. Make this the first lesson you teach in the module on formatting. If there are additional procedures that will be hard for your learners, make them the next modules.

Identify any remaining formatting procedures that may be easily confused with each other; plan to teach them together in a single module. Remember that the organizing principle is the difficulty that the learners will have; let the problems the learners must solve in their jobs—not an arbitrary preference you (or anyone else) might have—decide the order in which skills must be taught.

Two techniques can further help learners as you teach these modules. First, whenever possible, give the learners a mnemonic or a rhyme to help with recall. A *mnemonic* is something like the famous "People Can't Memorize Computer Industry Acronyms" to help recall the correct way to spell PCMCIA. A *rhyme* can be as simple as "Left, loose; right, tight" to help remember which way to turn a screw or nut.

Second, be sure that learners get continuous, *immediate* feedback on their progress in learning difficult material. Of course, if you use backward chaining, they get this feedback automatically.

Both backward chaining and teaching the hard things first have long, successful histories of application. Technical trainers have been using them as formal strategies since the late 1950s; lay people have been using them since the dawn of time. Use them with confidence in your courses.

Display Media

Being able to use a picture to explain something has always been an important need for instructors. With the computing world shifting to graphical user interfaces (GUIs), using a picture is essential. As technology progresses, there are more and more ways to display words and images to learners.

However, old, low-tech media are still important. In most cases, they are cheap, portable, and don't require a power source. In some cases, they can perform functions not practical to support with newer media.

What follows is a brief survey of both the old and the new. The following sections also contain some tips for the effective use of both kinds of media.

The Old Media (Boards, Newsprint, Overhead Foils)

The principle purpose of the old media is to put words and images up for continuous viewing by the students. In some cases, a secondary purpose is to provide a way to record ideas, questions, and other matters during the course. These records can be consulted and referred to as necessary during the rest of the program.

Boards—chalkboards, marker boards, whiteboards—are usually mounted at the front of the classroom or on the wall that serves as the backdrop for the *point of instruction*. The main function of boards is to give the *instructor* a convenient place to write or draw while teaching. They are never an acceptable substitute for a projection screen.

Newsprint—or a flipchart—is nearly always mounted on an easel. The humble flipchart is probably the single most useful tool an instructor can have. Flipcharts can be used by both instructor and students to record ideas and main points. The individual sheets can be torn off the pad and hung on the walls to record progress and points learned. They can also be used to record step-by-step procedures for reference by learners during the class. It is better to have two easels with pads and spare pads than to have just one. Always have a roll of masking tape available in the room so that you can post the torn-off sheets.

Some conference rooms have the flipchart mounted on a combination whiteboard/projection screen/cabinet. Such a flipchart is really useful only as a substitute marker board while the projection screen is in use. You still need an easel with newsprint pad in the room for your other work.

In using both marker boards and flipcharts, there are two important points to keep in mind about the lettering: color and size.

Although it seems most natural to use a black marker on the marker board and on the flipchart, there are better choices. Probably the best choice is a dark green marker (followed, in decreasing order of preference, by dark brown, violet, and blue). All these colors are easier to read against a white background than black. Some studies have shown that what is written in blue is forgotten quickly, which is why blue is listed last. The worst choice is red, which is hard to see and hard to read; in some countries, red may be associated with emergency instructions. Minimize the number of different colors you use on a single sheet or board.

8

> **Note**
>
> Be aware that about ten percent of males have a condition known as *color confusion*. This is not the same thing as color blindness (which is very rare). In color confusion, some men cannot distinguish blue from green; others may not be able to tell red from brown. If you want to use two different colors to contrast information or to highlight a diagram, avoid these pairs.

As for the size of lettering, the rule of thumb is to make your letters one-quarter inch high for every ten feet from the board or newsprint to the most distant viewer. If in doubt, make the lettering larger. It is easier to read text when both capitals and lower case letters are used. Printing everything in capitals makes words very hard to read.

You may want to prepare key flipcharts, posters, or easel cards ahead of time. Figure 8.5 shows the tips to keep in mind for these items. Although these are only suggestions, you should be very cautious about violating them. The most important tip is "keep it simple." Viewers should be able to get the point within five seconds.

Fig. 8.5
This chart gives the rules of thumb for visuals you prepare ahead of time.

Writing Good Visual Copy

- Keep it simple
- 5 to 6 lines of print
- 5 to 6 words per line
- Use large fonts
- Show only key points
- Make notation consistent

In the case of old-fashioned overhead projector foils, many of the same tips just given for flipcharts apply. Use Figure 8.5 to design layouts for foils. Color is very important in a projected visual but you have some additional flexibility. For example, you can obtain foils that are yellow or light blue as a means of reducing glare from the overhead projector screen. Use black print on these foils.

Lettering on an overhead foil should be 18-point to 24-point in size if your most distant learner will be no more than 35 feet from the screen. For distances of 35 to 75 feet, use 24-point to 36-point letters. If you ever have to teach such a large group that the most distant learner is 100 feet away, your foil should use 48-point letters. It is always better to use a sans serif type style, such as Helvetica or Arial, on overhead foils.

Pacing can be a problem with overhead foils. A typical overhead foil should stay up for three to five minutes. When you are done with the current overhead foil, turn off the projector to remove the distraction. The overhead is there to support you, not to carry the presentation.

The New Media (LCD Projection, Big Monitors, Networking)

With the new media, many of the tips presented in the last section are the same. On the other hand, the capabilities have increased. So has the price, unfortunately.

With LCD projection, you have a choice between the original LCD plate that sits on top of an overhead projector and newer self-contained LCD projector units. In at least one case, what seems to be a large LCD plate is actually an entire 486DX2 multimedia computer system, complete with hard drive, CD-ROM, speakers, and audio jacks.

In either case, you should observe the tips in the preceding section about type size, style, color, and number of words on the screen at any one time. If you are using a color LCD plate, you need an overhead projector with a light output of at least 400 lumens. If you have a gray-scale or monochrome plate, you can get away with a 300-lumen projector. With LCD plates and overhead projectors, you almost always have to turn off the lights in the front of the room.

With LCD projectors, especially the newer models, you may be able to leave all the lights on. The exception is if you place the screen directly under a light fixture (in that situation, turn off that light). Some LCD projectors have speakers built into them, which is a very handy feature if you are using multimedia.

An excellent alternative to projection in smaller classrooms is a large monitor. You can buy and permanently install up to a 33-inch monitor for about the same price as an LCD projector. Consider this alternative if there is no more than about 20 feet to your most distant learner. Big monitors are easy to see and you can leave the room lights up while you teach. If you have a lot of money and a big classroom, you can mount several monitors on the ceiling, aircraft-style, or on the walls, down the length of the room.

An LCD projector or a large monitor will help you pace your presentation. You can add elements to your visual as you need them by "flying" them on or by using an animated transition.

The one thing that takes a little planning when you are using LCD projection is the use of screen captures and scanned images. These tend to "break down" when projected because the pixel patterns become magnified and visible. The best plan is to use simple images that do not involve significant detail or high-color resolutions.

8

Other types of projectors work like a big-screen television. These are almost universally unsuited for training because the room lights have to be off or dimmed to the point that learners cannot take notes, may become disoriented, and have a tendency to fall asleep. In addition, these projectors are very expensive, hard to keep in adjustment, and have an unacceptably high failure rate.

An excellent alternative to all these options is one of the newer hardware and software systems that allow the instructor to control what is seen on the students' monitors. The instructor can send the video from his or her screen to an individual student or to all students. In some systems, it is possible to send the video from any student monitor to every student monitor in the room. Finally, the instructor can see what an individual monitor is displaying at any time.

Tip

Visuals are supposed to *support* instruction, not deliver it. Make sure that your visuals don't distract or call attention to themselves.

Avoiding Disaster: When (Not If) Equipment Fails

Were Ben Franklin alive today, he would have to amend his famous saying about death and taxes. "Hardware failure" is now the third certain thing in life.

In most classrooms, the weak link is the hardware. After that, the weakest link is the software on the instructor's system. As you plan your classes, keep this in mind. It is wise to have a Plan B for any eventuality.

The most commonly needed Plan B has to do with projector bulbs. If you are using an overhead projector or an LCD projector, have a spare bulb in the classroom where you can get to it quickly. Know how to replace the bulb. Remember to turn off the power to the projector before you make the replacement.

The most serious Plan B is the one that deals with the classroom network shutting down during the class. This is a Plan B you must think through carefully before every class. Will you cancel the course? Will you bring in a freestanding PC and a big monitor and continue to demonstrate until the system is restored? Will you shift to alternative media (a videotape or overheads)? You have plenty of choices, but they must be in place *before* disaster strikes.

From Here...

This chapter has dealt with the practical techniques on which every master trainer relies. You can add to your skills with further reading in other chapters of this book.

- For more about adult learners, see Chapter 3, "Adult Learning: What Do We Know for Sure?"

- To relate course delivery to course development, see Chapter 7, "Course Development."

- To relate the theory of course delivery to the techniques covered in this chapter, read Chapter 10, "The Flow of the Class."

- To learn how to deliver or reinforce learning outside the classroom, read Chapter 11, "Augmenting Classroom Training with Other Media," and Chapter 12, "Distance Learning on the World Wide Web."

8

Chapter 9

Housekeeping

by Gail Perry

Gail Perry has taught at lots of different computer sites—from formal, tiered classrooms equipped with the latest multimedia technology, to peering over partitions in offices while students sit at their desks. She knows it is the instructor's responsibility to make sure that the students are comfortable, the equipment works, and the coffee is hot.

Your students are in the classroom and you're ready to begin your instruction—right? *Wrong!* Try to imagine yourself as one of your students, sitting in strange surroundings, maybe confronted with unfamiliar equipment, not knowing what to expect in terms of breaks and lunch plans, wondering where to find the rest room....

Just as it's your responsibility to teach the subject matter to these students, you also have a duty to familiarize them with the surroundings. Unless your students work at the training site or have had other occasions to visit the site, you can't assume that they know their way around. And even if they *are* familiar with the classroom setting, they still need an introduction to your classroom style, your rules, and the equipment they will be using in class.

Not only do you have the responsibility to introduce your students to the environment, you have a vested interest in providing them with a sense of comfort and familiarity. The more "at home" they feel, the more they will relax, absorb the material they have come to learn, and respond and participate in class. Leave them feeling unwelcome and awkward and that attitude will carry over into their classroom performance.

The Classroom

Near the beginning of the class, before you begin actual instruction, introduce the students to the classroom itself. Indicate where students can place personal belongings they have brought with them such as coats, newspapers, books, and purses.

Describe the equipment to the students. If you plan to use a computer and display screen, point this out to the students. Tell students whether or not a network is installed in the room and what equipment they should expect to use at their stations (assuming that yours is a hands-on class). Let them know about the printing capabilities in the classroom. Specify what software is available on the machines.

Explain what students should do if they experience a problem with their equipment or their software: Do you want them to tell you about a problem or try to correct it themselves? Beginning students are usually afraid to experiment with their machines and will be quick to tell you if something doesn't seem to work correctly. More advanced students may not like to admit there is a problem they don't understand because they think it should be something they can fix—and they may try to do so!

In fact, you should encourage students to bring all problems to your attention so that you in turn can share these problems with the class. One of the most important lessons students can learn in your class is how to solve everyday problems associated with their computers.

As the instructor, you have the responsibility to maintain control over the equipment in your classroom. Equipment failures reflect negatively on you, particularly if the failures are persistent. And problems with equipment can slow down the class and break the flow of the material you are teaching.

Take the time to get to class early and turn on all the machines. Make sure that every student will be able to access the appropriate software, make sure that the printer functions properly, and try to achieve uniformity among the workstations.

The Environment

Your training should include breaks for the students; you should explain at the beginning of class when breaks will occur so that students can anticipate them. Encourage students to leave the room during breaks (if that is appropriate) or at least to get up and move around.

Explain the importance of breaks to the training. Students tend to absorb more information if there is a break in the flow rather than a constant barrage of data delivery. Although breaks provide students with an opportunity to experiment with skills they have learned in regular class time, you should still urge students to let their minds clear of computer information for a few minutes so that their approach to the training will be fresh when they return.

> **Tip**
>
> In addition, the physical demands of sitting still for long periods of time tend to be tiring and the mind begins to wander. Breaks provide an opportunity for a little physical exercise and a brief separation from the class material. Breaks also give students a chance to touch base with the real world, to place phone calls to office or home.

Be sure to let students know how long breaks will last and when class will reconvene. Especially in settings where students work in the same building as the classroom, students can disappear for long periods of time if they don't know precisely when class will begin again.

Let your students know if they are restricted to "official" breaks or if they can get up and leave the classroom when they need to. Adult students in particular appreciate the freedom of being able to get up and replenish coffee or use the rest rooms when they want to rather than waiting until you tell them it's break time. I've had pregnant women in class who find it difficult to sit for an entire day. Encourage students to get up and walk around the classroom during class if they want to stretch.

Refreshments

Refreshments should be available at the training site. Refreshments help maintain the energy of your students and provide a reason for students to get up and walk around at break time.

Make sure that students know your rules for bringing refreshments into the classroom. Do you want them to have food and drinks on the tables with the computers? Should drinks have lids? Have you provided napkins for foods that might be messy or sticky?

Atmosphere

Let your students know your expectations regarding their behavior. Do you encourage students to speak out in class? Do you want them to save questions for a specific question/answer time or do you want them to raise questions as they occur? Give students guidance about working ahead in the material or indulging in independent study.

Do you encourage students to work together or independently? If a slower student and a quicker student are seated next to each other, can the quicker one assist the slower one?

The way these issues should be handled may seem obvious to you—they are not necessarily obvious to your students. Your students may not have even considered how they should behave in class; your instructions will help their approach to the material and to each other.

9

The Surrounding Area

If students have traveled some distance to your classroom (as opposed to walking down the hallway in their office building), they will rely on you to provide them with information about the surrounding area—both inside and outside the building. Don't expect them to have knowledge about the environs before they come to class. It's fair to assume that your students have never before been to your building or your neighborhood or even your city.

Explain where facilities are located within your building. Students need to know where to find rest rooms, drinking fountains, and refreshments (if they are not provided in the classroom). Indicate appropriate areas for smoking. You should also tell students where to find telephones and how to access outside lines on the phones. If there is a phone message service available at the training site, be sure to let students know about this.

Note

One of the sites where I train has telephones in the classroom. Telephones this handy can be great for breaks and emergencies but calls during class can be disruptive. In a situation like this, students need to know the rules for use of the telephone.

For all-day classes, you should explain to students the arrangements for lunch. If lunch is available in your building, tell students where to get their food and where they will eat. If students are expected to get lunch on their own, provide maps of the area or give general directions to the local restaurants, noting which ones are more likely to provide speedy service.

Be sure to let students know at the beginning of class the time at which you expect to have scheduled breaks, including lunch. Your students may want to make plans to meet someone for lunch, or they may want to arrange a telephone conference for break time.

If students are in town for more than a one-day class, they will probably have already made arrangements for lodging. If the arrangements were made through you or the company for which you train, take a few minutes to find out whether students are satisfied with the lodging. Also make sure that all your students have secured their lodging arrangements; if they haven't, provide them with information about area hotels and motels. For students staying in town overnight, provide general information about restaurants and also let them know where they can find nearby drug stores or other establishments where they can secure necessities.

From Here...

As you make the training environment comfortable and personalize it to meet the needs of your students, your efforts will reflect positively on the entire training experience. Never discount the importance of meeting the needs of your students at a creature-comfort level.

- The classroom is ready, but what about your training material? See Chapter 7, "Course Development," for insights on what it is you're going to teach.

- Chapter 10, "The Flow of the Class," addresses what happens in the classroom once the show begins.

- Still a bit shaky on how to present your material in front of an audience? Turn to Chapter 8, "Training Techniques," for the basics on types of presentations.

9

Chapter 10

The Flow of the Class

by Peggy Maday and Carolyn Woodie

Peggy Maday owns Turning Point Training Systems based in Denver, Colorado. Carolyn Woodie owns Carolyn Woodie & Associates, a similar training company in the Washington, D.C., area. They both offer software training, office automation, conversion, courseware, and consulting services to corporate and government clients in most of the popular PC applications.

Now that you have read about training the adult learner, needs and skills assessments, course design, and training techniques, it is time to face the challenge of the actual training session. Over the years, we have noticed that although computer software has become more complex, the training time allowed is often less. As trainers, we must make the *best* use of the time we do have. Your training session may be four hours, one day, three days, or a week. This chapter addresses the training session, its structure, and how the session flows. The ideas expressed here may be applied to training sessions of any length.

The First Five Minutes

The classroom and computers should be ready at least 15 minutes before the class starting time. This allows you to personally greet the participants. You will have a few early birds, but the majority will arrive just five minutes before the class begins. Make the best of those first five minutes with the participants with these four tips:

- Have the title of the class written on the board, overhead, or easel. As people arrive, this information confirms that they are in the right location.

- Have a time schedule of the day written on the board, noting breaks and lunch times, so that people can take note of it.

- Greet each participant warmly. Many people come to a class with some apprehension. Your personal contact helps to diffuse their anxiety. Your warm and friendly greeting sets the tone for the day. It tells them that this is a friendly place. It is also a time to learn their names. Sometimes as I greet people, I write their name card for them. This reinforces their name in my mind (and I can be certain I can read my own writing on the name cards).

- Encourage people to find a comfortable place where they can see, hear, and easily participate.

The Front Seats Are the Best!

Everyone usually makes a beeline for the back seats. In one classroom, we had ten seats but only seven people in each class. The front seats were always empty. One day, I taped $5 bills to the front chairs. Needless to say, the front seats were filled fast. Word spread like wildfire and I had no trouble filling the front seats during the rest of the training sessions.—*Peggy Maday*

Keep Your Eyes and Ears Open

Your observations and interactions with the participants can provide insights on their readiness to learn; their interest and reasons for attending; additional "inside scoop" about hardware, computer, and network setup; and possible problems that might impact them back on the job.

These first five minutes are good for you, the instructor, too. They can help you make a natural transition into the training session. You have jumped the hurdle of meeting your new class and now you all are ready to learn together.

Introducing the Session

The official class begins with introductions. Many instructors tend to gloss over introductions. However, this period of time is very important because it is the framework for the entire training session.

Start on Time

Start on time even if everyone hasn't arrived. If you only have one or two participants when starting time has arrived, begin anyway. Do not penalize those who are on time by waiting for those who are late. Waiting for tardy students reinforces their tardiness. ("Good, they won't start until I arrive!") Also, starting late teaches those who are prompt to be later the next time so that they don't waste time sitting around. By starting on time, you tell the participants that their time is valuable to you. If you have only one or two participants, use a light-hearted tone to tell them that they are getting a private tutoring lesson because they arrived on time. Then begin. Your timely students will feel privileged.

Welcome Participants

Welcome the participants with a quick introduction including your name, the title of the class, and a brief background of your experience: "Welcome to *Introduction to WordMaster*. My name is... and I'm going to be your (instructor, facilitator, or whatever you call yourself) today." This introduction sets the tone for the day. It also clearly announces the class subject to everyone. ("Oh, this is *Intro to WordMaster*? I thought it was going to be *Advanced Excel Macros!*") A brief statement of your background or experience establishes your credibility. ("I have been teaching introductory through advanced WordMaster courses for over five years, and this my favorite version yet! I think you will enjoy learning more about it too!") It only takes a sentence or two to communicate the necessary information quickly.

Class Attendance Rosters

Many times, it is necessary for participants to fill in an attendance sheet. It may be appropriate to send the attendance sheet around the class during this time as the basic introductions of the day are made.

Introduce the Surroundings

This is the best time to note the location of the break areas and restrooms and to mention any rules of the classroom (such as whether food and drink are allowed). Many people need to know where the phone is located so that they can call their offices during breaks.

Help the participants feel comfortable. People have to feel comfortable in their physical environment before they can focus on their learning environment. Encourage them to tell you if they have any special needs or if the classroom is too hot or cold. For example, you can say, "I can't tell you how many times someone has said 'the room was too cold' on the evaluations. The evaluations at the end of the day are too late to change the temperature to make you more comfortable. The thermostat is right here. If you tell me, we can discuss it and change the thermostat accordingly." Allowing people input on temperature and sometimes lighting helps them feel that their physical comfort is your concern and that they have some influence on their environment. If control of the temperature or lighting is beyond your control, just say so. Then provide some alternative suggestions such as getting a light jacket or sweater on break or tilting the monitor to cut down on the glare.

Introduce the Schedule for the Day

Take a few sentences to introduce the time schedule for the day. Refer to the schedule previously written on the board. Everyone likes to know the time for breaks and lunch. It is difficult to keep the attention of people who had that extra cup of coffee that morning. They are much more interested in the time of the midmorning break.

Although it seems that there is a lot to be covered, a sentence or two is all that is necessary on each subject. Your introduction should take no more than three to five minutes. If it takes any longer, you will lose the interest of the participants.

Participant Introductions

The introduction of the participants doesn't take much time, but if you give some thought to *how* it is done you can glean a lot of information that will help you teach the group. People like to be where everybody knows their name. Take eight to ten minutes to introduce the participants to yourself and to everyone else. Properly done, this exercise can be one of the most important parts of the day. Each class has its own chemistry. I never skip introductions even if everyone knows everyone else.

Use Name Cards

Names are very important to everyone. It is very helpful to have participants' names on tent cards that sit on their desks or computers so that you can see them easily. Name tags worn by the participants are not appropriate because you cannot read the name if you are standing behind the individual. Name tent cards should have the participant's name on both sides so that you can read the card from both the front and the back of the room as you move around to help participants. Ask the participants to write their names on the cards. "Please write how you would like to be addressed on both sides of the name card."

Some professionals might balk at using name cards. It reminds them too much of school. An alternative is to draw a quick seating chart on a piece of paper as participants introduce themselves. This way, you have their names for easy reference during the class.

10

What's In a Name?

A few months ago, I was scheduled to teach the basics of using a particular word processor to a class of judges. Most of the judges were computer novices. Those planning the training were very anxious that everything be perfect. They had a rather long drawn-out discussion of whether or not to use name cards. If name cards were to be used, how should the names be printed on the cards: *Judge X*, *The Honorable X*, just the first and last name? It was a big decision for them.

I suggested that the judges be treated as any other participants and asked them to trust me as I handled the participant introductions. So when the judges came in, I said "Please write how you would like to be addressed on both sides of the name card." They made a few jokes to one another and put their names and some nicknames on the cards. One judge even wrote *Bill Gates* on one side of the card and his real name on the other side. They all laughed and this broke the ice and set the tone for the training. It was especially funny when I stood behind this judge and addressed him as *Bill* and wondered why he did not respond. We even tossed the Koosh ball around for quick introductions.

The training was relaxed, not stuffy or pretentious. It was the best thing for all of us. They relaxed and I relaxed too. I am scheduled to do another class of judges this month; the first class was so successful that I intend to follow the same modus operandi. In addition, I can now say that I know the judges in my state on a first-name basis.—*Carolyn Woodie*

Verbal Introductions

Here are some suggestions to make the introduction of participants a little more organized and timely:

- **Use a time limit.** Don't be shy about giving the participants a time limit. "Everyone has 30 seconds to introduce themselves." Or "Each person will tell us why they are here in 25 words or less."

- **Keep it fast paced.** Move along quickly to discourage lengthy biographies. Give participants one or two quick questions to answer. "Tell us your name, where you work, and one thing you are anxious to learn today."

- **Do something to keep people on their toes and listening.** Some instructors use a Nerf ball or a Koosh ball and have one person toss it to another person across the room. This helps to keep people alert because they never know when the ball will be tossed to them to give their intro.

- **Learn their names.** This is a good time to learn the proper pronunciation of a name. Nothing is worse than having your name constantly mispronounced. It is also the time to learn nicknames. Maybe his name is *Grant* but he has always been called *Bud*.

■ **Use this time to do an on-the-spot skills assessment.** Even if you did a skills assessment before the class, you may have substitute participants or false information. With a few well-chosen questions to answer, the participants will tell *you* why they are there, something about their background in the particular subject, and what they hope to get out of the class. Here are examples of some appropriate leading questions:

   ■ "How long you have been using Lotus?"

   ■ "What is *one* thing you want to make certain that you learn about in WordPerfect today?"

   ■ "What types of documents do you prepare using Word?"

   ■ "What can you do with a mouse besides play solitaire?"

   ■ "What is the most exciting thing you have done with Excel so far?"

Teaching a class of mixed experience levels is one of the greatest challenges of training. Yet it is quite common. As you know, you cannot please all the people all the time. A successful training session is a result of teamwork. Face this challenge with enthusiasm and your enthusiasm will be contagious. As introductions draw to a close, use this time to seek everyone's cooperation. Here are some examples of how to make the transition into the class time and also encourage everyone's cooperation:

■ "This is great! Everyone seems to have about the same level of expertise. I think this class is going to go far today! We may be able to cover more than we expected!"

■ "You've heard the same introductions I have. You can see we have a mix of experience levels. I'm going to ask those who are more experienced to be patient and remember when they were first beginning. I promise to throw you some great shortcuts that will make this class well worthwhile to you. You less experienced people will have to understand that some things will go over your heads, but you will understand them better later as you gain more experience. I promise I won't let you get lost!"

■ "Now that we have introduced ourselves, turn and shake the hand of the person on the right and then do the same with the person on the left. Make friends because you will work together, laugh together, and help one another today." (This is especially helpful if people are new to the subject and are feeling some anxiety.)

How To Handle Awkward Moments

The introduction time may provide some awkward moments. Experience helps you handle them; remember that light humor can sometimes help you move on quickly. Always be careful when using humor: it should *never* be at the expense of someone in the class. Here are a few common situations and suggestions on how to handle them:

- The students who don't want to be there and make it obvious. "I'm here because my boss made me come. I don't want to use WordMaster." At least they are honest. You don't have to take half the day to figure out why they are not too cooperative. Never deny their feelings. Being told that the world is going to be using WordMaster and they just better get used to it doesn't help. Reassure them that their feelings are common. Many people just need to be reassured that you will help make the learning process as easy as possible.

- Be aware that some people may come in angry that they have to learn *one more upgrade* or a different software package than the one they just became proficient at using. They haven't had the chance to vent their anger and they are ready to "shoot the messenger." Again, acknowledge their feelings. Agree that it may be difficult to change boats midstream but that you are there to show them easier ways to change boats. You are going to show them shortcuts that will make the transition easier.

- Students who say "I don't think I need *Intro to [blank]*, but they are making me take it anyway." Often people learn on their own but do not have a good foundation. They may know some advanced functions but have missed some of the basics. These individuals can be problems in the class, so address the situation early. Recognize that they probably know more than the average person and maybe even know some shortcuts you don't know. Promise that you will show them some shortcuts that they might not know so that their day won't feel wasted. If they are not disruptive, consider allowing them to explore a bit. However, don't be afraid to ask them to be cooperative and follow along with the class.

Diffusing the Anger

In recent months, I have been teaching many classes of individuals who are making dramatic changes from one computer environment into another computer environment. Production demands do not allow time to acclimate to the new environment. This has often caused resentment, especially if the changes have been instituted without any input from the end users.

If participants are angry, I have to diffuse the anger or the learning process is thwarted. I would much prefer to know about angry individuals before the class begins; at the start of the class, I take a few minutes to tell about my own experiences of having to change. I tell the participants how much I hated it in the beginning and almost

(continues)

(continued)

considered giving up teaching. Then I tell them how much I enjoy using it now that I am comfortable in the environment. I empathize with them and tell them that they are not alone. Many others are experiencing exactly what they are experiencing and it is tough.

Then I take a few minutes to demonstrate some whiz-bang features of what I will be teaching to try to win them over right from the start. I also check with them several times during the day to ask how they are doing and to offer a few additional words of encouragement. It is amazing how responsive people can be when they have a listening ear for their frustrations and someone who offers hope. —*Carolyn Woodie*

Using Ice Breakers

The longer your training session, the more time you can use for introductions and ice breakers. Ice breakers are used to help people relax and get to know one another better. Even a quick introduction can include an ice breaker. However, resist the urge to get involved in lengthy ice breakers unless they relate to the subject. If your training session is short, long introductions and ice breakers could be viewed as wasting time. Following are a few sample ice breakers that take only seconds to use along with your introductions:

- "Give one adjective to describe yourself."
- "If you were an animal, name the animal you would be."
- "What is your favorite season and why?"

Getting It Straight Up Front

It's important to get it straight right up front: what are your class objectives and how will you achieve them? Although, ideally, you want students to have an accurate picture of the training *before* they come to class, this is not always possible. Sometimes, people sent to class do not really know why they are there.

Objectives

Let the students know what to expect. This is an excellent opportunity to enthusiastically show the students "what's in it for them" and to increase their buy-in to the training. It creates anticipation for the rest of the class. If there are any unrealistic expectations, it's an opportunity to set the record straight.

Point out each objective and give a brief explanation or overview. Try one of the following ways to visually present the objectives as you speak:

- Write objectives on the board, easel, or in the handout. Save class time by doing this before class. Consider checking off objectives as you complete them. This gives everyone a nice road map and a sense of accomplishment as the day progresses.

- Refer students directly to the Table of Contents when your class parallels the training manual. Let the participants see where they can find each objective in the manual. When you complete a section (or periodically throughout the day) suggest to the group that they place a check mark in the Table of Contents next to each item accomplished.

- Create a slide show using software like PowerPoint, Freelance, or Presentations. You can be very creative and really grab attention with an attractive slide. Many presentation software packages allow you to highlight or check off items listed on the slide. You can load the same slide at the end of class and check off each objective accomplished throughout training.

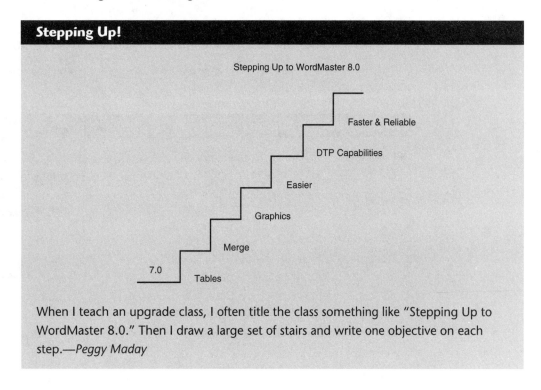

Stepping Up!

Stepping Up to WordMaster 8.0

Faster & Reliable

DTP Capabilities

Easier

Graphics

Merge

7.0   Tables

When I teach an upgrade class, I often title the class something like "Stepping Up to WordMaster 8.0." Then I draw a large set of stairs and write one objective on each step.—*Peggy Maday*

Training Technique

Explain how the students will learn and what they will be doing. Be specific about the format of the class and your training style. Will there be demonstrations, discussions, lab sessions, and so on? Take a look at the following examples, then formulate your own:

- **Explain the class format:** "We will work through hands-on examples together. Then you will be given a project to work on at your own speed to double-check your understanding of the technique."

- **Explain your training style:** "I encourage lots of interaction, input, and questions. Feel free to interrupt me by raising your hand whenever you do not understand or want to add something. If a question or comment can't be handled right then, I will arrange for it later in the presentation by writing it on the board." Explain the *House Rules* (see the following sidebar) and let participants know what you expect.

House Rules!

A popular, fun approach is to list your *House Rules* on the board or easel:

1. Have fun.

2. Be here (physically and mentally).

3. Participate.

4. Ask questions.

5. Cheat (help each other, look in the book, go to the help screens).

This really lets participants know this will be a fun, lively, interactive atmosphere.

OOPS! A Great Moment

I love it when my students make mistakes they are willing to share with the rest of the class. It is an excellent opportunity for all to learn. I often introduce incentives (like chocolate candy) at the beginning of the class for sharing these *great moments*. This sets a playful tone for the class that encourages mistakes, fun competition, and learning.

A special note here: Be careful with candy incentives. A little goes a long way. Too much candy can make the participants feel childlike—and they like to be treated as adults. Different groups seem to be more sensitive to this than others. Also, you can create a sugar high in the participants followed by a drop in energy. Like all things, play it by ear and adjust based on the group dynamics.—*Peggy Maday*

Training Manuals

Either place a manual at each training station before class or hand out the manuals as you speak. Consider the following items for your presentation:

- How to use the manual: as a classroom guide, an after-class reference guide, or both?

■ Is the manual's format the basis of the training? Let students know if you will not move page by page through the manual.

■ Will you cover everything in the manual? Are some of the topics optional? Tell students about the "extra bonus information" beyond the classroom material and you will not have any complaints.

■ Is there an index? Show students how the manual is organized.

■ Is there a place for notes? Show participants where to write their great insights.

The Middle Five Minutes

As the class progresses, make sure that you are on track with the students and that the students are on track with the class objectives. You may have to adjust your technique or materials while there is still time to make changes. Then let the students know how they are progressing. Experienced trainers become quite expert at reading their students, but even this "sixth sense" is not adequate or accurate enough. Try to find out how the class is progressing from the student's perspective with some of the following techniques:

■ Talk to participants as they return from break or lunch. "How is it going? Learning any new information?" or "How is the speed? Too fast or too slow?"

■ Talk to your contact person if someone has arranged the training. "How are we doing? Are we presenting the information you feel is necessary?"

■ Keep your ears tuned to comments as students go out or return from breaks and lunch.

■ Pass out confidential index cards at break or lunch. Ask students to write a number from 1 (I don't understand) to 10 (I understand it all) indicating their comfort level with the new concepts. This works well and is quick when you suspect you are not on target and are considering modifying your game plan.

■ Have the students fill out a progressive evaluation form as you complete each segment. Give them room to rate their ability to complete the task just presented with a simple check mark and a place to write comments. This works really well in longer sessions and in pilot training sessions. Of course, you have to plan for this ahead of time by having a form for students to fill in.

Do not hesitate to make slight modifications at this point. Perhaps the participants want more practice before going on. Perhaps they think the training is moving too slowly. Making even slight adjustments can turn the class around and make the training more successful for the group.

Approximately half way through the training, make a quick comment on how the students are doing. Someone often asks if they are on schedule. Although every group is a little different, it helps participants to know that they will be complete the class on schedule.

- If objectives are on the board or easel, point out the progress you have made.

- When teaching several small features near the end of the class, students become concerned if they think they are behind. Let them know when they are still on track.

On the other hand, if you are running short on time, tell students that, too. Ask them to vote on which of the remaining topics they want to cover in the remaining time. This allows them to learn one or two topics instead of rushing through all of the topics and failing to learn anything.

The Last Five Minutes

Do not rush through to the last minute without adequate closure. Many speakers and trainers make the mistake of just trailing off. Above all, *never end late*. A solid wrap-up is necessary to help people effectively take this new information back to the workplace. Keep the following points in mind when planning your closing:

- Ideally, begin tying things together 15 minutes to a half hour before the end of the session.

- When you do not end on time, you have lost your students anyway once the closing time has passed.

- If you are running later than expected, do not try to cram an hour-and-a-half's worth of training into the last 45 minutes. It's like trying to pour just one more glass of water into an already full pitcher.

- When using evaluation forms, allow the students a few minutes to think through any comments or suggestions they might want to make.

- Recognize the importance of the participants' time and the importance of each person who has attended. Thank them and quickly say good-bye to each participant as they leave.

The *Aha!*

The closing is another great opportunity for students to reiterate in their own words something they have learned. I often go around the room and have each person share something they have learned and how they will implement it back on the job. I often refer to this as an *Aha!* This technique often sparks ideas in the whole group and helps bridge the gap between what students have learned and how they will use it to improve their productivity.—*Peggy Maday*

10

Everything in Between

Assisting the participants to gain new knowledge or refine existing skills is a challenging job. The trainer needs adequate preparation and planning, skill in handling problems, properly spaced breaks, and strong skills in planning a successful training class.

Planning

You should start by creating a plan to serve as your framework for the day. The plan can help you pace yourself throughout the training and can keep you on track. Every class is just a little bit different. It is easy to forget to present certain points regardless of how well you know the topic.

Make your plan as complete as possible, including all the features to present, analogies, overheads, demonstrations, exercises and page numbers, practical applications, questions, additional props, and so on.

Make Your Plan as Complete as Possible

Include the following elements in your plan:

- Features to present
- Analogies
- Overheads
- Sample questions
- Practical applications
- Demonstrations
- Exercises
- Page numbers
- Props
- Filenames

Create your plan in some sort of organized fashion such as an outline (see fig. 10.1), a table (see fig. 10.2), or by making your instructor notes directly in the training manuals.

Fig. 10.1

A training plan in outline format.

**Training Outline
Word Master 8.0
Secretary Training**

1. **Help**
   a. Brief demo inserting date into document
   b. Hand out question cards for teams
      i. Make sure that each person figures out their questions
      ii. Have them present to class
   c. Pg 35–37
2. **Bits and Pieces**
   a. Demo ways to select text—bonds.mmo
      i. Mouse
      ii. Keyboard
   b. Edit selected text
   c. Delete selected text
   d. Cut, copy, paste
      i. Toolbar
      ii. Edit menu
      iii. Drag-and-drop if it's a fast class
   e. Pg 39-40
3. **Speller**
   a. Demo [md] baths.exr
   b. Discuss proofreading
4. **Do CHALLENGE Exercise #2 (20 minutes)**
   (cut, copy, paste, delete, hard page, print single pg, speller, hard space, hyphen, help)

Fig. 10.2

A training plan in table format.

Concept	Props	Activities	Instructor Discussion
Conversion to WordMaster 8.0 Instructor Guide			
Help	Cards with questions Pg 35-37	Scavenger hunt in teams, then present solutions	• Demo with date text • "An encyclopedia at your finger tips"
Bits and pieces	Pg 39-40 bonds.mmo		• Demo selecting with mouse and keyboard • Edit selected text • Replace selected text • Cut, copy, paste — toolbars, menu, and drag and drop if time
Speller	baths.exr		• Demo • Discuss proofreading
Challenge	Exercise #2	Complete exercise Questions and answers	• Cut, copy, paste, delete, hard page, print single page, speller, hard space, hyphen

Handling Problems

You must be quick on your toes to handle problems as they occur.

Late arrivals can interrupt the class no matter what. It's best to politely acknowledge latecomers as they walk in the class and let them know when you will get with them. Sometimes, it's easy to bring them up to speed with a few comments. Other times, you may have to ask them to just observe until the next break or the next exercise. Then you or another student can get them started. Do not disrupt the entire class for them. Often, they are as uncomfortable as you are with being late and appreciate a couple of minutes to catch their breath and become oriented. When you are missing someone at the beginning of class, lay out their manual, any supplies, and registration forms.

Equipment and installation problems are frustrating to you and the students. Try not to let a whole class sit while you try to solve hardware or software problems. Instead, try to keep them productive or give them a deserved break while you attempt to solve the problem. Try one of the following solutions:

- If only one machine is having a problem, let the participant move and share a machine until break time.

- Give the class a quick break.

- Have the whole group work together informally answering questions or practicing difficult material previously covered.

- Let the students work in small groups on a backup exercise instead of having each person on his or her own machine.

- Modify the class flow creatively based on the software and hardware available.

Modify the Class Flow Creatively

I was training at a law firm, running on a Novell network, when the network went down. The word processing software was on the local hard drives, but the document management software we were using was available only on the network. We elected to keep the class running and just learn the word processing part of the course. Later when the network came back up, we went back and covered the document management part of the training. The participants came away with a stronger understanding of how the document management software integrated into the word processing software and did not seem to suffer for the inconvenience.

Quite honestly, the participant's involvement in making the best of the bad situation seemed to set a spirit of cooperation and working together throughout the entire class.—*Peggy Maday*

Sometimes, no matter how hard you try, the class is dragging and people are losing interest. Always have a few fun, short exercises to pull out. Something lively for a few short minutes can turn the course of the day. See the following sidebar for a fun example with a monkey.

Fun with a Monkey

I learned an excellent way to energize students and provide text for a word processing document at the same time. The class builds a story together similar to a game I used to play at slumber parties as a child.

Each student starts out in their word processing software at a blank screen. Recite the first sentence and ask the students to type while you dictate. *"Once upon a time there was a little boy with a monkey."* Each participant types this sentence on their own computer. Then, call out each student's name at random and ask them to dictate the next sentence (which they are creating on the fly) as the group types. I often wrap it up quickly by throwing out, "And the moral to this story is...."

It is a sure way to get lots of laughs while everyone gets a break from the tedium. For novice groups, we talk about not pressing Enter at the end of lines and word wrap. For more advanced groups, I often use the text for part of my demonstration in creating text borders. This energizer only takes five minutes.—*Peggy Maday*

Breaks

Frequent breaks are important. They are energizing and give the participants and instructor time for refreshing. Consider the following rules of thumb when planning your breaks:

- Limit each period of instruction to an hour. Taking even a five-minute break—just long enough to run down the hall or to grab a drink—is helpful.

- Consider providing one longer break for people to take care of phone messages. Try one 10 to 12 minute break in the morning and a similar, longer break in the afternoon. Then intersperse a couple breaks of the five-minute variety, just to energize the students.

- Be specific about when class will resume. Write it on the board. If there is a wall clock, make it the *official time*. Use an odd time, like 1:58. Participants will remember the time and are more likely to take you seriously.

- Always start promptly at the announced time. Waiting to start class until the stragglers show up perpetuates the problem of the tardy student.

Impromptu Breaks

Many years ago, when I had just started training, I learned a very important lesson: *When all else fails, take a break.* I walked into a training session where one thing after another went wrong. There were several equipment problems. There were two versions of the same training manual with exercises on different pages. My frustration level grew and grew. I have since learned to take quick breaks to regroup when I am smack-dab in the middle of chaos. Even a couple-minute break can give me time to formulate a plan, take a deep breath, and move forward.—*Peggy Maday*

10

Vital Training Tips

Respecting and motivating students is key to the learning process. Always keep in mind the following **12 Basic Keys for a Successful Training Class** and your training experience will be rewarding for the participants and for you as well:

1. **Express genuine enthusiasm and sincerity.** You cannot expect excitement about learning if you are not excited about teaching. Do not be phony. You must be sincere.

2. **Repeat each new idea in as many ways as possible and then move ahead.** Try overviews, demonstrations, listing the steps, and having students read help screens or the manual. Let students discuss the concept and relate it to a project or situation back at the office. Allow them to do it on their own or with the help of another student. The key here is to repeat the information in several ways, but not so that they notice. Allow participants enough time to master the new information, but keep moving ahead at the same time.

3. **Keep the class interactive.** Allow the participants to give you as much information as possible through questions and their own observations. Give them time to answer your questions. Do not just jump in with an authoritative answer. People will not argue with their own facts. Allow time for discovery. What they discover on their own will be remembered longer.

Instead of Telling Them, Let Them Tell You

Challenge students to find as many different quick menus as they can in a program that uses the right mouse button for context-sensitive menus. We usually demonstrate one menu and then let the students discover the rest. Give a small prize or candy reward to the person or team who came up with the most menus.

(continues)

(continued)

Have a Help Scavenger Hunt. Divide the group into teams and give each team a different set of questions. Have them answer their questions using the Help feature. Again, we start out by showing them one item in the Help system. Let each team present their findings to the rest of the class.

4. Respect the student's space. Never grab a keyboard or mouse and just fix a problem. Most people need to actually do it themselves to experience understanding. If you absolutely must take their keyboard or mouse to figure out the difficulty, ask their permission and then explain thoroughly.

5. **Recognize and respect the different learning styles.** Present each topic and allow for individual learning styles. When you give instructions, make them verbal *and* written. "Turn to page 15. I would like you to do the exercise at the top of the page regarding formatting your document." Write the page number on the board as you speak. For more information, see Chapter 3, "Adult Learning: What Do We Know for Sure?," and Chapter 8, "Training Techniques."

6. **Answer the student's questions from their perspective.** Try wording your answer differently or asking another student to explain in their words.

7. **Try to answer all the questions.** If the question is not relevant to the entire class, maybe you can take the time to answer it at a break or at the close of the class. If you do not know the answer, tell the student you will try to find the answer and get back to them.

8. **Be careful not to criticize or talk down.** Do not tell a student, "We just covered that five minutes ago." Be especially careful when you become frustrated. Even displaying negative facial expressions like rolling your eyes back in amazement can be noticeable. Expect to give complete and thorough explanations and still have some misconceptions.

9. **Recognize students for their contributions.** When someone shares a valuable observation or idea, genuinely thank him or her and recognize the merit of the contribution. You want to set the stage so that others feel comfortable in the interaction.

10. **Make mistakes great moments for all.** Often, several participants will make the same mistakes or have the same misconceptions. You can turn their mistakes around by asking them to share them with the group or have the first person making the mistake help the others. Be gentle here and proceed with caution.

11. **Admit your own mistakes.** If you give erroneous information when answering a question or when you stumble in presenting an idea, be graceful in admitting your mistake. Do not try to cover up or make excuses. Remember that you do not have to be the "sage on the stage" who knows the ins and outs of everything. Your role is to provide information, valuable learning experiences, and opportunities for people to solve their own problems.

Digging a Hole

When I was an inexperienced instructor, I always feared those awful moments (and everyone has them) when I would make a mistake that would send the entire class down a wrong path. Whenever that happened, I would get tense and then the class would tense up as I tried to straighten things out. Sometimes, I would make things worse before they got better. Once when I started to explain something incorrectly, I just chuckled and said "Well, you have just observed the instructor digging herself a hole. Now, let's see if she can climb out!" Everyone laughed, including myself. It took the edge off of the situation. The laugh cleared my own mind and gave me a few extra seconds to mentally regroup. Then I was able to clearly explain the mistake I had made and set everyone straight. Now I have that phrase handy to use whenever I need it.
—*Carolyn Woodie*

---

12. **Use only appropriate humor.** There is certainly a place for some humor in the classroom, but make sure that your joke or comment is appropriate. Politics, sex, and religion jokes are typically taboo.

From Here...

We've covered a great deal in this chapter. Every bit of the training session is important. If used properly, each component from the preplanning and the introductions through the content of the class and on to the closing has a purpose. All these elements fit together like an interlocking puzzle presenting the final picture of a very fruitful training course for everyone.

Supplement what you have learned here with information from these chapters:

■ Chapter 3 "Adult Learning: What Do We Know for Sure?," and Chapter 8, "Training Techniques," give you the proper educational techniques you will need to execute a successful training session.

■ Chapter 6, "Post-Class Evaluation," helps you determine whether all your hard work has paid off.

Chapter 11

Augmenting Classroom Training with Other Media

by Bill Brandon

Bill Brandon has managed, developed, and delivered instruction since 1968. His company, Accomplishment Technology Unlimited, provides clients with systematic ways to train, guide, and motivate employees to higher levels of accomplishment. Recent projects include development of computer-based training and multimedia facilities, performance support, documentation, and training materials.

When it comes to improving people's ability to use computers and software, training is sometimes too much. It is also nearly always too little.

Many managers see training as time consuming and expensive. At the same time, simply training people in the use of their computers often does not result in the levels of skill required to support the success of their organizations. Can this paradox be solved?

Given the high rate of change in technology, systems, and applications, formal classroom training probably could not keep people up to date even if it were done perfectly. Most trainers are aware of the Consultant's Mantra: You can have it good, cheap, or fast—pick any two of the three. Is there a way to work around this problem?

Fortunately, the answer to both questions is *yes*. By delivering all or part of the instruction on selected content outside the classroom, you can save time and money and at the same time ensure quality learning.

Available methods for instruction outside the classroom range from the traditional correspondence course to delivery of content using CD-ROM and the Internet. This chapter presents a wide selection of media and formats you can mix and match in many different ways to build a solution that fits your needs.

A simple catalog of methods and technology by itself does not address the actual learning issues. Therefore, this chapter provides guidelines for applying adult learning principles to alternative delivery methods. It also addresses administrative factors and other matters you should consider when the learners are outside the classroom.

General Guidelines for Alternative Delivery Methods

The delivery methods discussed here are used outside the classroom. However, the conditions of adult learning and principles of teaching still apply. These principles continue to influence the quality of your program results.

Note

Good designs involve the learner in an active way even though an instructor is not mediating the experience. Furthermore, alternative delivery methods are not "secondary" delivery methods. They are valid means for helping adults learn.

A complete learning program consists of both classroom and other experiences. A program that consists of classroom experiences alone is not complete—and is almost always ineffective in the long run.

There is a significant up side to using alternatives to classroom training. When you consider what it costs to develop and deliver a classroom course, other media are almost always cheaper in the long run. Busy people (and their managers) like it when they aren't taken out of the office all day to attend a class. Some things (practice and teaching executives to use computers, to name two of them) may be best done completely outside the classroom.

Tip

Despite the clear benefits of using alternatives to seat-based training, you must consider the downside. Getting people to do training work outside the classroom is not always easy. Getting supervisors to let people do training on the job can be a challenge, too. If you assign pre-work before a class begins, you must decide what to do when the learners walk into class without having done the pre-work. Computer-based training and materials on CD-ROM and videotape may involve fees and capital expenses. Finally, you have the expense of maintaining the materials.

Much of the work in designing a successful alternative delivery program consists of maximizing the up side and minimizing the downside. You can do two things to make it easier to accomplish these ends: The first is to apply the principles of adult learning. The second is to deal effectively with the issues of administration and execution.

Applying Principles of Adult Learning Outside the Classroom

Table 11.1 suggests how features of self-paced or alternative materials can support the ways adults learn best. The list in the right column is not exhaustive.

Table 11.1 Applying Adult Learning Principles to the Use of Alternative Materials

Adults Learn Best If They:	Alternative Materials Create These Conditions When They:
Feel a need to learn	Include self-assessment.
	Show learners new possibilities.
	Help learners set goals.
Identify with the goals of the learning experience	Involve learners in setting their own objectives for the learning experience.
Participate in the planning of the learning experience	Provide learner options for using the materials: amount, sequence of learning, and so on.
	Offer more than one delivery medium (book, CBT, videotape, and so on) for each set of objectives.
Participate actively in the learning experience	Offer a variety of choices for additional learning, group work, and so on.
	Put learners in touch with each other.
Feel the learning process makes use of their experience	Offer several entry points; if experienced, skip the basics.
	Suggest possible ways to apply what they learn.
Have a sense of progress toward their goals	Provide a progress map and self-evaluation criteria.

Adult learning does not happen in a vacuum. It takes place within a social context that includes other learners. Because time for learning must fit into the learner's schedule, it makes sense to design the program in ways that recognize and support the learner's autonomy.

Many of the suggestions in Table 11.1 seem familiar because they are common practice in instructor-led classroom courses. All you need to do is figure out how to implement these in a self-paced program. For example, helping the learner set goals and objectives for the learning experience is a pretty ordinary feature of training programs. To implement this in an alternative format can involve having the learner write out the things he or she hopes to learn and how these goals apply on the job. The employee can then discuss this list with a supervisor or manager.

Another easily translated feature is the skills self-assessment. A simple check list at the start of the workbook or at the beginning of a computer-based training program can serve the purpose. And any alternative program must have a "motivation" section that invites the learner to consider the benefits of adding new knowledge.

Some of the features suggested in Table 11.1 have no parallel in classroom courses. These are very powerful features, however, and can make the results of self-administered training better than the results of classroom training.

For example, offering more than one delivery medium is not something you can do easily in a classroom. But you can easily obtain and offer instructional materials on common application software and operating systems in many formats: books, videotapes, audiotapes, computer-based training, and so on. The learner can choose the form that best suits his or her learning style and work situation. The objective is to have employees who can use the company's word processing and spreadsheet software, not to have everybody go through the same course.

Another suggestion in Table 11.1 ties into this multiple-delivery mode. You should arrange the administration of the program so that learners know who among their co-workers is also taking training (or has already had training) in the same application. In this way, they can help each other and compare what they learned from their own experience with a different medium of instruction.

In a training program conducted outside a classroom, it is possible that different learners may enter the training at different points, take different paths, use different materials, and still arrive at the same set of learning objectives. This is the idea behind the "course map" in Figure 11.1. Course maps can apply to a single course on a single application or they can apply to an entire curriculum.

Fig. 11.1

A course map lets a learner create a customized route to the completion of a set of learning objectives.

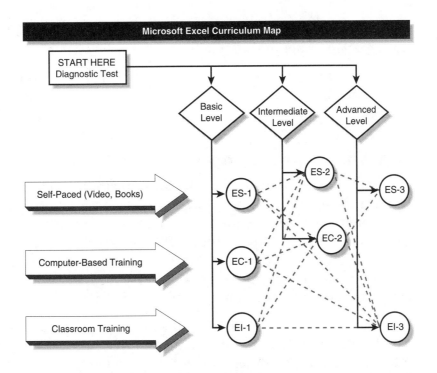

Note

The alphanumeric designations on the course map in Figure 11.1 indicate that the course modules deal with Excel (E). Other designations identify the medium of instruction: self-paced (S), computer-based (C), and instructor-led (I). Finally, they state the level of the module: 1 (Basic), 2 (Intermediate), and 3 (Advanced). Any designation system that makes sense to users can be applied here.

The learner receives this course map at the beginning of her training. She uses diagnostic tools to choose her entry point. For each course, she selects the medium that best matches her situation. After each course, she refers to the map to decide what course to take next. Prerequisites and required courses are clearly identified on the map. The result is that the employee gets the skills she needs, the way she needs them, when she needs them.

Finally, it is important to provide the learners in an alternative program with some means of judging their progress. This can be as simple as checking off modules completed on the course map, it can involve self-evaluation checks, or both.

Dealing with Issues of Administration and Execution

Although alternative approaches can provide excellent results quickly and at low cost, some special requirements apply. Many of these are not self-evident and are covered in depth in "Creating a Successful Alternative Program," later in this chapter.

Six of these requirements are worth mentioning now, however. You can be thinking about them as you read the descriptions of the various methods.

Get Management Support

First, get support for the use of alternative methods from management. Not just the manager in the information systems or human resources department, but the staff and line managers whose employees are going to use the materials. Most of these officials are accustomed to training that takes place in a classroom. Most will also accept the idea of training that takes place on the job, while the employee is performing work within the scope of their job function.

But training that takes place while the person is sitting at his desk, during working hours, but which takes that employee out of "production" for 15 minutes at a time is a different story. The same is true of training that requires the employee to go to a computer learning lab and work alone and unsupervised for an hour or two. It is even true of training that consists of attending user group meetings.

All these formats may be resisted or rejected by managers who do not understand the adult learning model. Depending on the culture in the organization, you may have to convince managers and supervisors that alternative approaches are valid, effective ways to train employees. Be sure to involve the managers in the planning, implementation, and evaluation of your alternative curriculum.

Make an Early Decision about Grades

In general, grades have no function in adult education. There are only two reasons why you would need to give grades:

- To meet requirements for a Continuing Professional Education (CPE) program

- To meet mandated requirements of a regulatory body, such as part of a licensing program

However, you may find yourself under pressure to give grades. This pressure may come from management or it may be the custom in your organization. If at all possible, resist this pressure. There are a number of very sound reasons why you should not give grades.

First, grades promote a spirit of competition with co-workers. Because the desired model within an organization is cooperation, why provide another program that drives people apart?

Second, grades carry with them the connotation of school, an experience regarded as painful by many adults. Why associate your training program with something people prefer to avoid?

Third, being judged by another adult is a distinctly unpleasant and demeaning experience for most of us. If it is important to involve adults as equal partners in their own learning, isn't the grading process inconsistent with this belief?

Fourth, the only evaluation that makes sense in adult education is whether the adults have learned what is important to them. Why not have the learners measure their own progress against this standard?

Knowing early whether or not grades will be given, and how progress will be evaluated, is important to the course developers. It is better to make an explicit decision early about these matters than to develop the course and discover during implementation that a decision made by default is unacceptable to the organization or the learners.

Formalize Enrollment

Entering an employee into a formal classroom training program is normally so effortless as to need no special attention. Getting the right kind of start in an alternative program, on the other hand, takes some explicit activity. Formalized enrollment is important because it raises the credibility and importance of the course at the same time that it supports and empowers the employee.

If at all possible, an individual in the training department should administer and coordinate all training done outside the classroom. This person's job includes the following duties:

- Contact each enrollee by phone or by mail and welcome him or her to the program

- Respond to the learner's concerns and questions about the program

- Assist in the assessment of entry-level skills and readiness and suggest where to start in the program and how to proceed

Taking these simple steps helps improve the completion rate for the course and also improves the results. In a classroom course, the instructor can provide these services. In a self-paced course, the three small actions listed above perform two vital functions. They tell the learner that the course is important and they encourage the learner's participation.

Provide Incentives to the Learners

In addition to raising the importance of the course, you must answer the question most adults have at the forefront of their concerns most of the time: "What's in it for me?" There is plenty of evidence about what's important to people, and you can use this information in the design and delivery of your alternative programs.

As you look over the incentives for adult learning in Table 11.2, you should see a number of possibilities. These incentives were selected from Malcolm Knowles' book, *The Modern Practice of Adult Education*, as most applicable to teaching adults to use computers in the 1990s. The more of these incentives you can provide with programs outside the classroom, the more you motivate people to participate fully.

Table 11.2   The Right Answers to the Question, "What's in It for Me?" for Adult Learners

Adults Want To Have More:	*Adults Want To Be Seen As:*
Time and money	Smart and up to date
Praise from other adults	Creative
Comfort and leisure	Influential
Pride in accomplishments	Efficient
Success in business	Highly effective
Self-confidence and prestige	Authorities
Adults Want To Have Less:	*Adults Want To Be Able To:*
Expense and wasted effort	Express themselves
Drudgery, discomfort, doubt	Be independent of others
Worry and risk in the future	Answer their own questions
Chance of embarrassment	Be like people they admire
	Improve their lives
	Advance themselves

Provide Learners with Support

Provide continuing assistance to your enrollees throughout the time they are involved in the classroom alternative. This involves four kinds of activities:

■ Communicate with the learners periodically as they go through the course or curriculum

■ Affirm the learner's decision to take the course and encourage them to stay in it

- Provide assistance and counseling as needed by the learner
- Continue to promote the course and its follow-up programs

These activities replace the normal social support of the classroom. They also help to counteract the forces that cause learners to fail to complete self-study programs. Learners should at least have a phone number or an e-mail address from which they can obtain help when they are stuck.

Recognize Factors Affecting Interest and Participation

There are a few factors you can't do much to avoid. Instead, you must recognize their effects and do what you can to either take advantage of or offset them. These three factors do not affect all training and alternative approaches in the same way. They are highly audience dependent.

First, the subject (for job-related courses) has some effect on the level of interest. In general, training seen as developing technical or general office skills, or dealing with business administration and management, get the most interest. Training that seems to be narrow in focus gets the least interest.

Second, the interest in work or career-related training decreases after about age 40. It is important not to confuse this decreased interest with reduced capacity to learn or with fear of computers. Research shows that the capacity to learn remains fairly constant with increasing age.

Older people do tend to be less inclined to simply accept what the instructor says in an uncritical fashion. In addition, very few people are actually afraid of computers. Usually, adults just don't see why they should have to change the way they've been doing things for years.

Finally, interest and participation in alternative forms of training tend to increase with higher socioeconomic status. However, people at lower socioeconomic levels are extremely interested in concrete skills that help them improve their earnings and status.

Electronic Performance Support Systems (EPSS): Changing Performance without Training

Training, even the kind done outside the classroom, is always relatively expensive. It is a good idea to ask one special question before you decide to use training to solve your performance problems. Can these problems be fixed without doing any training?

In many jobs, it is common to see job aids, checklists, or cheat sheets in use. These are ways to get the desired performance without requiring training. In other jobs, by simplifying the work or redesigning the tools, training requirements have been reduced or eliminated.

In the late 1980s, observations like these led to the notion that human performance could be supported with the help of electronic and computer systems. Gloria Gery, who is given credit by most practitioners for getting the idea of the *electronic performance support system* (EPSS) off the ground, often says that "training is just compensation for bad design."

What does an EPSS look like? It has a thousand faces. Simple forms of EPSSes are so familiar they are easily overlooked. The "Intellisense" built into Excel and Word are very basic electronic performance support. So are wizards and coaches. A more advanced EPSS may have its own microprocessor built into a complex system.

In some cases, the EPSS works invisibly to correct errors made by the system operator. In other cases, it becomes more active and offers references, coaching, or short segments of computer-based training.

How do you get an EPSS? Generally, you build your own or contract to have it created. The tools used range from Microsoft Word (used to create Windows help files) to CBT authoring systems and specialized software for EPSS development.

Note

An EPSS is a good solution when the system in use is highly complex and when safety is a primary concern. Large EPSSes tend to be expensive to create and maintain—and it is very difficult to show a return on the investment. Well-made help files and intelligent software are worthwhile investments for less complex systems and reduce the amount of training required. You will probably still have to deliver some instruction, either in the classroom or out, to ensure the desired performance.

Formats for Learning Outside the Classroom

Training outside the classroom can be delivered to individual learners. The training can also involve groups of learners in activities that help the individuals learn from each other.

For Individuals

There are four common patterns for individual learning experiences. In increasing order of scope, they are coaching, distance learning, directed study, and apprenticeships or internships. In coaching, the scope of the learning objectives is usually very small. The employee is to learn how to perform a limited number of tasks or job duties. In an internship, the scope of the learning objectives is often very large and complex, encompassing the whole of a career field. All four methods can potentially develop the individual's particular skill.

Coaching

Generally, coaching is an informal arrangement in which one employee assists another in learning specific software or system features. This is usually an association of brief duration.

> **Tip**
>
> Coaching is a good strategy for limited purposes but is a bad idea for use in teaching an employee an entire software package or system. You should be very selective in choosing people who do the coaching. In fact, it is worth considering the creation of a training program to help coaches coach.

Distance Learning Courses

This big category includes correspondence courses and using CBT or any sort of materials mediated by workbooks, audiotapes, or videotapes in a "course" format. That is, distance learning courses employ lessons and progress checks and have some sort of expectation that learners will complete the course within a given period of time. The objectives are set for each module ahead of time.

Although it is possible for an employee to choose which modules to complete or which materials to use, the employee normally cannot tailor the objectives of the program. Distance learning is much like a classroom course in most respects, and the scope of the objectives is very similar. Chapter 12, "Distance Learning on the World Wide Web," treats this subject in depth.

Directed Study Programs

In a directed study program, the learner works out the objectives of study with an advisor, who then prescribes a course of study that may involve a number of different resources. The learner may be expected to complete projects or work assignments that use what has been studied.

There are scheduled meetings between the learner and the advisor. During these meetings, they review and assess progress, work out the particular needs of the learner, and possibly redirect the learner. The scope of the learning objectives is quite a bit larger than in distance learning. A programmer who is learning a new language, for example, may be a good candidate for a directed study program.

Apprenticeship/Internship Arrangements

In contrast to the other individual learning formats, the apprenticeship or internship is usually a long-term program with a very wide scope. It may be part of an employment agreement between the learner and an organization. Such an arrangement often includes learning experiences on the job, in the classroom, or in the other three formats just described. An internship can also include formal academic study.

A person learning to be an animator, for example, may become involved in an apprenticeship program that takes a couple of years to complete. At the end of a program this complex, a learner should have technical mastery of the subject and be highly proficient.

For Groups

It also makes sense to involve the work group in the learning process. Even though individuals may get the training they need to use the new software themselves, this is often not enough. When changing the software changes the nature of the work or the relationships between individuals doing the work, it is time to involve the entire work group.

In addition, groups can handle much of the actual teaching-learning process. This relieves the training organization of the burden and can be an effective, enjoyable experience for the learners.

Action Projects

In an action project, the system or application users figure out the answers to group problems such as the use of e-mail, Lotus Notes, and so on. Action projects usually bring the group together and establish an objective. Resources outside the group are identified, and a schedule is negotiated. In some cases, the group may be assigned to document the solution they create.

Tip

In a sense, the action project is the group equivalent of directed study. A typical action project may require one to three months to complete. The important factor in an action project is making the objective very specific and providing adequate time during the work day for the team members to meet.

User Groups

A user group is a more-or-less independent body. It may be composed of individuals from more than one organization. User groups can be very broad in scope, including many different systems and applications under their umbrellas. For example, Dallas has the Dallas Xchange Corporation. This huge user group grew up in the 1980s and now fills the Infomart the third Saturday of each month with over 90 hour-long meetings on different computer systems, applications, and disciplines.

Another example is the Southwest Notes Users Group (SNUG); their monthly meetings start off with a new users tutorial. Membership includes users, developers, administrators, executives, and business partners. A well-run users group brings in guest speakers from outside, practitioners as well as vendors, and often runs an annual technology fair.

If you have a local "computer newspaper" (usually given away free near the front door of chain bookstores), check its calendar section to see what is available in your locale.

11

Setting Up Your Own User Group

Organizations often set up their own user groups in house. Here are some guidelines if you want to try setting up your own user group.

The singlemost important thing is for the user group itself to decide the important issues. If a manager (or anyone else) tries to control this decision or the meeting agendas, the user group will dry up and blow away.

The best and most informative user groups seem to do five things:

1. They publish an agenda early for each meeting and stick to it.

2. They let the users decide how to be organized, when and where to meet, and how often to meet.

3. They get as many volunteers to help as possible.

4. They poll the users regularly to find out their needs.

5. They don't waste their member's time. The agenda is fast-paced in design and execution.

In a large group, consider breaking into small groups by interest periodically. Some groups have a specific time in each meeting called "birds of a feather." This allows people to pursue particular needs that they have, exchange ideas, and so on.

Another form of user group is worth mentioning. This is the *online user group* seen on services such as CompuServe and America Online. Most major software publishers sponsor forums or user groups on these services. In addition, a number of independent forums flourish on the commercial services.

Online forums offer a place where users of a product or system can come together with each other and with the software publishers. Users can ask questions, trade tips and ideas, and learn how to do things better. The only drawback to this approach in the past has been the expense of the commercial services. However, as competition with each other and from the Internet drives online prices down, the expense is getting much more reasonable. The commercial services offer a big advantage over the Internet in that the conversations and the forums are *moderated*. This means a much better "signal to noise" ratio: fewer flames, whiners, and impostors.

Conferences, Conventions, and Fairs

Another excellent format for groups is similar to a very large user group meeting. In many metropolitan locations, vendors and other groups sponsor events such as NetWorld and Windows Solutions. Many of these venues include hands-on demonstrations and tutorials that can be useful in your training program. In addition, you can often get free passes from vendors.

Larger organizations may conduct annual in-house technology fairs for their end users. These last a day or a week, and consist of demonstrations, short tutorials, and informational presentations.

One of the best examples is the annual fair run by Mona Davis at the Federal Reserve Bank in Dallas. New users are introduced to the systems and software in use; experienced users are exposed to possible applications they may not have considered. This is a good opportunity to get people to sign up for both classroom and alternative learning programs.

These fairs seem to work best in organizations in which the cost of training is charged back to the departments that use the in-house services. If you are competing with outside training organizations, a technology fair can help you put your best foot forward and keep the business.

Large Meetings or a Series of Meetings

This large-meeting format seems to be used most often when launching a new system that affects large numbers of employees in an organization. By bringing learners together, it is easier to give an overview, explain the reasons for the change, and generate support for the new approach.

A well-conducted meeting can reduce resistance and help create a positive sense of anticipation. You may have had the experience of having your office software peremptorily changed by the IS group without any preparation. If so, you can appreciate the wisdom of using a large meeting or a series of meetings as part of the launch strategy.

Delivery Vehicles for Training Outside the Classroom

Within each of the formats just outlined, a number of different methods and media are available to deliver the content and to facilitate learning. These formats can be offered individually or they can be used as learner-selected options. Table 11.3 shows some possible combinations to consider.

Table 11.3 "Mix and Match" Possibilities for Learning Formats and Delivery Vehicles					
	Learning Formats				
Delivery Vehicle	**Coaching**	**Distance Learning**	**Directed Study**	**Internship**	**Action Projects**
For Individuals					
Print	✓	✓	✓	✓	✓
CBT		✓	✓	✓	
Online	✓	✓	✓	✓	✓
For Groups					
Delivery Vehicle	**User Groups**	**Conference or Fair**	**Large Meetings**		
Print	✓	✓	✓		
CBT	✓	✓			
Online	✓	✓			

When selecting among the various media or between different materials done in the same medium, work with the learner population to come up with a list of selection criteria. If possible, have actual users review the alternatives.

The temptation may be to go with the cheapest product or the one that most closely resembles what the trainer or the IS department thinks is acceptable. However, this temptation ought to be resisted. The cheapest way is often not the best way, and the best way is usually not the most expensive. Remember that you are trying to match the students' learning style, not the management's.

Books, Self-Instruction, and On-Your-Own Workbooks

Print is the classic medium of instruction and was around long before computers supported classroom instruction and self-instruction. One of the earliest self-instruction manuals was the Egyptian *Book of the Dead*, essentially a tutoring program for the afterlife.

Despite its long history, the print medium can easily be misused. Many people do not learn well from books. They may require additional coaching and hands-on help to succeed. It is a good plan to make help (preferably from a human being) available to the learner who is using printed materials as a primary medium of instruction.

Where Do You Get Print Materials? Should You Write Your Own?

For standard, commercially available application software and operating systems, many sources for print materials exist. In fact, the biggest problem may be simply dealing with the volume of these items.

For "plain old books," major publishers can provide a seemingly endless array of alternatives. You can browse the shelves in any large bookstore to perform an initial screening of current titles. You may want to establish a library of books that can be sent out to learners. Or you can have learners buy their own books (perhaps from a list of suggested or approved titles).

In either case, all publishers will send lists of titles in print and new books to interested managers. On the back of most title pages is a statement giving an address or phone number for inquiries about prices for bulk quantities. This is the best place to start the process of getting on the mailing list. The back of the title page often contains other information, such as the availability of the book in translations. Every publisher will make it easy for you to order from them.

For workbooks and self-instruction materials, it may be a little more difficult to get a comprehensive list of suppliers. One of the best places to find out about such texts is the Internet. Another good place is the Computer Training and Support forum on CompuServe. These online resources offer the additional advantage of putting you in touch with others who have tried various solutions. A list of some of the best online resources appears at the end of this chapter.

Software publishers may also make self-instruction materials on their products available for free or at low cost. You can usually find out about such tutorials by contacting your local sales representative or by calling the company's marketing or sales department.

You may want to (or have to) consider writing your own materials. If this is the case, study the formats and layouts used in the commercial products. These generally work well. Remember that it is a serious violation of copyright law to copy commercial products. Test your materials with a small sample of users before releasing the manual for general use. Be sure to spell-check and proofread your product carefully.

You will find that you get better results by having a skilled writer prepare your in-house text materials. Programmers know everything there is to know about the custom software they have created, but most cannot write satisfactory user manuals or self-study materials. Many technical writers have the same problem. The difference in quality obtained by bringing in a good writer is significant and saves money in the long run. You get what you pay for.

Augmenting Printed Material

The information in print can be supported by more information on disk or tape. This additional information may be used as reference material, exercises, or a conceptual overview.

Here are some common ways to deliver this added information:

- **Demonstration and Reference Materials:**

  - CD-ROM

  - Audiotape and videotape

  - Formatted files, read by Adobe Acrobat or another viewer

- **Exercises and Examples:**

  - Lotus ScreenCam movies

  - Floppy disk

You can mail all these media. You can send ScreenCam movies and formatted files over a LAN, commercial information service, or the Internet.

When To Use Print Media

Of all the available media, print is probably the most familiar to learners and the most flexible. It is not necessarily the cheapest, especially when you consider the cost of revisions. The augmentations suggested in the preceding section can help you work around limitations or special cases.

Consider print media when the learners do not have access to alternatives such as online delivery. Books are useful as references after the learning experience, which can help reduce support costs and so offset the cost of the materials.

Print works well with older learners and with individuals who have the academic experience and discipline to learn well from it. Print may not work as well as other methods with the youngest workers or with persons who have learning disabilities or attention deficit disorders. Finally, learners should have a choice between print materials, augmented print materials, and other media.

Computer-Based Training

Computer-based training, or CBT, is often a better way to deliver instruction outside the classroom. CBT is frequently cheaper than using print media.

From the learner's point of view, CBT is just more software. As a result, it is important to provide the student with a user guide and help desk support just as you would for an application program. This is true even if you are distributing information over a network so that the user does not have to install the CBT on his or her system.

You can obtain CBT on nearly any commercial application or operating system, running on any platform. The quality of CBT in 1995 is, in general, much better than the quality of the same kind of materials published as recently as 1993.

Where Do You Get CBT? Should You Write Your Own?

Computer-based training can be obtained directly from some software publishers, from courseware publishers, and from independent developers. As with print materials, it is a good idea to inquire on the Internet or on CompuServe's Computer Training and Support forum about titles and the experience of others with the various products.

In the case of popular commercial applications, it does not make sense to develop your own CBT. Computer-based training is time consuming and expensive to prepare but very cheap to purchase. You may want to consider developing EPSS, such as custom help files, wizards, coaches, or other macro forms to make it easier for users to employ infrequently used features.

Developing your own CBT may be the only option you have if you are dealing with an in-house application. You still have the choice of employing a consulting firm to do the actual development and testing. To repeat a point made earlier, CBT is just another piece of software. However, it requires special tools and knowledge to create CBT, expenses you may want to avoid if you do not have a frequent need to do this sort of work.

There are as many formulas for estimating time and cost of CBT development as there are developers. A good rule of thumb for in-house development is that your first CBT tool with a given authoring tool takes six months and about $60,000 to $100,000 to finish.

This estimate includes the time it takes to learn to use the authoring tool and the costs of the authoring tools and the computer system you use to do the development. It also incorporates the salaries of the author, the instructional designer, and two or three other persons to assist in development. These assistants include a graphic artist and possibly a C programmer. It does not include any allowance for other costs (benefits, insurance, office space, and so on). This estimate also assumes that little or no video or audio will be shot specifically for the production.

Your mileage may vary, as they say. The numbers are high, but if the CBT is satisfactory, it will show a positive return on investment (ROI) that should meet your chief financial officer's criteria. CBT that replaces part of an existing classroom course nearly always has an even higher ROI.

What Should a CBT Program Include?

A computer-based training program should include a user manual and help desk support. Most of the other requirements are less tangible.

Remember that, in the minds of many users, your CBT is competing for critical acclaim with computer games and animations that required millions of dollars and months to develop. It is also competing under the standards for television broadcast quality. This isn't fair because there's no way any ordinary CBT is going to win either of these contests.

Fortunately, computer-based training doesn't have to outshine the competition. It *does* have to be good enough to look credible. This means that CBT can't cut many corners in the sounds and image areas. It also means that you should check any CBT product carefully for typos, bugs, and grammatical errors.

> **Tip**
>
> Be sure that the segments of the CBT take an average learner no more than 10 to 15 minutes to complete. This allows learners to fit the segments more easily into their work schedules. Measure the average time to complete a module by having several representative learners actually complete some modules before you release the CBT. Learners should be able to stop at any time and pick up again exactly where they left off.

Finally, a good CBT system should be capable of reporting progress both to the student and to the student's advisor.

When To Use CBT

Computer-based training is a good choice when you have a lot of learners who need instruction. It is also a good choice when the learners are spread out geographically. If the learners are not the kind of folks who do well learning from books, consider using CBT. But most of all, you should use computer-based training when the financial return on investment is between 85 percent and 500 percent. These are perfectly reasonable numbers, and many applications can support them.

Online Education and Training

The number of ways to deliver training online is increasing. You can provide the course materials on a server or other system that the learner can dial up. In some cases, audio and video portions of the materials can be supplied to the learner on a CD-ROM or downloaded to the learner's system. This approach offsets the time required to send audio and video files (which are very large) over a network or telephone line.

Another version of the online course is one in which there are audio and video links between the instructor at one location and the learners at remote locations. The learners may be miles away from the instructor and from other learners. This is practically returning to the classroom, but without the time and expense of travel.

There are three different ways to accomplish online delivery. Two of them are analogous to the old-fashioned correspondence course; one operates in real time.

E-Mail, Client–Server, and Bandwidth: Correspondence School in the Computer Age

Learners in any location, given a workbook and an *electronic mail* (*e-mail*) account, can complete practical exercises and return them to a centralized location for feedback. Depending on the nature of the e-mail connection, a lot more may be possible as well.

Network Solutions   If the training material involved is mainly text and a few still images, delivery of learning materials over a network is fairly straightforward. When the module materials are all text, sample files, and simple executables, it may be possible for learners to access them directly from the server without affecting the rest of the network. Plain text materials can also be sent to the learner's hard drive a module at a time. The learner completes the module, returns the assignments using e-mail, and the next module is sent.

When there are images or audio files in the module, the module can be sent to the learner's workstation at night. In some cases, this arrangement minimizes the effects of sending large amounts of data on network speed and on other network users. Of course, in many organizations, the networks are in full use 24 hours a day, every day.

At this point, things get a little complicated. The network system in each organization is different from every other network, so this section deals in generalities. If you think you want to use your network system to deliver instructional materials, talk to the system staff in your MIS department. This is especially true if you want to send video or multimedia CBT across your network.

New *local area networking* (*LAN*) and *wide area networking* (*WAN*) technologies make it more practical to consider using multimedia and video. These technologies include *Fast Ethernet, frame relay, asynchronous transfer mode* (*ATM*), and new *data switching methodologies.*

The challenge is to make the best use of the network's *bandwidth.* A computer network is like a pipeline for data. Images, sound, text, and graphical user interfaces are just data on the network. Bandwidth is the amount of data that can flow through the pipeline. The transmission capacity of the lines determines the kinds of applications practical for a given network.

Bandwidth is affected by many factors, including the type of cabling used for the lines, the transmission technology, and the transmission protocol. LANs typically have greater bandwidths than WANs. However, technology is helping speed up WANs as well.

Organizations take different approaches to the bandwidth problem. Some try to minimize traffic between the server and its clients. This is the rationale behind sending the instructional materials to the learner's workstation. However, as pointed out earlier, it is hard to predict the amount and pattern of traffic on a network.

Other organizations have a policy of avoiding any application that requires a lot of bandwidth. This may mean that you have to use only text-based applications. Such a policy can have a serious effect on plans for using the network to deliver instruction.

In many organizations, remote workers dial up the server using ordinary telephone lines. These users have access speeds much slower than the LAN speed. This is caused both by access speed limits imposed by the telephone system and by the speed of the remote user's modem. Compare the remote user's top transfer speed with a 28.8 Kbps modem to what is enjoyed by someone on a system using standard Ethernet: 10 Mbps. Dial-up users are normally not good candidates for instruction involving a lot of video or audio.

There are some options to help the remote user, however. Telephone companies in some areas offer different types of digital circuits. One type of digital circuit, *point-to-point* or *T1*, provides 1.544 Mbps. The *T3* circuit runs at 45 Mbps. Finally, the *integrated services digital network* (*ISDN*) runs at 64 Kbps per channel; by using multiple channels, speeds of up to 1.5 Mbps can be attained.

Other options include even faster technologies such as *frame relay* (384 Kbps) or *ATM*. ATM has the advantage of being scaleable, and it currently offers speeds up to 622 Mbps. At these speeds, it is possible to handle voice, data, and video simultaneously.

With the addition of a video server (such as StarWorks from Starlight Networks, Inc.), it is becoming practical to send video signals over an enterprise LAN. With Lotus Notes, a system may be able to use Video for Notes to accomplish the same end. At this writing, Starlight and Sun Microsystems are about to release Training on Demand: multimedia networking software.

Although the technical means are at hand to deliver multimedia training and video to multiple sites, it is still very expensive to do so.

Using the Internet and Commercial Services

A large number of organizations are beginning to use the Internet as a means of providing instruction outside the classroom. Although this approach certainly has its limitations, it also has a number of advantages.

For example, in most cases, the Internet is only a local phone call away for employees and learners around the world. Internet traffic has no effect on the company's internal network. With proper course design, this method is at least as effective as traditional correspondence courses.

Training and Cyberspace

Two examples of using the Internet to deliver instruction may give an indication of where online education and training are headed in the immediate future. The first example is the EASI Online Workshop on Disability Access to Information Technology. This is sponsored by EASI (Equal Access to Software and Information, an affiliate of the American Association for Higher Education) and the Rochester Institute of Technology. You can see a preview of the workshop on the World Wide Web at the time of this writing.

One of the goals of this workshop is to "demonstrate that e-mail is the little giant of the Internet." Participants in the workshop are urged to be active, in either or both of two ways. First, by using the reply command to a given assignment; all replies are rebroadcast to the entire class, where they become part of the group interaction. Second, learners can send personal e-mail to the instructors.

A syllabus and introduction are sent to participants before the start of the seminar. A regular schedule that involves sending out lessons each Monday, Wednesday, and Friday for three weeks, is established. A registration fee is required, and the Rochester Institute of Technology awards a completion certificate or Continuing Education Credits (CEU). Over the Internet, this seminar has already been delivered to 500 participants in 21 countries on six continents.

The second example of online instruction—this time using a commercial network—is the Microsoft Online Institute (MOLI). MOLI is an online interactive learning and information resource on the Microsoft Network (MSN) online service. It is available only to Windows 95 users with MSN accounts.

The model for MOLI is a college campus. On this campus, learners have online access to learning materials, instructors, product information, reference materials, user forums, and other resources. Microsoft's stated mission for this arrangement is to provide the flexibility of self-study while maintaining a relationship between the student and instructor.

MOLI is initially serving computer professionals who need information or training on Microsoft Back Office products, developer tools, desktop operating systems, and related technologies. By early 1996, Microsoft expects to expand MOLI offerings to include information and training for general business users of Microsoft Office products and vertical markets.

Much like the EASI course just described, MOLI seeks to pair electronic self-study learning materials with online instructor expertise. Learners choose courses from an online course catalog and then purchase class tuition from the third-party learning organizations (Online Classroom Providers, or OCPs) offering the courses. The OCP sends the electronic course materials and the learner completes the exercises. Interaction with the instructor and fellow students occurs with e-mail, bulletin boards, and forums mostly "on" the MOLI electronic campus.

Online class length is determined by the OCP and, to some extent, the learner. Online Classroom Providers set a time limit for their students based on the complexity of the material to be covered. Currently, the average online course length is estimated to be five weeks. Fees for MOLI courses should be about half what is charged for classroom courses by the OCPs.

Developments in technology and in the battle between the telephone service providers and the cable television service providers will probably shape this alternative in the long run.

Video Conferencing: Classrooms without Walls

Other technology is putting the real-time classroom online. Desktop video conferencing has started to come into its own, supplementing older and more expensive technology.

Beginning in the late 1980s, land-line and satellite transmission costs dropped to the point that organizations ranging from the United States Government, General Motors, and Electronic Data Systems to the Southern Gas Association were able to use them to bring training to large numbers of people scattered across the United States and the world. Microsoft uses the same technology to support its Developer Network broadcasts.

In a large-scale video conference environment, the link from the instructor to the learners usually involves video and audio; the link from learners back to instructor is only audio. Sometimes, the learners are each provided with a responder unit and can be given "pop quizzes" so that the instructor can figure out whether the learners are understanding what is being said.

These video conferencing systems are usually very expensive and practical only when very large numbers of people "attend" so that the cost per person becomes reasonable. Another disadvantage is that such broadcasts usually require learners to go to some central location and remain there for several hours during the course of a day. Other than being able to reach huge numbers of people at many locations simultaneously, broadcasts offer no particular advantages over classroom instruction.

With the limitations on learner participation inherent in the systems, broadcasts can easily be less effective with adult learners than traditional classrooms. Broadcasts may be best for the large-group format described earlier for program launches.

A cheaper, though less capable, technology is becoming available as *desktop video conferencing*. This technology links two workstations or sites together using ordinary telephone lines or the network cabling in the organization's system.

With desktop video conferencing, it is possible to have a virtual meeting in which participants can see and hear each other, make presentations using familiar software such as Astound, PowerPoint, or WordPerfect Presentations, and show objects, sketches, or other materials without scanning them. The Starlight video server software mentioned earlier in this chapter is often chosen to support desktop video conferences.

Desktop video conferencing is a useful tool for coaching and one-to-one instruction. It permits both parties to stay at their workstations and can be set up as simply as a telephone call. Bringing in more than two parties may be difficult or impossible for some time to come, however.

When To Use Online Education and Training

There is no simple answer to this question. The correspondence course format provides low-cost, flexible instruction at the expense of effectiveness and interaction. Providing online education and training on a LAN or WAN or to dial-up learners can require a large capital investment, especially for new cabling. Using the organization's client-server system can also have a negative impact on system performance. On the whole, however, the use of e-mail-based or computer-based training is likely to become more cost-effective and common as time goes on.

Creating a Successful Alternative Program

As you have seen in the preceding pages, there are many options, formats, and methods to consider in setting up an alternative to classroom instruction. Yet as in so many other efforts, it is not the chosen technology alone that determines success. Critical decisions are to be made, and the trainers, managers, or administrators who design the overall training and education system must themselves find support and resources.

11

Critical Decisions

At the beginning of the chapter, the section "Dealing with Issues of Administration and Execution" outlined a half-dozen key issues to consider. In addition to good instructional design, these six issues are the ones that must be dealt with simply to get an alternative approach to work at all:

■ Get management support

■ Decide about grades

■ Formalize enrollment

■ Provide incentives to learners

■ Provide support to learners

■ Recognize factors affecting participation

There are four more factors to consider. These make the difference between programs that merely work one time and are then forgotten, and those that are truly successful. A truly successful program generates more opportunities to use alternative approaches.

■ Provide a complete learning system.

■ Clarify the relationship between the alternatives and the classroom.

■ Involve the boss in the learning process.

■ Evaluate the program for effectiveness.

Provide a Complete Learning System

Although the title of this chapter refers to "augmenting" classroom instruction, everything addressed in this chapter can produce learning. Instruction, whether in or out of the classroom, is part of a complete learning system. For adults, this system includes experiences on the job and experiences involving other people.

Designers who approach the business of putting together adult learning programs from the perspective of the classroom instructor sometimes overlook this point. No part of the program is more or less important than any other. Some methods fulfill certain functions better than others, but each has its place.

Designing computer training for working adults means designing a series of learning experiences that ultimately lead to attainment of a set of objectives. The designer should look for ways to provide a well-rounded program that offers something for every kind of learner.

Figure 11.1, earlier in this chapter, showed a curriculum map. In addition to being a handy tool for the learner's participation, the curriculum map represents a complete learning system. All the elements that lead to attainment of the final objectives are parsed and grouped across the width of the map. All the choices available to the learner appear vertically down the map. Where a sequence of prerequisites is important, it is laid out. Where a learner has the option to do additional study to improve mastery, it is indicated.

Develop your computer training curriculum and its parts with the curriculum map in mind. If you take the map as a model of the outcome of your design process, it is much easier to offer a complete learning system.

Clarify the Relationship to Classroom Efforts

Mapping also helps make the relationship between classroom training and other formats clear to all parties. It is vitally important that managers and learners understand that a classroom course alone is not all that is required to master an application or a system.

Even if you do not use a curriculum map, try to clarify what is provided by the classroom course and by the other elements. It must be clear that you are not developing redundant programs for their own sake.

Involve the Boss

You need the managers of the learners to act on what they now understand about the process of training. There are four things a manager can do to help improve the payoff from the investment in training:

- Before the training experience starts, the manager should meet with the learner to explain what the learner will be able to do after the training. That is, the manager must tell the learner that training is important.

- If at all possible, before the training experience, the manager should provide the learner with the system or software. The objective is for the learner to "fool around" with the system and identify questions to investigate during the training.

■ After the training experience, the manager must provide the learner with dedicated time to practice using what was learned. This may take as little as a half-hour a day for a week. This practice time results in additional learner effectiveness in using the system or the software.

■ The manager should interview the learner after the training. The purpose is to verify that the objectives negotiated in the first step have been achieved.

Evaluate the Program

11

Every learning experience and every training program should be evaluated. The principle is to find out what works and what doesn't. Do more of the former and less of the latter. The evaluation should include the following efforts:

■ Follow-up interviews with learners about six weeks after training

■ Review of help desk logs to see what changes took place

■ Discussions with the managers of learners, to assist in rediagnosing the learning needs

Support for Designers, Administrators, and Managers

None of the work it takes to create a successful computer training program for adults outside the classroom is necessarily easy.

> **Tip**
>
> You may be able to attend courses at universities or local colleges on the subject of creating and maintaining adult learning programs. Some commercial seminar providers also offer courses on the subject. One especially excellent source of public seminars covering a wide range of adult computer education skills is SkillTech Professional Seminars (call 1-800-34-TRAIN for a list of seminars and their public schedules).

A lot of help and support are available from other sources as well. Some of the best is provided by the professional organizations for trainers, such as the International Society for Performance Improvement (ISPI) and the American Society for Training and Development (ASTD). These groups have many local chapters as well as robust national organizations and excellent professional journals.

Another excellent source of training for those who lead the training effort is the Computer Training and Support Conference, sponsored each fall by SOFTBANK Institute. It has a companion in the spring, called the

Interactive Learning Conference. Either or both of these conferences can put you in touch with thousands of professionals in the computer training industry.

Finally, you can have the equivalent of a year-round conference by using the resources available to you online. The following sections list a few that I have found especially valuable.

Support on CompuServe

The Computer Training and Support forum (GO DPTRAIN) has been around since 1986. Its message areas (a total of 24 of them) are set up to organize discussions about topics ranging from general training techniques to conferences and professional associations, and from 32-bit operating systems to mainframe training concerns. This is probably the oldest ongoing online service for the computer training profession. It is certainly the largest such service, with thousands of members, hundreds of whom are active at any one time. DPTRAIN also offers a large number of libraries with downloadable files and utilities of interest to trainers and support staff.

A Personal Note about CompuServe

CompuServe is close to my heart. I've been the System Operator (Sysop) of the Computer Training and Support forum on CompuServe since 1987, shortly after Elliott Masie founded the forum in 1986. Both new and experienced trainers post literally hundreds of messages each week on DPTRAIN (as the forum is known). You'll find it easy to get answers to even the thorniest questions related to training. At the very least, you can be sure to find a sympathetic ear when you have a training tale to bemoan. And you'll also find a lot of support for your training successes, too. Frequent threads address topics ranging from evaluations of different LCD projection devices to trainer salaries to going into business for yourself. You'll find discussions of the newest training methods, such as TDL (technology delivered learning) as well as reiterations of traditional approaches that still work. If you're new to training, this is the place to come for advice, direction, and support. If you're an old hand at the training business, you'll want to swap war stories and look for fresh approaches to training adults in the use of computers. You'll also find several of the authors of *The Computer Trainer's Personal Training Guide* online from time to time in the Computer Training and Support forum on CompuServe. See you online!

Support on the Internet and World Wide Web

As you might expect, vast resources are available on the Internet and the World Wide Web. The problem is finding and keeping track of them. Although the landscape is always changing, here are several newsgroups and Web sites (as of early fall, 1995) that are worth checking out and that should be fairly permanent:

11

AEDNET (Adult Education Network)
Includes subscription to the quarterly *New Horizons in Adult Education Journal*, sent electronically. Send the command SUBSCRIBE AEDNET *FirstName LastName* to listserv@pulsar.acast.nova.edu.

Computer-Training
Moderated discussion of issues and techniques in computer training. Send the command SUBSCRIBE COMPUTER-TRAINING *FirstName LastName* to listserv@bilbo.isu.edu.

COMPINST-L
For computer instructors. Send the command SUBSCRIBE COMPINST-L to listserv@netcom.com.

MMEDIA-L
Multimedia discussion mailing list. Send the command SUBSCRIBE MMEDIA-L *FirstName LastName* to listserv@itesmvf1.rzs.itesm.mx.

MEDIA-L
Media in education. Send the command SUBSCRIBE MEDIA-L *FirstName LastName* to listserv@bingvmb.cc.binghamton.edu.

EDTECH
Technology in education. Send the command SUBSCRIBE EDTECH *FirstName LastName* to listserv@msu.edu.

NETTRAIN
Training in use of the Internet. Send the command SUBSCRIBE NETTRAIN *FirstName LastName* to listserv@ubvm.cc.buffalo.edu.

HELP-NET
For new Internet users. Send the command SUBSCRIBE HELP-NET *FirstName LastName* to listserv@vm.temple.edu.

NEWBIENEWZ
New users looking for training. Send the command SUBSCRIBE NEWBIENEWZ to majordomo@io.com.

Lifelong Learning
A Web site on adult education at the University of Tennessee: //http://web.ce.utk.edu/.

Educom
A training and development Web site: http://educom.edu/.

Authorbase
A database of CBT authoring systems, maintained by the U.S. Army and the National Institutes of Health: http://wwwetb.nlm.nih.gov/authorb/irx/index.html.

Introduction to Multimedia

An actual online seminar: `http://info.mcc.ac.uk/CGU/SIMA/seminar/toc.html`.

InfoVid Outlet

Offers videotape instruction materials on computer training topics: `http://branch.com:1080/infovid/c100.html`.

From Here...

This chapter has dealt with the additional formats and media available to you for creation of a complete adult training experience. By adopting these methods for your computer training curricula, you add value to every course.

- For more information about adult learners, see Chapter 3, "Adult Learning: What Do We Know for Sure?"

- Chapter 6, "Post-Class Evaluation," contains some additional information about course evaluation you may find valuable. Look in the section entitled "How Did You Do?"

- If you want to know about specific techniques you can incorporate into learning experiences outside the classroom, read Chapter 8, "Training Techniques."

- Additional information about training outside the classroom can be found in Chapter 12, "Distance Learning on the World Wide Web."

- Some provocative ideas about where some of the methods and media discussed in this chapter are leading can be found in Chapter 15, "The Future of Computer Training."

Chapter 12

Distance Learning on the World Wide Web

by Bernard J. Dodge

Dr. Bernard J. Dodge is involved in the Pacific Bell Education First initiative as an advisor to the three PacBell/SDSU Fellows who are developing state-of-the-art applications of telecommunications for schools, community colleges, and libraries. He has a doctorate in Instructional Design and Development from Syracuse University and is a Professor of Educational Technology at San Diego State University, where he has taught since 1980.

For years, those of us who use technology in our teaching have been promising that technology such as programmed instruction, video, and computers would revolutionize the way people learn. And for years—in all innocence—we've been kidding ourselves. More recently, however, things seem different. The arrival of the World Wide Web signals the beginning of some fundamental changes in how teaching, training, and self-directed learning will occur at all ages and stages of life.

Chapter 11, "Augmenting Classroom Training with Other Media," outlines some strategies for integrating Internet use into the classroom. This chapter offers much more detail on that topic. Specifically, you learn how to use the World Wide Web as a vehicle for disseminating course materials and for creating active learning experiences within a classroom-based course. You also learn how to build on those experiences and incrementally move towards delivering your courses to those beyond your classroom walls.

To pursue the ideas described in this chapter, your company or campus must be connected to the Internet. Throughout this chapter, I refer to

Bernie Dodge wishes to thank June Dodge for her nimble help in researching this chapter.

resources available on the World Wide Web. These resources appear in `monospaced type`. The full addresses of these resources are listed at the end of the chapter.

Distance Teaching: The Old Paradigm

Farhad Saba, an experienced researcher and implementer of distance education, refers to the traditional form of distance teaching as "talk, chalk, and a hairy arm." Even today, you can still tune in on your local instructional cable channel and see examples of this approach: the expert stands before a chalkboard writing brief phrases and elaborating on them. Students in the studio classroom dutifully take notes and occasionally ask questions. Those viewing at a distance might be able to phone in a question or comment if the class is broadcast live—but more often than not, their only role is to listen and retain what's said.

It doesn't sound exciting, does it? And yet, it doesn't sound extreme or outlandish, either, because it replicates the format of many classes we've all sat through or given. Lecturing works (at least for some situations) and lecturing to distant learners has pretty much the same effect as lecturing to those in the back of the room. It's an efficient way to get content across, as long as the content is well organized and the learners are sufficiently motivated to pay attention.

What happens, though, when the content is so rich and multifaceted that it resists being reduced to a well-packaged presentation? Have you ever tried to teach principles of good page layout to a room full of novice desktop publishers? Would a lecture about software piracy and intellectual property rights change anybody's attitudes or behavior? Can you really teach someone to troubleshoot their Excel macros by talking them though a sequence of bulleted lists?

These are examples of situations that call for higher-level thinking than the usual lecture. What's lacking in traditional distance teaching (and in traditional same-room teaching)? There are at least two things: active participation and meaningful, higher-level thinking. What makes the World Wide Web exciting as an educational environment is that it is tailor-made for both.

How Quickly Things Can Change

It goes without saying that technology is changing our personal and professional lives at an ever-quickening pace. I've experienced this first hand recently. Late in 1993, a colleague said to me at a conference, "Have you seen Mosaic? It's amazing." I didn't know what he was talking about, so I filed the word *Mosaic* in the back of my mind and resolved to look it up when I got a chance. My chance came two months later when I visited a colleague on another campus. He had Mosaic running on his computer. In a matter of minutes, he was showing me illustrated pages of information from all over the world. My jaw dropped. This truly *was* amazing. Finally, someone had made the Internet pretty to look at and easy to use. On that day, my professional life changed direction because I could see that this was going to radically affect the way I teach and the way many of us will learn.

A few months later, I had installed Mosaic on my computer and evangelized about it to anyone within earshot. I visited Web sites that described how to set up your own Web server and write in HTML. On my own birthday, September 5, 1994, I was ready to give birth to EdWeb, the Web site for the San Diego State University College of Education. With the help of my laboratory staff, I added page after page of content. Our first attempts were spartan or ugly (or both). Later on, we got better at it and I gave a few workshops on HTML development. The price of admission to the workshop was that attendees had to volunteer 10 hours of their time putting more of the College's resources on EdWeb. By bartering HTML skills for free labor, I widened the number of Web developers at our site to over 20 in a short time.

EdWeb is thriving today as we begin to put more and more of our courses on the Web. In less than two years, I've gone from "What's Mosaic?" to Webmaster. I look forward eagerly to the technologies of audio and video delivery coming soon.

12

Why Active Learning?

More and more, educators at all levels, from kindergarten to adult training, are drawing a distinction between two fundamentally different approaches to teaching (see fig. 12.1).

Fig. 12.1
The Knowledge Transfer model: Replicating a fully formed system of concepts in the mind of the learner.

In one, the goal is to transfer, as effectively and efficiently as possible, a concise and coherent block of information from the teacher or computer into the minds of the learners. Most existing computer-based training for adults has been designed with *knowledge transfer* in mind. Extraneous information is left out. The content is simplified. The emphasis is on individual learning—and learners have a limited number of paths through the lesson.

This approach works well for the training of basic skills in areas of knowledge that are well defined and stable. For most of us, however, the world just isn't that way. As adults, we face one ill-defined problem after another. The specific facts we have to know change so quickly that some knowledge becomes obsolete almost as soon as we master it. The knowledge-transfer approach doesn't prepare us well for a messy world in constant motion.

An alternative way to think about teaching and learning is called *constructivism*. A constructivist trainer doesn't strip away the natural complexity of a subject. Instead, multiple perspectives are brought to bear. The goal of a constructivist learning environment is not the accurate transfer of content from the instructor to the learner. Instead, the learners are given tasks and opportunities, information resources and support; the learners are encouraged to construct their own version of the content—subject to revision through feedback. Many paths through the lesson are allowed; collaboration with other learners is stressed over lonely individual learning. A constructivist use of technology presents information to the learner in multiple forms from multiple sources and invites the learner to make sense of it.

The learner can acquire the information needed from several sources with the computer and from offline sources including his or her own previous experience, from information gathered while collaborating with other learners, and from references and other sources of expertise found somewhere far away from the computer screen.

In general, a constructivist approach is *more learner focused* and less teacher focused. The emphasis is on making a set of tasks and resources available to learners and creating an environment in which the learners can actively create their own meaning in that context rather than passively absorbing knowledge structures created by the instructor. In the learner-focused approach, the instructor's role moves toward being a coach and orchestrator of resources and away from being the sole source of information. The emphasis is on case studies, problem solving, and the creation of meaning.

In the last two years, a new technology has grown enormously in importance and accessibility. This technology, the World Wide Web, lends itself beautifully to constructivist, active learning.

Introducing the World Wide Web

The World Wide Web is the fastest growing part of the Internet. Before we get into the educational uses of the World Wide Web, let's define some of the terms commonly used in discussing the Web.

Mosaic was the first of the graphical user interfaces for the World Wide Web. Later, another program, Netscape, added more features and faster speed (see fig. 12.2). Both Mosaic and Netscape are *browsers*—software tools installed on your computer that let you look at documents on the World Wide Web.

Fig. 12.2
A typical Web page as displayed by Netscape, a very popular Web browser.

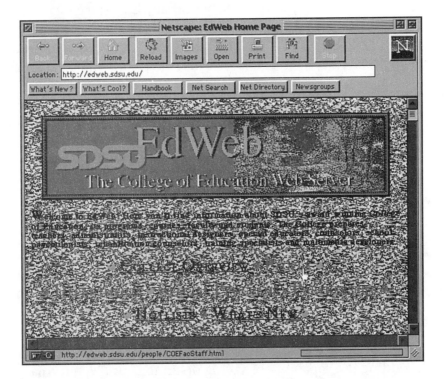

Figure 12.2 shows a typical document on the Web. This *Web page* includes graphics both as a source of information and as decoration. Notice that some of the text is bold and underlined. These underlined words are called *anchors* or *hot text*. When you click an anchor, the browser sends a request off to a distant computer asking it to send the information for a different page. If you click an anchor in figure 12.2, the screen would go blank for a moment and then very quickly change to a new page.

Each page you are looking at resides on a computer called a *server*. A Web server can be run on a personal computer or a UNIX workstation. The server need not be a fast, expensive machine. In fact, I set up my first server on a six-year-old Macintosh SE/30. When the traffic grew to the point of justifying the investment, we upgraded to a faster machine. Setting up a server is a fairly simple task; corporations, university departments, and even elementary schools are doing it every day.

Every document on the Web has an address called a *URL* (Universal Resource Locator). A typical URL looks like this:

```
http://edweb.sdsu.edu/people/COEFacStaff.html
```

Here's a breakdown of each part:

`http://`	This indicates that the URL is a Web page. Other possibilities include `ftp://` (for a file to be downloaded) and `mailto:` (for an e-mail address).
`edweb.sdsu.edu`	This is the name of the particular Web server on which the file resides. The `edu` suffix tells you that it's in the education domain, which means it's at a university.
`people`	This is a folder or directory on the server.
`COEFacStaff.html`	This is the particular Web page to be displayed.

What makes the World Wide Web especially exciting is that it also allows you to create anchors that download files for you or send e-mail to an individual. The Web makes it easy to gain access to data, software, and people. It's a user-friendly front end to almost everything on the Internet.

Creating and Publishing Web Documents

Within a year or so, the mechanics of creating documents on the Web will become transparent. Most publishers of word processing software are adding the capability of saving documents in Web format to their ever-growing list of features. So far, however, using a word processor to create Web pages directly may not give you the end result you had in mind. An active Web writer will want to know how to tweak the appearance of the documents; for the moment, that requires some familiarity with HTML.

The Basics of HTML

HTML (HyperText Markup Language) is easy to learn. To prepare a page for the Web, you just embed special characters, or *tags*, in the document to tell the browser how to display a given word. To show the phrase *San Diego* in **boldfaced** text, for example, the HTML looks like this:

```
The phrase <b>San Diego</b> is in bold.
```

For a computer trainer, learning the basics of HTML should take no longer than a weekend. Excellent resources for learning HTML can be found on the Web, indexed in *A Primer for Creating Web Resources*. The *Web 66 Internet Server Cookbook* contains recipes for putting pictures and sounds in your pages, serving downloadable files, and maintaining a server from a distance. If paper is still your preferred medium, a very well-written book is *Teach Yourself Web Publishing with HTML in a Week* by Laura Lemay (published by Sams Publishing).

An alternative method for displaying content on the Web is the *Adobe Acrobat* format. Acrobat lets you create complex page layouts, but users of your materials must have the proper helper application installed on their machines. In a corporate environment with software standards in place, this shouldn't be a problem.

Once you create your pages, simply upload them to the server you are using. Most medium-sized to large-sized corporations have already established a Web presence—and so have many smaller companies. Whether you purchase space on the machines of an Internet provider or set up your own Web server, you need not be physically near the server itself. Most maintenance can be done from a distance.

12

Teaching and Learning with the Web

The Web is a particularly appropriate vehicle for computer training for several reasons:

- Computer trainers (unlike teachers of cosmetology, for example) are up to the challenge of Web document preparation and running a Web server.

- Those being trained in computer skills are already seated at a computer, so the Web is accessible to them at any point while they're learning.

- Computer skills are particularly susceptible to the "use it or lose it" phenomenon. Making course materials available at a user's workstation on the job allows for just-in-time training.

- Because new versions of software appear regularly, it's useful to disseminate courses in a form that can be updated routinely.

- Because the one thing that everyone on the Web has in common is a certain level of familiarity with computing, there is a wealth of material available in Webspace on the topic of computer use.

Transitioning to Distance Education

Moving your classes from the classroom to being available at a distance on the Web isn't an overnight affair. Rarely will you be given the resources to drop what you're doing and create a distance-education endeavor entirely from scratch. Fortunately, you can make the transition in several gradual steps. Think of it as a four-phase process, with each phase building on the one that precedes it:

Phase 1:   Distribution
Phase 2:   Activity Development
Phase 3:   Automation and Interactivity
Phase 4:   True Distant Delivery

Phase 1: Using the Web To Distribute Materials to a Non-Distant Class

Most distantly delivered classes start out as face-to-face sessions delivered in a classroom. To move towards distance delivery, begin by making the Web a storage and dissemination medium for a traditional class. Assignments, syllabi, reading lists, worksheets—all these elements can be placed on the Web and viewed at the trainee's computer. The first task is to convert your existing materials to a format readable by Web browsers. Word processed materials must be translated to HTML or Acrobat format. Overhead slides and other graphics must be converted to GIF or JPEG format or to Acrobat's PDF format.

There are several advantages of moving paper to the Web:

■ By trial and error, you'll settle on whatever process is most efficient for making the conversion in your situation. Once that's done, you can train someone to do it for you.

■ You'll use less paper—and perhaps feel free to make more "handouts" (the electronic kind) than you would otherwise.

■ Once put in electronic form, your materials can be easily updated as your course changes.

■ You can augment your course materials by pointing to resources elsewhere on the Web.

■ You can publish a class list with e-mail addresses to make it easier for members of the class to communicate with each other. Clicking a name calls up a window into which students can type their messages.

■ Graduates of your course can refer back to the latest versions of your materials as they need them on the job.

■ Your course may attract new students as other people surfing the Web stumble across your information.

■ If your course materials are accessible to those outside your class or clientele, you'll be discovered by others elsewhere teaching similar material. This opens the door to professional idea-sharing that wouldn't otherwise happen.

■ The Web is platform independent. Mac users, Windows users, and UNIX users can all view the material from their favorite machines.

Figure 12.3 shows a typical course Web page listing a variety of course materials.

Fig. 12.3
This Web page shows the kinds of information you can make available to students.

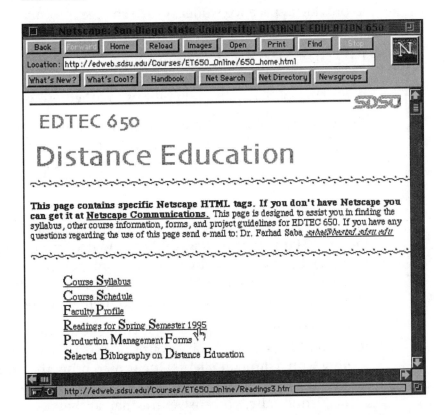

Phase 2: Adding Web-Based Activities to a Classroom-Based Course

Once the use of the Web as a way to distribute course materials is second nature to you, the next phase is to take advantage of all the material that's out there beyond the walls of your usual turf. The more you incorporate such activities into your course, the more your course becomes transformed into a learner-centered environment and the less often you'll find yourself holding forth on center stage.

Here's a partial list of the resources you can tap into:

- **External experts**. Brilliant though you are, you probably don't know all there is to know about the domain of your course. If you can get friends and colleagues, both inside and outside your enterprise to volunteer to answer questions, you've broadened the pool of experience available to your students.

- **Newsgroups**. What if you have a question and don't know who to pose it to? Newsgroups provide an invisible college of people helping people. They are a great source of up-to-the-minute news about software releases, bugs, and workarounds. If you have your own news server, you can also set up internal newsgroups specific to your course to provide a space for students to exchange information on an ongoing basis.

- **FAQ files**. Most newsgroups maintain a list of frequently asked questions (FAQs) that have come up within that group. These can be a rich source of materials and pointers to other resources on the Web.

- **Technical notes**. Most major software publishers (such as Microsoft, Novell, Claris, and Adobe) have placed their technical notes on the Web. You can make links to these as reference material and create activities that require your students to access them.

- **Software archives**. Patches, applications, utilities, documentation…there are many sources of useful wares ready to be downloaded. FTPing (that is, *downloading*) and decompressing this software is handled transparently by your Web browser. If you place an anchor on a page that refers to a file, all your users have to do is click the anchor to have the software delivered to their desktops.

- **Simulated people**. Suppose that you're teaching a course on desktop publishing and you want your students to have the experience of dealing with a difficult client. One way to bring that kind of encounter into the classroom is to set up an e-mail address with a fabricated name. Periodically, you answer the mail at that account while acting like someone else.

How do you create activities that make use of resources like these? The first step is to become a knowledgeable Websurfer yourself. Keep an active list of what's out there and think constantly about how you can make use of it. Figure 12.4 shows a simulated Web page that incorporates several kinds of resources (note that this figure does not show a real URL).

Fig. 12.4
A simulated Web page that provides students with exercises that access other Internet resources.

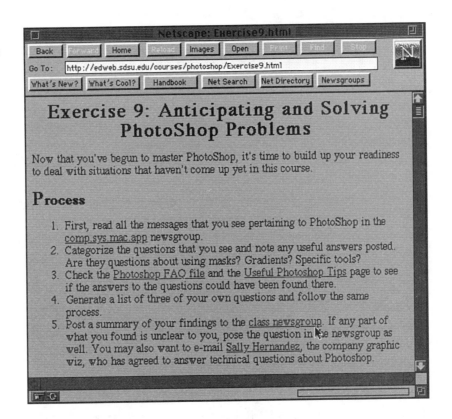

The Importance of Structure

Having access to the World Wide Web is like suddenly having the largest library in the world move in next door to you. For many people who are new to the Web, the temptation to browse and pursue one link after another is so strong that they spend countless hours glued to the screen. In an educational or training situation, however, we don't have the luxury of spending all our time that way. As much as we value curiosity and exploration, it's necessary for us to find ways to get the greatest learning benefit from the Web in the shortest possible time. At San Diego State University we've been thinking about how to do that; toward that goal, one of the lesson formats we've developed is called a *WebQuest*.

WebQuest

A WebQuest is an activity of guided inquiry in which learners are given a task that requires Internet access to complete. WebQuests can be designed as short-term or long-term activities. At the end of a short-term WebQuest, a learner will have grappled with a significant amount of new information and made sense of it. A short-term WebQuest is designed to be completed in one to three class periods.

WebQuests are deliberately designed to make the best use of a learner's time. There is questionable educational benefit in having learners surf the Net without a clear task in mind—and most educational and training institutions must severely ration student connect time. To achieve efficiency and clarity of purpose, WebQuests should contain at least the following parts:

1. An **introduction** that sets the stage and provides some background information.

2. A **task** that is doable and interesting. The task can include a series of questions that must be answered, a summary to be created, a problem to be solved, a position to be formulated and defended, a creative work, or anything that requires the learners to process and transform the information they've gathered.

3. A set of information **resources** needed to complete the task. Many (although not necessarily all) of the resources are embedded in the WebQuest document itself as anchors pointing to information on the World Wide Web. Information sources can include Web documents, experts available through e-mail or real-time conferencing, searchable databases on the Net, and books and other documents physically available in the learner's setting.

4. A description of the **process** to follow to complete the WebQuest. How should the groups organize themselves? In what order should they attack the materials? What do they do if they have questions?

5. Some **learning advice** on how to organize the information acquired. This advice can take the form of guiding questions or directions to complete organizational frameworks such as timelines, concept maps, or cause-and-effect diagrams.

6. A **conclusion** that summarizes what they will have accomplished or learned by completing this WebQuest.

You can read more about the underlying rationale of WebQuests by browsing the About WebQuests document (the address is given at the end of the chapter).

My First WebQuest

One example of a short-term WebQuest is an exercise I gave to a class of student teachers a few months ago. My goal was to give them an understanding of how Archaeotype, a computer simulation of an archaeological dig, was conceived and implemented at two very different school sites. Because of hardware constraints, I couldn't actually demonstrate Archaeotype for them. That wasn't a problem, however, because the important thing for them to focus on was how the Archaeotype software was used, what kinds of benefits and problems were encountered, and what kinds of second-order effects it had on the teachers and the students who used it. I wanted my student teachers to get a systems view of Archaeotype—a higher-level vantage point that would be impossible for me to convey to them through a lecture.

The exercise took about two hours and involved students working in groups to answer a series of questions. In the front of the room were paper copies of part of the Archaeotype documentation. We set up a video conferencing unit in an adjacent room through which the students could interview a California teacher who had implemented Archaeotype in his classroom. In the back of the same room was a speakerphone with which another group could interview one of the designers of Archaeotype who was at home in New York City.

The WebQuest document itself was placed on the San Diego State University Web server so that the students could look at it from any computer in the building. As part of that document, there were anchors that led them to a number of project reports and theoretical papers on the Web.

Each student team met to divide among themselves the labor of accessing each of these resources; then they split up. After an hour and a half, they reformed their groups. The final step of their task was to communicate to each other the insights they'd gathered and to teach each other so well that I could walk up to anyone in the group and elicit a complete explanation of what they learned.

As an educational experience, this first WebQuest worked extremely well. Everyone in the class was actively engaged for those two hours, and each came away with a depth of understanding that I could not have given them by lecturing. Rather than standing on center stage as the only source of information, my role instead was to walk from group to group and serve as a learning coach. It's actually a more enjoyable role!

Phase 3: Adding Interactivity and Automation

Moving through Phases 1 and 2 requires only a bit of technical skill. There is a larger leap in sophistication needed to accomplish Phase 3—which is why most online courses as of this writing have stopped at Phase 2. Phase 3 involves taking better advantage of the power of your Web server and using it to store, process, and display information provided by your learners.

Think about all the things you do as an instructor that are repetitious or clerical. If you move those things to the Web server's plate, you'll have more time to create a better learning environment in other ways. Here are several possible tasks that are appropriately delegated to the computer:

■ **Interactive FAQs**. In any course, 20 percent of all possible questions come up 80 percent of the time. Instead of taking up class time dealing with repetitive questions, place them in a database of pages organized by a branching tree of questions and subquestions.

- **Testing**. As you move towards distant delivery of your course, you lose the ability to sense which students know what just by watching their body language. Frequent small-scale tests can provide the information you need and let you focus your attention on those who need extra help.

- **Tutorials**. The Web lends itself well to one-frame-at-a-time tutorials that have been the staple format of computer-based training since the 1960s. For well-defined, stable content, you can move parts of what would have been a lecture into this more interactive format.

- **Meeting scheduling**. Outside of class time, you'll want to make yourself available by phone, video conference, or in person. The Web can provide a way for individuals in the class to sign up for a particular time slot so that your time and theirs is well spent.

- **Course evaluation**. The best instructors don't wait until the end of a course to find out how it was perceived by the learners. Putting an anonymous evaluation form up on the Web and encouraging its frequent use allows you to make midcourse corrections quickly.

- **Feedback database**. In providing feedback to learners on their performance of complex skills such as programming, page layout, or spreadsheet design, you find yourself making the same kinds of comments repeatedly. A Web-based feedback *template* allows you to pick and choose from among common comments and edit them into a personalized reply efficiently.

It is a simple matter to place a form on the Web that collects information from your learners. To actually send that information to the server and process it, however, goes beyond simple HTML and into the realm of CGI (the Common Gateway Interface). Most Web developers stop at this point because creating CGI programs requires the ability to program in C, Perl, or AppleScript. In the future, ready-made CGIs will be available to accomplish most tasks, but currently, the learning curve here stops most people.

Tip

If you don't have the programming resources in-house to add Phase-3 automation to your course, you should at least keep your eyes open for packages of CGIs to appear on the market. The `comp.infosystems.www.authoring.cgi` newsgroup is an excellent resource to watch.

Phase 4: Making a Course Available to Distant Learners

Once you complete Phase 1 and put all necessary course materials on the Web, and complete Phase 2 by building in constructivist activities that make use of resources available in cyberspace, you can begin to allow distant learners to participate in your course.

Note

If you ask anyone who has conducted a course over the Internet what it's like, the first thing they'll tell you is how much time they spend answering e-mail. It's for that reason that I strongly recommend implementing Phase 3 before you move your class to distance education. Creating tools that allow for efficient testing, question-answering, and feedback allows you to scale up your course to many additional learners at a distance without breaking your back.

12

The transition to Phase 4 can be as quick or gradual as you like. I recommend first allowing just a few distant participants to join a classroom-based course. Pay attention to the gaps in what they learn by not being physically present and fill that gap by adding more materials to the Web or more activities that bring them into interaction with the nondistant students in the course.

Once the bugs are ironed out, you can make your course "partly virtual" on a routine basis. Your class list will include people you'll never physically meet.

The final stage in Phase 4 is optional: making a class completely virtual. If your course is so completely articulated and automated that a motivated learner can do it all from a distance, you're ready to detach it from the traditional face-to-face class that served as its starting point. At this stage, if you are working within an institution that involves itself in course credit, registration, and starting and ending times, you'll have to wage a battle to add flexibility to that infrastructure. If you can accomplish this, you will have created a course that people can take when they need it and where they need it. Your course will have transcended both time and space!

The Future of Net-Based Training

Face-to-face classes have a history going back to Cain and Abel being home-schooled in the suburbs of Eden. They have an immediacy and richness that isn't easy to replicate online. However, the Net world is moving quickly towards greater interactivity and sensory engagement. There are several developments worth watching:

- **RealAudio**. Some Web sites allow you to click a picture and hear a greeting or introduction in the form of a sound file. You have to wait for the file to download before hearing anything, however, which tries the patience of all but the most fervent Web surfers. RealAudio is different. It begins to stream audio to your workstation almost immediately. It's like radio on demand. For distance education, the usefulness of RealAudio is obvious. All the spoken communication that makes up the bulk of a traditional class can be digitized and made available as needed. As long as this doesn't lead back to the "talk, chalk, and a hairy arm" tradition, RealAudio can become a standard feature of distance education on the Web.

- **VRML**. Virtual Reality Markup Language (pronounced *ver'-mul*) is an embryonic set of tools and conventions for portraying three-dimensional space on the Web. Instead of seeing a static picture, you can hold your mouse down over a graphic and see it from multiple perspectives, zooming in for detail and veering in any direction. For distance education, VRML allows for a more intuitive depiction of content: imagine seeing bubbles labeled with all the major concepts in your course. Lines linking the bubbles represent the relationships among them. Zoom in on a bubble and you arrive at a Web page describing it in more detail. You might also use VRML to create a simulated learning environment with a reference room, laboratory, and help desk.

- **HotJava**. Most of what's available on the Web is inert. You can admire it but not interact with it. HotJava is a language for writing small programs (called *applets*) that are downloaded as part of a Web page. HotJava allows the Web to take on most of the characteristics of the interactive multimedia you find on a CD-ROM.

- **MOOs**. *MOO* stands for MUD (Multi-User Dimension) Object-Oriented, which doesn't at first convey much about its meaning. A MOO is a shared virtual space that people can help create from their own computers. You can set up a conference room the way you like it and invite others to join you there. Currently, most MOOs are text based. When they begin to become more graphical (soon), they will become the most popular places to be in cyberspace.

These developments, and others, will make distance education more and more practicable on the Web as time goes on.

Resources

This chapter can provide only a springboard for your own future learning on this topic. The resources listed here can help you to continue your learning in more depth. One disadvantage of the fact that this list is on paper is that it will become outdated almost immediately. To alleviate that problem, I'll keep an up-to-date version on the Web at the following URL:

`http://edweb.sdsu.edu/people/bdodge/CTPTG-Bib.html`

Paper-Based Documents

Dodge, B. J. (1995). WebQuests: A technique for Internet-based learning. *The Distance Educator*, 1(2), 10-13.

Jonassen, D. H., Wilson, B. G., Wang, S., & Grabinger, R.S. (1993). Constructivist uses of expert systems to support learning. *Journal of Computer-Based Instruction*, 20(3), 86-94.

Lemay, L. (1995). *Teach Yourself Web Publishing with HTML in a Week.* Sams Publishing.

Montgomery, J., Campbell, R., & Moffett, C. (1994, Oct-Nov). Conducting and supporting a goal-based scenario learning environment. *Educational Technology*, 34(9), 15-20.

Schank, R. (Graham, W.) (1994, Oct-Nov). Goal-based scenarios and business training: A conversation with Roger C. Schank. *Educational Technology*, 34(9), 27-29.

Documents on the World Wide Web

About WebQuests: A document outlining the definiticn of this approach to Web-based instruction.
`http://edweb.sdsu.edu/courses/edtec596/About_webquests.html`

Adobe Acrobat: The Acrobat format is becoming more widely adopted as a way to display complex page layouts. You can download free reader software from this site:
`http://www.adobe.com/acrobat.html`

ChibaMOO Papers: This collection of papers on Multi-User Dimensional Object-Oriented environments provides some glimpses of how to create virtual spaces for collaborative learning.
`http://sensemedia.net/papers`

CS330, Concepts of Programming Languages: This course is taught at Brigham Young University by Dr. Phillip J. Windley. It is fairly complete, containing the complete text of the lectures, assignments, a newsgroup, and pointers to other resources.

http://lal.cs.byu.edu/cs330/homepage.html

EdWeb: The Web site for the San Diego State University College of Education.

http://edweb.sdsu.edu

Engines for Education: Roger Schank's vision of a new model of education and training.

http://www.ils.nwu.edu:80/~e_for_e/

HotJava Home Page: HotJava is the next leap forward for the Web. It will add a new degree of interactivity by allowing small programs, or *applets*, to be included in a page.

http://java.sun.com/

How To Grow a Web Server: A presentation about both the mechanics and the social technology of creating a community of Web publishers.

http://edweb.sdsu.edu/people/bdodge/growweb.html

Introduction to Common Lisp Programming for Artificial Intelligence: This course is taught at the British Open University and can be taken entirely at a distance. Tutorial groups function through e-mail Listserv groups and selected live MUD/MOO/Chat sessions, partitioned into specific topics.

http://kmi.open.ac.uk/courses/dmzx863.html

LRNG731: Advanced Object Technology: This is another course like the preceding Lisp programming course, taught at the George Mason Program on Social and Organizational Learning in Fairfax, Virginia.

http://gopher.gmu.edu/bcox/LRNG731/00LRNG731.html

Primer for Creating Web Resources: This is an excellent index of tutorials and guides for HTML and CGI development.

http://www-slis.lib.indiana.edu/Internet/programmer-page.html

New Tools for Teaching, by James J. O'Donnell at the University of Pennsylvania: Professor O'Donnell has gone all the way to Phase 4 and has conducted several courses on the classics to learners spread over the globe. An inspiring read.

http://ccat.sas.upenn.edu/teachdemo

RealAudio: The first practical demonstration of audio streaming, which allows users to click and hear audio almost immediately as it downloads.

http://www.realaudio.com/

VRML (Virtual Reality Markup Language): An extension of the Web that allows users to manipulate three-dimensional graphics on Web pages.
`http://www.vrml.org/`

Web 66 Internet Server Cookbook: A readable guide to specific techniques for Web development.
`http://web66.coled.umn.edu/Cookbook/contents.html`

WebQuest Template: A structure for creating WebQuests.
`http://edweb.sdsu.edu/courses/edtec596/webquest_template1.html`

WebQuest1: An example WebQuest through which student teachers learned about the Archaeotype program.
`http://edweb.sdsu.edu/courses/edtec596/webquest1.html`

WEST: Web Educational Support Tools: This new company provides server-based tools that automate the creation of tutorials and tests, monitor student progress, and facilitate interaction with instructors.
`http://west.ucd.ie/`

World Wide Web Workbook: A useful tutorial that introduces new users to the conventions of the Web.
`http://sln.fi.edu/primer/primer.html`

12

From Here...

It's not easy to see where the rapid development of the Internet is going to take us. One thing *is* certain: each week, new sources of information and tools that have the potential to enhance learning for all of us crop up. The first challenge facing trainers is to develop a usable connection to this wealth of resources and to fight the budgetary, political, and technological battles required to open cyberspace up to our learners.

The second challenge is more pleasant. It's a challenge to our imaginations. If you could open up your classroom to the world, and the world to your classroom, what would you do differently? Over the next few years, most educators will have to answer that question. Personally, I'm eager to see what we come up with.

For now, you can start your adventures by referring to the following chapters in this book:

■ Chapter 1, "The Challenges of Training in the 90s," which discusses some of the new methods of delivering training.

■ Chapter 11, "Augmenting Classroom Training with Other Media," for additional insights into using non-traditional methods for training.

■ Chapter 13, "The Internet and Trainer Support," which provides more information about using the Internet and its famous child, the World Wide Web, for distance training.

■ Chapter 15, "The Future of Computer Training," which provides a glimpse of what the future of "over the Net" training may look like.

Part IV

Trainer Assistance

Chapter 13

The Internet and Trainer Support

by Patty Crowell*

*For the past six years, **Patty Crowell** has been responsible for computer training for the staff and faculty at the University of Kansas School of Medicine. She provides technology updates and product demonstrations and often speaks to computer user groups about topics ranging from the Internet to Windows applications.*

Every day, references to the Internet reach the general public through television, newspapers, magazines, and radio talk shows. Where bookstores used to display multiple titles on DOS and PCs, they now display multiple titles on the Internet. The Internet is the part of computer technology that is reaching the widest range of the public—in a very short period of time. As a trainer, you may have already experienced the impact of, interest in, and confusion over the Internet. If you're not currently an expert on the Internet and training users on the topic of the Internet, you may be one of those who is interested and confused by it.

This chapter addresses Internet training for those new to the Internet and to Internet training. It is also for those who are planning or now conducting training on the Internet. For trainers, the Internet is a resource for preparing for a class and a resource to use during class; for learners, the Internet is a resource after taking a class. This chapter discusses how you can effectively use the Internet to plan for Internet training sessions, use the Internet during class, and motivate learners to use the Internet after class.

* Que Education and Training would like to thank Laureen Davis and L. Daniel York for some of the ideas in this chapter, which came from their presentation, "World Wide Web: Essentials for Computer Training and Support," at the 1995 Computer Training & Support Conference.

This chapter assumes that you and your learners have the tools to fully exploit the capabilities of the Internet—obviously, Internet access and e-mail. Also, with the widespread use of graphical Web browers (such as Mosaic and Netscape), this chapter assumes that you will want to structure your Internet training around the use of a Web browser.

The Levels of Internet Training

Training users on the Internet involves three levels of instruction. First, because the technology of the Internet is so new to most people, you will need to teach learners the basic concepts of the Internet. You don't have to dwell on the hardware technology behind the Internet, but you should present an overview of the concepts. Second, you will need to introduce users to the purposes of the Internet—the wide range of information resources available on the Internet and its powerful capability to communicate around the world. This second level of instruction also includes introducing users to the software tools necessary for accessing information and communicating on the Internet. The third level of instruction focuses on getting users to apply the Internet to their own needs: their own organizations and their own jobs. This chapter recommends that your Internet training includes having users search the Internet for information related to their interests and jobs and having users communicate to groups with similar interests and knowledge. The more you have learners use the Internet in your class, the more quickly they can begin teaching themselves and the more quickly they can discover how the Internet fits their needs on the job and in their organizations.

No matter what level of Internet training you are conducting, Internet trainers agree that giving learners hands-on interaction with the Internet is the most effective way to teach. Incorporating "live," hands-on use of the Internet in your class, however, is risky. At any moment, an Internet connection can go down or delays in accessing sites can bring your class to a halt. If you decide to incorporate live, hands-on interaction with the Internet into your class, be prepared to train your class without depending on the live connection (see "Planning an Internet Class," later in this chapter).

Depending on the goals of your Internet training, you may want to combine these three levels of instruction into one class. One class, however, will not give you much time to enable learners to search for information or communicate with others on topics related to their interests and jobs. If you are training for an organization, you may have to develop a long-term Internet training program that stretches the three levels of instruction over multiple classes. To accomplish this, organizations must develop long-term training plans that focus on what they want to accomplish. Classes must shift from *Beginning Internet, Intermediate Internet*, and *Advanced Internet* to topic-specific training such as *Managing Databases, Using Graphics To Enhance Documents*, and other productivity-related courses. Users need a base level of knowledge and the ability to know how to use certain Internet tools.

The First Level of Internet Training

In the 1980s, a computer trainer spent his or her time teaching users the basics of the computer and the basics of DOS. Because of the newness of the technology, computer training for beginners included showing users a basic "map" of the technology and showing them how to understand the concepts of PC technology. Today, teaching users about the Internet presents a similar situation. The newness of the technology of the Internet to many people requires that training begin with a basic map of Internet concepts. This section presents the fundamental concepts to introduce to your Internet class. Because the information in this section assumes that training people on the Internet includes teaching them about the World Wide Web, we begin with a simple explanation of the World Wide Web. Second, we cover the basic concepts you must present to learners to help them learn how to navigate through the World Wide Web. Third, we suggest how to introduce learners to the many ways they can find information on the Web. Finally, we introduce learners to the concept of downloading files from the Web.

13

What is the World Wide Web?

Your learners have probably heard the terms *the World Wide Web, the Web*, and *WWW* mentioned often with reference to the Internet. Some may think these terms are synonymous with the Internet. To help them understand the concepts of the Word Wide Web and the Internet, use the following simple explanation.

Although the Internet is a worldwide system of networks that are all connected, the World Wide Web is a system that links the information available on the Internet and lets users jump from one document to another. To take advantage of this system, users must have *Web browser software*. This software makes it possible to click a word in one document and jump to related information in another document (see fig. 13.1). The document you jump to may exist in the same location where you started using the Internet or it may exist at another location anywhere in the Internet system—another city, another state, or another country. Web software and the World Wide Web system let you jump not only from one piece of text or numerical data to another, but also from one graphic to another, from text to a graphic and vice versa (see figs. 13.2 and 13.3), and also from a graphic or text to a video or sound clip. Of course, your ability to view graphics and video clips and listen to audio depends on your hardware setup.

Fig. 13.1
Web browsers let users click a highlighted word to access information located at another Internet location.

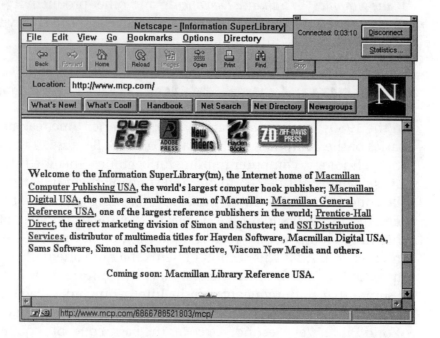

Fig. 13.2
Click any one of these lines of highlighted text to access a graphic like the one in figure 13.3.

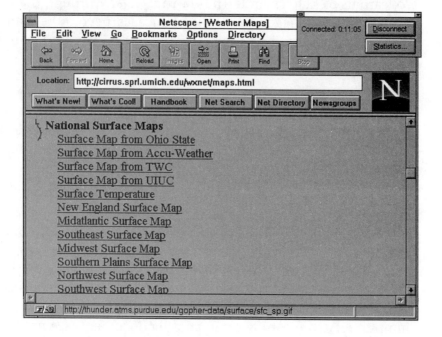

Fig. 13.3
The graphic that appears when you click one of the lines of highlighted text in figure 13.2.

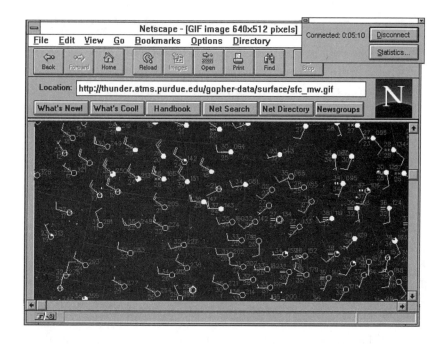

The World Wide Web (also called WWW or W3) is a hypertext-based distributed information system created by researchers at CERN in Switzerland. Users can create, edit, or browse hypertext documents. Clients and servers are freely available, and information on just about any subject imaginable is available online. Traffic on the Web grew over 1,700 percent in 1994 and the trend has continued. In March 1995, the World Wide Web became the greatest source of traffic on the Internet!

13

The Internet Is a Library; The Web Is the Signposts

To clarify the concepts of the Internet and the World Wide Web, use an analogy such as the following. Think of the Internet as a library: the physical building, rooms, shelves, aisles, hallways, staircases, books, videotapes, records, and cassette tapes give you access to millions of pieces of information. Like networks connected to other networks in the Internet, the physical layout of the library enables you to get from one body of information to another. The World Wide Web, on the other hand, is the system of signposts that help you access connected information quickly. Just as the tools in a library that help you get to connected information quickly are complex, so is the World Wide Web. In a library, for example, you can use multiple methods to access connected information—you use the card catalog, ask librarians to direct you to information, use the labels on bookshelves and areas of the library to find topics, or use indexes to find books, periodicals, videotapes, cassette tapes, and so on. Just as the library has various tools for accessing information—computers, card catalogs, and workstations to view video tapes or hear cassettes—the Web browser software has tools that enable you to read text, view graphics, and access video and sound clips.

Navigating Through the World Wide Web

Once you clarify the concepts of the Internet and the World Wide Web, introduce the features that will help learners understand how to navigate the Internet. These features include the computer screen elements that indicate a hypertext link, icons, buttons, and menus that are part of Web browser screens. You should also introduce the naming convention (Universal Resource Locator, or URL) that identifies the location of the information users are accessing.

Teaching learners to navigate a Web browser is fairly simple. With Web software like Netscape, you need to concentrate only on a few key screen items (see fig. 13.4):

- The hypertext links

- Icons for moving from one document to another

- Buttons for searching the World Wide Web

- The naming convention for getting from one Web site to another

- The Web software menu

Fig. 13.4
With the Netscape Navigator Web browser, there are only a few items you have to explain.

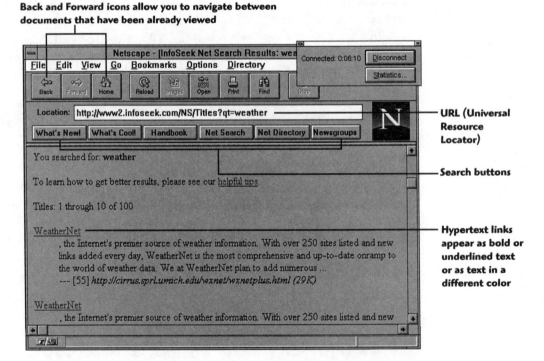

Hypertext links in the World Wide Web appear as bold, underlined text, or as text in a different color on a color monitor. One click allows you to move from the current document to information about the link you selected. With graphical WWW browsers like Netscape, links can be added to pictures on the screen as well as to plain text. With a graphical link, clicking a defined region of the picture activates a link to more information. Back and Forward icons allow for easy navigation between documents that have already been viewed. Net Search and Net Directory buttons provide access to search tools and subject indexes. The **G**o menu lets you select a site you have been to during the current session of Netscape.

A URL (Universal Resource Locator) describes the type of resource and where it can be found. URLs allow users to access most types of Internet resources, including hypertext documents (HTTP or HyperText Transfer Protocol), Gopher, FTP, and so on. In a general sense, the format of a URL is as follows:

```
<resource_type>://<pathname>
```

In more detail, a URL may consist of the following parts:

```
<resource_type>://<host_name>:<port>/<directory>/<filename>
```

This method is the most efficient way to access a site for which the URL is known.

Finding What You Need

In addition to showing learners how to use hypertext links to access information, your Internet training should introduce the methods available for searching the Internet: the "telephone books," the "card catalogs," and the "tables of contents" of the Internet. An alternative to navigating through endless hypertext documents in the hopes of finding useful information is to use one of the many powerful search tools (also known as *search engines*) available on the World Wide Web.

Many useful search tools are available. They can be accessed from the Netscape Internet Search page, or accessed directly using their URLs. The URLs for a number of search tools and subject directories are listed here:

- **CUI W3 Catalog**

   http://www.winc.com/W3Catalog.html

- **EINET Galaxy**

   http://galaxy.einet.net/www/www.html

- **Harvest**

   http://harvest.cs.colorado.edu/Home.html

- **Lycos**

   http://www.lycos.com

- **W3 Search Engines Meta-Index**

   http://www.lib.ncsu.edu/meta-index.html

- **Web Crawler**

  http://webcrawler.com

- **Yahoo**

  http://www.yahoo.com

Accessing Gopher with Netscape

Gopher servers contain information stored in a hierarchical format. There are folders that contain more information, documents that can be viewed on-screen, and search icons that allow the user to search either the current Gopher server (or, in the case of the Veronica search tool, to search all Gopher servers). Gopher servers can be accessed with one of the following methods:

- Click a link to a Gopher server in any World Wide Web document

- Use the Gopher's URL to access the Gopher directly

Downloading Files with Netscape

Downloading files using FTP (File Transfer Protocol) is simple through Netscape. Occasionally, a home page contains a link that automatically lets you download a file. In other cases, selecting a link to an FTP server displays a list of directories, which you can navigate to locate the desired file. You can also use FTP to download a file from within Netscape by constructing a URL with the provided information. For example, the URL to access the Netscape client software is as follows:

    ftp://ftp.netscape.com/netscape1.1/windows

The Second Level of Internet Instruction

Once you introduce learners to the tools of the Internet and the World Wide Web, you should structure your training session so that learners use the Web to communicate and search for information. You will particularly want to introduce learners to mailing lists so that they understand the practical benefits of the Internet as a communication tool for business.

Introducing Mailing Lists

Using the Internet for sending messages is one of the greatest benefits the Internet brings to organizations. The second level of Internet training should include introducing learners to communications by subscribing to mailing lists. You can introduce mailing lists and have learners begin to use the Internet by having them access a Web site where they can search for list groups by topic. One such Web site is at Indiana University:

```
http://scwww.ucs.indiana.edu/mlarchive/
```

This Web site enables users to query a database of list groups and receive information about the nature of the particular groups they have searched for. If you, as a trainer, searched for list groups related to training, some of the list groups returned from your search would include these:

- A discussion group focusing on computer based training:
  ```
  listprog@bgu.edu
  ```

- A discussion group focusing on Internet training for beginners:
  ```
  majordomo@world.std.com
  ```

- Training and Development Managers issues:
  ```
  listserv@uccvma.ucop.edu
  ```

If you have the students in your class access the Indiana University site, have them search for groups focusing on topics of interest to them. If, for example, a learner searched for discussion groups on marketing topics, he or she would find more than 25 entries.

Other ways to access mailing lists include downloading a file containing a list from this site:

```
ftp://sri.com/netinfo/interest-groups.txt
```

You can also request a list from `listserv@dartcms1`. Once you have downloaded a list, make the file available to your learners and have them search the list using the word processor available to them. Also provide your students with recommended books that contain mailing lists, such as *The Internet Yellow Pages*, from New Riders Publishing.

Subscribing to Lists

After learners have selected a topic of interest, have them record the addresses of the list groups, using whatever method is best suited to your training lab situation. The fastest method is to have them print their selected list from the Web browser (if they are searching for lists at a site like the Indiana University site) or to print the addresses of groups from a word processor (if they are searching a text file they have downloaded).

Next, have each learner subscribe to the discussion group. Stress the importance of saving the first note received from the discussion list (this note indicates that the user's subscription has been accepted). Show the learners samples of notes from several sites. (Rather than taking the time to visit several sites, you may want to download sample files before class, save them in a folder, and then retrieve some of the samples during class to show students the types of discussions that occur in mailing lists.

Internet Etiquette ("Netiquette")

If your learners access the Indiana University site (where they can search a database of lists groups), they will see some of the primary rules of Internet etiquette—*Netiquette*, as it is commonly referred to on the Internet. The Indiana University site, for example, tells users to delete old mail frequently, turn off mailing lists when they are away for a long period of time, and know the difference between addresses.

You may choose to prepare a short overview of Internet etiquette and refer learners to sources providing more detail. You may want learners to access sources on the Internet where Netiquette is covered. One of the training resources on the Internet can take you to a site that focuses on Netiquette. The `itcs.com/topten/Internet` training resources page links directly to this site:

```
http://www.fau.eud/rinaldi/net/index.html
```

This page provides information on such topics as *Electronic Mail and Files—User Responsibility* and guidelines for participating in discussion groups. The information on these topics is an excellent resource; you can cover this information in class or have learners access the information and print the guidelines for their own future reference.

The Third Level of Internet Training

As the number of Internet users has increased dramatically, so has the need for the third level of Internet training. This level of training addresses those users who want to learn how to efficiently and effectively apply the use of the Internet to their work and organizations. The third level of training assumes that users are experienced with the tools and capabilities of the Internet (the topics of the first and second levels of training discussed in the first part of this chapter).

Once learners understand the tools available to take advantage of the Internet and the World Wide Web and know how to search for information and communicate on the Internet, you can structure your training class around a specific topic or topics related to the learners' jobs or personal interest. If for example, you plan to train a group of managers to implement Total Quality Management (TQM) techniques in their company, you can search the Web before class to find the types of information and interest groups focusing on the topic of TQM. If you use the Net Search tool available with the Netscape browser, for example, you get 100 entries under the topic TQM. Although some of the sites listed are on the Internet to advertise their consulting services, these sites often provide valuable information in addition to promoting their businesses. One such site that provides useful references to TQM is the TQM Library, available through David Butler Associates (see fig. 13.5):

```
http://www.zoom.com/dba/library/index.html
```

This site provides a directory of topics that link to sites at which TQM articles and case studies are available.

Fig. 13.5
The TQM
Library site.

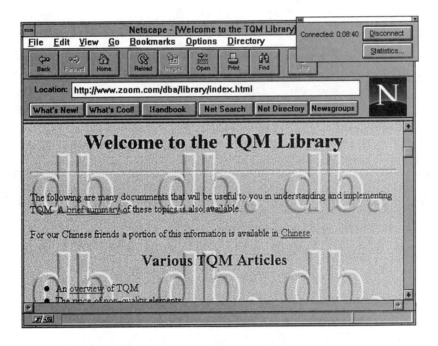

Before class, prepare tasks for learners that give them the opportunity to use different search tools, to download information, and even to look up and subscribe to mailing lists. On the topic of TQM, for example, learners can access a list of TQM groups through the Online Quality Resource Guide at this URL:

```
http://www.casti.com/qc/lists/online.resources.guide.txt
```

In addition to mailing lists, this site references other sites of interest and bulletin board services, including TQM discussion groups on America Online and CompuServe.

Planning an Internet Class

Planning an Internet class can be quite different from planning a class on any other computer-related topic (such as Excel or Microsoft Word). First, if you are able (that is, if it is possible) and you decide to make the class interactive by having learners access Internet sites, join discussion groups, and so on, you must survey those who will attend your class. Second, you must test the access to certain sites related to your class's interest. Both of these tasks add to your normal preparation time but you will be rewarded by the effectiveness of an interactive class.

Have a Backup Plan

As mentioned earlier, the most effective Internet training classes are those that include your own demonstrations and hands-on exercises of live searches and actual communication through mailing lists. Obviously, access to the Internet in the training class depends on the setup and type of connection to the Internet available in the training lab. But even with the best setup for accessing the Internet, you should be prepared with a backup plan so that you can keep the pace of the class moving as planned even in the event of an emergency.

Inevitably, some site you want to access will be down the day you give training. Or the traffic will be so high that the pace of your class will be slowed as you or learners wait for files to load or be downloaded. Be prepared with two types of backup plans:

- If your demonstration of using the Internet is slowed down or halted, be prepared to instruct learners how to find alternate sites.

- Be prepared to show examples of sites and mail from discussion groups using a slide-show or transparency presentation of the sites you intended to visit during class. Be prepared to either structure your whole class around a prepared *demonstration* of Internet sites or to structure your class so that you have the option of showing a *slide or transparency* instead of actually connecting to a site.

Being prepared for your Internet class with screen captures of Internet pages not only provides a backup in case of Internet access problems but also provides you with working materials for conducting the class. Use printed copies of screen shots or printed Internet pages you have accessed during class preparation to record notes for your class presentation.

Using Information about Your Learners

Knowing how your learners might integrate the Internet into their jobs and interests is essential with Internet training. If you know your audience, you can plan and practice for the class. Find out your students' interests, job assignments, and areas of expertise. Use this information to find appropriate sites before class. Getting information about your class to help you structure an Internet session does not have to involve many questions. Simply asking learners why they are taking your Internet class can uncover enough information to help you prepare the class appropriately for those students.

Understand how to use information about learners during the class. Once you know the topics in which members of your class are interested, teach learners the techniques for using search tools, Internet directories, online bulletin boards, and discussion groups to get the information they want.

13

Using the Internet To Teach the Internet

If the members of your class have access to the Internet, consider using various Internet sites to do the teaching for you. Numerous sites exist containing text information that explains the Internet or providing online tutorials learners can follow at appropriate times as you introduce concepts and techniques for using the Internet. If you use the Internet to teach the Internet, you motivate learners to continue their own learning after class by returning to some of the sites you introduced or by finding new sites.

Internet sites containing instruction about the Internet range from information for beginning users to information for advanced users—including instruction on programming and development for the Internet. If you are teaching a beginning level class, for example, you can send learners to some of the following sites:

- *Internet Survival Skills* at the University of Hawaii:

  `http://kawika.hcc.hawaii.eud/iss101/101mods.html`

  This site introduces the Internet and covers the World Wide Web and such topics as e-mail, FTP, newsgroups, Gopher, locating information, and getting connected to the Internet.

- ROADMAP:

  `http://www.brandonu.ca/~ennsnr/Resources/Roadmap/Welcom.html`

  This multilesson tutorial presents information on Listservs, e-mail, Netiquette, Internet security, the World Wide Web, and other topics for new users.

- *Internet Tutorial* by Karen Schneider:

  `http://www.intac.com/~kgs/pps/welcome.html`

  This tutorial answers such questions for new users as "What can I do on the Internet?," "What do I need to know to use the Internet?," and "What are the best Internet tools?"

- *Where To Start*:

  `http://lawlib.slu.edu/newusers.htm`

  This tutorial for new users is from Jim Milles at St. Louis University.

Many of the tutorials available on the Internet present information in text format. When using these tutorials, learners can select topics from a main page and proceed to other pages to learn Internet concepts, tools, and user techniques. Apart from these text-based tutorials, some interactive tutorials are available. One such interactive tutorial is the *Escort Internet Tutorial* at the following site:

  `http://www.pointcom.com/escort/txt/learn/learn.htm`

This site provides six interactive tutorials learners can use. Topics covered in these tutorials include *Introducing the Internet*; *Electronic Mail Tour Package*; *Mailing Lists Tour Package*; *UseNet Newsgroups Tour Package*; *FTP Tour Package*; *Gopher Sites Tour Package*; and *World Wide Web Tour Package*. Each tutorial presents learners with a pop-up tutorial that contains step-by-step directions to lead them through practice sessions using Internet tools and software.

Motivating Use of the Internet after Training

There are a number of ways in which you, as a trainer, can motivate members of your classes to continue using and learning about the Internet. One such method is to direct learners to the tutorials on the Internet that can help them continue to learn (refer to the preceding section in this chapter). Motivate learners to subscribe to list groups and search for information related to their interests and jobs following the class.

Other methods of motivating learners to use the Internet after class include the following:

- If you or your organization has its own Internet home page, use the page to communicate with learners.

- Inform learners of sites you have found that can help them use the Internet.

- Suggest to members of your class that they create their own list groups so that employees at other locations within the same organization can communicate on specific topics of interest.

- If you or the training department of your organization has its own Internet page, use it to post notices about upcoming classes, share technical tips, or provide solutions to technical problems related to your training expertise.

Making Your Learning On-Going

13

To retrieve Internet information during any class, you must have a very broad understanding of what is available on the Internet. Develop the habit of keeping information about new sites, list groups, and so on in a simple database. My own database—called the "trainer's toolbox"—can be customized to meet my needs and the needs of any organization.

The trainer's toolbox enables you to track sites you can then use in classes or demonstrations. To create a trainer's toolbox, develop a database in either a spreadsheet or database program that will be easy and handy for you to use. In the database, include such fields as the rating, topic, address, comments, author, and alternative address of sites and resources.

For the rating, devise some system to help you identify sites ranging from your favorites to those you don't ever want to visit again. I recommend leaving the poor sites in your database so that you don't waste time in the future going to the site because you forgot what it contained. You'll appreciate not wasting your time and your equipment's time accessing a useless site. In my own database of sites, I use the following simple rating system:

- **A is absolutely worth the time**: The site has useful, easy-to-understand, and well-organized content. The site has more or better content than any other site. The site has excellent references and links to other sites. The format of the content is excellent. The site is easy to use. The site makes good use of graphics—graphics are pertinent to the site. The site does not contain needless graphics causing long, unnecessary access time.

- **B is better than most sites**: The site has very good, easy-to-understand, and fairly well-organized content, but does not have all the references and links to other sites that an A site may have. Also, the graphics may not be as professional or useful as those on an A site, or the format of the content may not be as good as that of an A site.

- **C is common:** The site offers nothing more than most other sites covering the same topic; in fact, it duplicates the content of most other sites. The site also offers no advantages to users in its references and links to other sites. The site's use of graphics and format is weak or common at best.

- **D is a dog site:** The primary weakness of this site is that the content is useless for your needs or the needs of others (if you are rating a site for learners or someone else). The graphics and format of the site may be excellent; however, you or others gain little from spending time reading through pages or downloading information. Sites with the primary purpose of advertising products or services may well fit this rating.

In addition to the rating, include a topic to help you remember what the site is as well as its importance to you. The *topic* field can help you sort sites when necessary. Under a *comments* field, include any special login commands or passwords. You may also want to include a column to identify whether the site is FTP, Telnet, e-mail, or WWW. Finally, categorize sites by subtopics. For example, because I train medical students and professionals, I include in my database a field that categorizes medical sites as medical school sites, research center sites, or sites focusing on specialties.

I recommend that you include in your trainer's toolbox not only sites of interest to you as a trainer or related to your training classes, but also entertaining sites you may want to include as examples in your classes. CityNet, for example, is a site that provides travel information for popular cities around the world (`http://www.city.net/`). Remember, however, that if you introduce a site like CityNet to your class, you will have members of the class who will want to access city sites around the world.

Tables 13.1 through 13.5 are charts taken from my database of sites. Ratings for sites are not included so that I do not bias you for or against any particular entry. I recommend that you visit these sites—particularly those containing resources about and for Internet training—so that you can determine how the sites best fit your needs.

Table 13.1 E-Conferences or Lists

Topic	Address	Message	Author	Alternative Address
Help Desk	`listserv@wvnvm.wvnet.edu`	`subscribe hdesk-1`		
Help-Net (questions from new Internet users)	`listserv@vm.temple.edu`	`sub help-net <fname> <lname>`		
How To Start and Manage a BITNET-LISTSERV Discussion Group	`listserv@uhupvm1.uh.edu`	`get kovacs prv2n1`		
Info-IBMPC	`listserv@arl.mil`			
Info-Mac	`listserv@vmd.cso.uiuc.edu`	`subscribe info-mac <fname> <lname>`		`listserv@cearn.cem.ch` or `listserv@`
KIDLINK about online life for parents and educators	`opresno@estern.uio.no`			
List of all electronic magazines (e-zines) on the Net	`e-zines-request@netcom.com`			
MS WinNews Electronic Newsletter directly from Operating System Division	`majordomo@microsoft.nwnet.com`	`subscribe WinNews <ADDRESS>`	Microsoft	
On women and information technology	`listserv@bitnic.educom.edu`	`subscribe educom-w <lname> <fname>`		
Scout Report—What's new on and about the Internet, focus on researchers and educators	`majordomo@is.internic.net`	`subscribe scout-report`	InterNIC Information Services	`majordomo@is.internic.net/subscribe scout-report-himl`

(continues)

13

Table 13.1 continued

Topic	Address	Message	Author	Alternative Address
Training	listserv@psuvm.psu.edu	sub trdev-l		
Windows	listserv@wicvm.uic.edu	subscribe win3-L <fname> <lname>		
Women in Computers	systers-request@pa.dec.com	mail goes to list owner		
WordPerfect Lists	listserv@ubvm.cc.buffalo.edu	Sub wpwin-L, wpcomp-L, wp51-l, or wpoffice <fname> <lname>		

Table 13.2 Learning about the Internet

Topic	Address	Login/Comments	Author	Alternative Address
Gopher-It Workshop	ror@netcom.com	Free; mail Copley	Thomas P. Copley	
List of service providers; tax funded	gopher.internic.net			
New User FAQs	FTP to ds.internic.net/rfc	login: anonymous password: guest		
Roadmap: Internet Training Workshop	listserv@ua1vm.ua.edu	get map package f=mail	Patrick Douglas Crispen	pcrispe1@ua1vm.ua.edu
Roadmap to Internet Services Online Class	Telnet sunsite.unc.edu	login: lynx		http://www.itcs.com
The Hunt	ftp.cni.org/pub/ net-guides/i-hunt	login: anonymous	Rick Gates	gopher.cic.net or ftp.cic.net

Table 13.3   Resources

Nonelectronic Resources

Title	Publisher
Using the Internet, Special Edition, 2nd Edition w/CD-ROM	Que
Official Internet Yellow Pages, 2nd Edition	New Riders Publishing
Internet Starter Kit for Mac, 2nd Edition	Hayden
Internet Starter Kit for Windows, 2nd Edition	Hayden
Teach Yourself Web Publishing w/HTML in a Week, 2nd Edition	Sams.net
Internet Unleashed, 2nd Edition	Sams.net
Using the Internet, Special Edition	Que
Using the Internet, Special Edition	Que
Using HTML, Special Edition	Que
Navigating the Internet, Deluxe Edition	Sams.net

Organizations

InterNIC (Official Source of Information about the Internet)
Mission: To provide Internet information services
To supervise the registration of Internet addresses and DNS names
To develop databases that serve as white and yellow pages
Contact: `www.internic, gopher.internic.net, ftp.internic.net, info@internic.net`

Coalition for Networked Information
Mission To make Internet information resources more accessible
To increase knowledge about networked resources
To enhance and increase these resources
Contact: `joan@cni.org` (files available at `ftp.cni.org` by anonymous FTP)

Electronic Frontier Foundation
Mission: To protect civil liberties for the networked community
To support educational activities related to networking
To develop an awareness among policy makers regarding networking issues
To encourage and support the development of new tools to help networks
Contact: `eff@eff.org`

The Internet Society
Mission: To provide assistance and support to groups and organizations interested in the use, operation, and evolution of the Internet
Contact: `isoc@nri.reston.va.us`

13

Table 13.4 Supporting and Teaching about Computers

Topic	Address	Login/Comments
Distance Ed (evaluation group)	`listserv@unlvm.unl.edu`	`sub asat-eva`
Distance Ed (international)	`listserv@psuvm.psu.edu`	`sub deos-l`
Distance Ed (research)	`listserv@ryerson.bitnet`	`sub disres-l`
KUFacts	`telnet://kufacts.cc.ukans.edu`	`login: kufacts`
Listserv List	`listser@bitnic.cren.net`	`message = list global`
Listserv List	`mail-server@sri.com`	`message = send interest-groups`
Listserv List: Network Information Systems Center	`ftp://sri.com`	`/netinfo/interest-groups.txt`
Listserv List: Dartmouth's List	`listserv@dartcms1`	`message = send listserv lists`
Masie Center	`courses@masie.com`	automated server will reply
Net-happenings	`listserv@is.internic.net`	`sub net-happenings <your name>`
Net-resources	`listserv@is.internic.net`	`sub net-resources <your name>`
Nettrain	`listserv@ubvm.cc.buffalo.edu`	`sub nettrain <your name>`
New Electronic Discussions	`listserv@vm.1.nodak.edu` or `sub new-list`	
New International Internet Resources	`listserv@itocsivm.csi.it`	`sub newnir-l <your name>`
Top 10 Internet Training Resources	`http://www.itcs.com/ telnet-sunsite`	
Training and Development Discussion List	`trdev-1@psumv.psu.edu`	
Training and Development FAQs	Gopher to `hub.terc.edu/ education/training`	
Training Materials Online Course	`trainmat.ncl.ac.uk`	Gopher to `hub.terc.edu/ education/training`

Table 13.5 Training and Support Sites on the WWW

Topic	Address	Comments
Hdesk-L archives available from Roman Olynyk's personal home page	`http://wvnvaxa.wvnet.edu/~roman/roman.html`	
CERN European Particle Physics Lab; responsible for development of WWW	`http://www.cern.ch`	
Guide to Cities	`http://www.city.net`	
Microsoft	`http://www.microsoft.com`	
MindVax	`http://www.phantom.com`	
The WELL	`http://www.well.sf.ca.us`	
Internet Resources	`http://www.brandonu.ca/~ennsnr/Resources/`	
American Universities	`http://www.clas.ufl.edu/CLAS/american-universities.html`	
The Macmillan USA Information SuperLibrary	`http://www.mcp.com/`	
Ziff-Davis Publishing	`http://www.ziff.com/`	
Novell	`http://www.novell.com/`	
Pulse	`http://www.kumc.edu/`	

13

From Here...

So, what is the best of the Internet for trainers? Only you can define that. Hopefully, this chapter has provided you with the tools to get started in defining that for your environment. If you need additional direction in your quest for Internet information, turn to the following chapters:

■ Chapter 11, "Augmenting Classroom Training with Other Media," has additional suggestions for how you can use the Internet as well as other media to supplement that more "traditional" classroom training.

■ Chapter 12, "Distance Learning on the World Wide Web," helps you move your class from the lab (in which students are all physically present in one location) to the Web (in which students access prepared information whenever it is convenient for them).

Chapter 14

Certification of Trainers

by Carolyn Woodie and Peggy Maday

*Carolyn Woodie and **Peggy Maday** have both seen the favorable results of certification in their own businesses. Carolyn, owner of Carolyn Woodie and Associates in the Washington, D.C., area, has been a WordPerfect Certified Instructor since 1989. Peggy, owner of Turning Point Training Systems in Denver, Colorado, has been a WordPerfect Certified Instructor since 1988 and a Microsoft Solution Provider since 1992.*

Certification and skills assessment are here to stay. In the mid-1990s, we are witnessing an ever-increasing focus not just on technical people being certified but on users being certified. Certification of skills and expertise gives customers of training services and products some measure of certainty about the quality of instruction. And with the trend toward outsourcing of training services, businesses need some sort of assurance that their training needs will be met appropriately.

This chapter deals specifically with certification for technicians and trainers. You will read about several real certification programs and their requirements, benefits, and pitfalls. These programs are ever evolving. Although you will read about actual programs, check the current requirements and benefits of a program by calling the software vendor.

The History of Software Certification

In the early days of the PC, many software companies began certification programs. Companies needed representatives out in the field to support their products. Some of the users' guides and manuals were so bad that the technicians and trainers acted as missionaries carrying effective techniques, procedures, and answers to end users. You could purchase certification or authorization status for a fee if you were a legitimate training business. Requirements for certification did not include much actual skill assessment testing.

Much of this is changing today. There is a stronger emphasis on skill assessment and less on purchasing certification for a fee.

Novell: One of the Early Pioneers in Certification

Novell began a certification program in 1988 for their network products. They initially designed this training and assessment program for their own internal technicians. The training brought the technicians up to speed before they were put out on the floor. The design of the lab testing ensured that the trainees did the installation correctly and reported, on a step-by-step basis, what they encountered and learned. This training for the internal technicians was quite successful.

Before long, the internal technicians were complaining about customers who did not have the knowledge and information they needed. The education department at Novell created the Certified Novell Engineer (CNE) program, modeled after their own internal program. Today there are over 65,000 CNEs in the field. There has been a lot of discussion about whether this credential makes you an excellent technician or not. Regardless, not too many companies will hire a network technician who does not have a CNE certificate.

Microsoft: Created an Entourage of Problem Solvers

Microsoft began their Solutions Provider program in late 1989 and early 1990. Resellers, developers, consultants, technical support people, and training organizations work with Microsoft to solve business software problems such as integration, custom development, training, and technical support.

There are currently more than 2,500 Microsoft Solution Providers nationwide. This program is worldwide and extends to Australia, Canada, France, Germany, Japan, and the United Kingdom.

Certification Trends Today

Increasingly, many leading software companies are turning toward certification as an indicator of expertise. People carrying a software vendor certification stand out to the general public as "experts in the field." This credibility can benefit you, your organization, and your customers.

Certifications are available for the many different kinds and levels of computer support professionals:

- Consultants
- Installation technicians
- Trainers
- People who train trainers and computer support personnel

Opportunity for New Trainers!

If you are just starting out in the training field, certification provides an excellent way to set yourself off from the pack. Start researching certification by contacting the software vendor for the specific requirements. Then create a plan to satisfy those requirements. Again, the software vendor will have some suggestions about how to get the education or training you need to satisfy the technical requirements. Try going to your local training centers: many of them offer training courses specific to the certification process. Make sure that you understand the vendor requirements thoroughly and that the course meets those requirements before spending any of your hard-earned dollars.

14

Certification Requirements

Each certification credential has its own requirements designed to measure your competency. You have to meet a combination of requirements based on the particular certification process you are looking at. These requirements include the following areas:

- Professional qualifications
- Technical or product testing
- Training and presentation requirements

Professional Qualifications

Some certification credentials recognize the individual; others recognize the organization. For example, you might be applying, on your own behalf, to become a Certified WordMaster Instructor. On the other hand, you might be applying on behalf of your own company or a company you work for to become an Authorized WordMaster Training Center.

Most certification programs require you to fill out an application form. The application typically requests company and personal profile information. Whether you are a large business or a small independent, you must provide proof of legitimacy.

Expect to provide *some* or *all* of the following information:

- Business name (typically, you must be employed or representing your own business as an independent)
- Ownership of the company you represent
- Address
- Phone number
- Electronic Mail IDs such as CompuServe or Internet addresses
- Business licensing or ID
- Contacts (shipping, marketing, sales)
- Business focus
- Size of business
- Specialty areas or vertical markets
- Description of products and services
- Company revenue information
- Employment totals
- References

Some programs request resumes from the individuals applying. Others require minimum levels of experience in computer technical areas or in training.

Who Can Be Certified?

Many of these requirements point to the company as well as to the individual. Even as independent contractors, we have had to provide proof of being legitimate business organizations. Certification is not a process for someone between jobs; it is more a process that recognizes competent business entities, large, small, or independent.
—*Peggy Maday and Carolyn Woodie*

Technical or Product Testing

There is usually a test or exam. This process provides a measurement of your technical expertise.

Nature of the Exam

The typical tests are closed-book, computer-based exams. The exams usually feature multiple-choice and true/false types of questions. Some questions are factual in nature; others measure your problem-solving abilities.

There has been much discussion about whether the exams measure true proficiency. The organizers of the various certification programs write some exams better than others. This can lead to lots of frustration for you in satisfying the requirements. Possible sources of frustration include the following:

- Some of the facts are strict memorization and can be somewhat exotic

- Ambiguous questions

- Repetition of obscure questions and not testing key areas

- Unfair scoring (not giving partial credit on multiple, multiple-choice questions)

Some of this frustration is inevitable in computer-based testing. Most software vendors do their best to minimize these problems. Nonetheless, you may encounter many frustrations. In the end, the frustration usually pays off when you receive your certification.

14

Frustration *Does* Pay Off

In looking back, we feel that perseverance and tenacity are the most important elements in completing a certification. We have both failed certification exams and felt like giving up. Some of the information we had to learn to pass the exam did not seem that important in the real world. In spite of the discouragement, we decided the certification was worth it for us. If you really want the certification, you must make the commitment and stick with it! —*Peggy Maday and Carolyn Woodie*

A nationwide testing service like Drake Prometric or Sylvan Learning Systems may administer the exam. You must register with the testing center before taking the exam. Payment is necessary before you can take the test. Bring your photo ID on the day of the exam for identification. Exams are usually pass/fail. Depending on the credential, you may have to pass the test at a specific level of proficiency.

How To Prepare for the Exam

Adequate preparation for the exams is essential. Start by using the product and becoming familiar with the reference guide. Here are some other possible sources of preparation material:

- Outlines from the software vendor

- Other training references (for example, Microsoft suggests their Resource Kits)

- Sample tests

- Certification courses (these can be expensive and lengthy but are often your best bet)

- Self-paced study materials

Most software vendors offer comprehensive lists of how to prepare along with the certification program specifications.

Training and Presentation Requirements

Some certifications measure just technical expertise, no more. Other certifications go a step further and assess your training or presentation skills. You may have to do one of the following to fulfill your training requirement:

- Produce a training video of an actual training class

- Perform a live teaching presentation

- Provide teaching and training references from stand-up training classes

- Attend "Train-the-Trainer" seminars

- Hold another accredited training certification

Training and presentation requirements used to be very vendor specific. For example, WordPerfect required you to submit proof of your training expertise by producing a video specifically for them. Now, software vendors allow you to use other training vendors' credentials to satisfy their requirements. Again, using WordPerfect/Novell as an example (Novell recently purchased WordPerfect), you can now satisfy your training requirements if you have a valid training credential with Lotus or Microsoft. In fact, there is a movement towards worldwide accreditation called the CTT (Certified Technical Trainer). The next three sections describe the evolution of training and presentation requirements.

WordPerfect's Videotape Requirements

From 1987 through 1994, WordPerfect required both live videos and training references for their Certified Instructor certification program. You chose a topic from an approved feature list. WordPerfect's Instructor Services rigorously evaluated this video of a live training segment in the areas shown in Table 14.1.

Table 14.1 WordPerfect Corporation Criteria for the Evaluation of a Training Video	
Criterion	**Requirement**
Communication skills	Clear and audible speech, correct grammar.
Product knowledge	Inspires confidence, technically correct information.
General demeanor	Positive learning environment, adapts to students' needs, appropriate energy, pace, and attire.
Teaching techniques	Introduction Content and objectives Scope Identifies students' initial understanding Encourages contributions Teaches to objectives Defines vocabulary Restates questions Provides clear and concise answers Logical lesson flow Completes concepts before moving on Monitors students' understanding Provides simple exercises and examples Monitors students' screens Uses visual teaching techniques in addition to lecture Summarizes/reviews Identifies final understanding

As Table 14.1 shows, this evaluation was a very comprehensive training assessment. It took both experience and commitment to successfully complete.

Novell's Application Trainers Training Requirements

When Novell purchased WordPerfect, many of the requirements changed. In 1995, Novell modified the training portion of the requirements to allow training credentials from other programs. You can satisfy the teaching portion of the certification by choosing from the following options:

- Hold current certification as a WordPerfect Certified Instructor, a Lotus Notes Certified Instructor, or a Microsoft Certified Trainer.

- Pass a Novell Instructor Performance Evaluation.

- Successfully complete Educational Testing Service's (ETS) cross-industry, Certified Technical Trainer Program for technical instructors (see the next section for more information on the CTT program).

Certified Technical Trainer Program (CTT)

The Certified Technical Trainer program provides a credential recognized worldwide to designate proficient technical trainers. Educational Testing Service (ETS) is developing this cross-industry program, available in November 1995. The software industry sponsors and supports CTT. To be certified, you must take a knowledge test and a performance test:

- Instructional Skill Knowledge: A two-hour exam of 100 to 120 questions in multiple-choice and scenario format. The test is administered by Drake Prometric and Sylvan Technology Centers.

- Performance Test: A videotaped presentation for a live audience is sent to ETS for scoring.

Costs Associated with Certification

Many costs are involved with certification. You must weigh all costs carefully when determining whether becoming certified is worthwhile. Consider the following costs in becoming certified:

- Application and annual renewal fees
- Certification courses
- Test costs
- Other materials
- Loss of productivity

Application and Annual Renewal Fees

Initial application fees and annual renewals vary widely with the various programs. However, higher fees sometimes reflect more tangible benefits (a high cost is not always a negative). Carefully check out the corresponding benefits when evaluating costs. Table 14.2 shows a sample of some current (1995) costs for some of the popular programs.

Table 14.2 Initial Application Fees and Annual Renewals for Popular Certification Programs		
Software Vendor	**Program Name**	**Program Fee**
Novell	Novell Applications Instructor	$200 initial fee $100 annual fee
Novell	Novell Applications Training Provider	$1,700 initial and annual fee
Microsoft	Microsoft Solution Provider	$1,995 initial and annual fees

Certification Courses

Certification courses offer hands-on training consistent with the certification requirements. Frequently, software vendors authorize a professional education center to provide the training. In other cases, the software vendor itself provides the certification course. In either case, these courses often include exactly the information you need to pass your test. Cost for this high-end training is usually substantial, averaging in excess of $500 per day. If you have to travel to a city offering the course, you must also consider travel costs.

Test Costs

The costs for the tests themselves average around $100 per test. Consider that you may have to take the test more than once to pass. Some people actually take the test before spending too much time studying so that they have a clear idea of the level of detail involved.

Other Materials Costs

Some programs offer self-paced study guides instead of or in addition to the authorized courses. And of course, there is always the cost of third-party books and resource kits.

14

Loss of Productivity Costs

Last but not least, you are going to need some time to prepare for your certification. Loss of productivity can be your most substantial cost. You may already have substantial experience, but you can spend a good deal of time fine-tuning and increasing your skills in a couple weak areas.

Benefits of Certification

There is a myriad of benefits to becoming certified. First and foremost, certification provides industry recognition of your knowledge and proficiency. Table 14.3 provides a sampling of the more tangible benefits from some of the major programs.

Table 14.3 Benefits of Certification			
	MS Solution Provider	**Novell Application Instructor**	**Lotus Notes Certified Instructor**
Industry recognition	✓	✓	✓
Vendor logo	✓	✓	✓
Technical information mailings	✓		✓
Dedicated e-mail forums	✓	✓	✓
Invitations to events	✓		
Referrals	✓		
Internal use software	✓		
Training software	✓		
Priority support	✓		✓

As Table 14.3 shows, different programs provide different tangible benefits. Microsoft sends each Solution Provider a monthly mailing with a box full of technical information, CDs, software, marketing materials, and on and on. Many technicians certify just to keep up-to-date on what is happening and to receive the licensing for the Internal Use Software. Microsoft certification also costs $1,995 per year. Are the benefits worth the costs? This is a very individual matter. Evaluate it carefully. Be sure to refer to the next sections on "Certification and the Employee," "Certification and the Employer," and "Certification and the Independent Contractor" to explore benefits beyond the tangible benefits you see here.

Please note that the software companies listed here may have other programs that offer the benefits you desire. The programs and benefits are changing all the time. Check the current requirements and benefits of a program by calling the software vendor.

Certification from Various Points of View

Now that we have looked at some of the history of certifications and some of the requirements, consider how the various training roles can view certification. First, we will look at certification from the perspective of the employee.

Certification and the Employee

Some training companies and training departments of corporations require their trainers to hold certifications in various software products. This is their way of ensuring the quality of the training. Some employers may require certification to help them meet standards to become approved as an "Authorized" or "Certified" training center. Are there direct benefits for the employee?

There are some possible benefits of certifications for trainers who are employees. Certification is one way to increase your skills and can set you apart from other trainers who are not certified. Certification may provide personal respect and recognition in the training field. Achieving a certain certification can be a confidence builder and a personal affirmation of your skills and knowledge.

It is very helpful if your employer considers certification advantageous. Your employer may consider covering your expenses to attend training conferences or seminars. Your employer may even agree to pay for study materials and time to study and prepare for the required tests. This can be a real advantage for you as an employee and is something an independent trainer does not have. Certification can be a wise investment in your future and can provide additional credentials for future employment.

On the other hand, consider some of these possible difficulties. What if your employer does not see any advantages to you becoming certified? Finding the time or funds to attend training sessions can be difficult. Working through the certification process on your own time can be costly. A few employers view certifications in a negative light. They have noted that some individuals, once they attain certification, leave their employment to work independently or to move to the competition. If

14

your employer has a negative perspective on certification and you want to work toward a certification, you may have to do some negotiating or provide reassurances that your employer's investment is worthwhile. In the next section, "Certification and the Employer," take note of the comments regarding possible formal agreements you can try to negotiate with your employer to satisfy both your needs and the needs of the employer.

Certification and the Employer

For the employer, hiring certified instructors may be a way to ensure the quality and consistency of the members of your training staff. If your goal is to become an "Authorized" or "Certified" training center, having instructors certified in the products can be an asset. Some software companies may *require* that the training staff have a certain number of certified instructors before awarding the "Authorized" or "Certified" training center designation.

Quality of Certified Instructors

One employer's views about current certification programs:

"In the past, I specifically sought to hire certified instructors. My clients responded well to certified instructors. The best certification by far was the WordPerfect Certified Instructor program. Microsoft and Lotus certification programs did not give me the same confidence. I was never disappointed when I hired WordPerfect Certified Instructors. Not only were they tested for product knowledge but they were also tested for stand-up training skills. Since then, no other certification program has given me the same confidence. Most certification processes today emphasize knowledge but not teaching ability. It seems that certification has become a profit source for the software companies. If you can pay the fees, you can usually get the standard. Therefore, today's certification does not have the same value to me as an employer."

The training marketplace has become more knowledgeable about training certifications. Some government and corporate training contracts now require that training be led by certified instructors. Having certified staff members may make your training center one step above the competition.

Can you charge higher fees? Will certified employees request higher salaries? Sometimes that is the case but not always. As certifications become more commonplace, higher fees for training and higher salaries for certified trainers may not be feasible. However, if becoming certified requires a great deal of effort and invested dollars, it is only reasonable that it should be reflected in the training fees charged and the salaries paid.

Some employers have found that some employees who achieve certifications then leave their employment for greener pastures. Employers need not use this as a reason to view certification negatively. They can develop written agreements to cover the needs of both parties. Some employers have agreements that they will subsidize certification costs. Often, they pay for preparation time if the employee agrees to remain with the employer for a minimum amount of time (usually at least a year). Additionally, if the employer has paid for study materials, some agreements require that if the employee leaves, the materials are owned by and remain with the employer. Proper agreements can make certification a win-win solution for both employer and employee.

Certification and the Independent Contractor

Certifications for an independent trainer may be a very good investment. Certifications can provide recognition in the industry and a definite marketable credential. Some software manufacturers provide direct referrals to instructors certified on their products. However, not all certification programs provide referrals. Even when they provide referrals, the referrals may be overrated by the manufacturer. If receiving referrals is a strong reason for becoming certified, it is wise to research the true value of the benefits. Check with those who already hold the specific certification and see what their experience with direct referrals has been.

Certification can be a personal confidence builder, affirming your knowledge of the product. If the certification requirements also test training ability, it is an added credential.

Certification as Self-Enhancement

One certified independent trainer stated that "Certification gave me the confirmation that I was doing a good job. I knew I was doing a good job, but preparing for and passing the written test and the teaching review assured me that I was indeed one of the top trainers in my specialty. It was a real confidence booster!"

Some software vendors provide significant software discounts to certified individuals either for their own use or additional copies for training purposes. One great benefit may be the additional technical help a certified individual receives as a benefit of the certification. This may include special access to the software vendor's technical staff, electronic forums for exclusive certified users, CD-ROM-based troubleshooting databases, or seminars. Some certifications provide priority support so that the independent contractors can provide better support for their clients than noncertified competitors.

Certification To Expand Technical Resources

"I have attained and maintain a certification for the chief benefit of the increased technical support available to me as a certified individual," says an independent technical consultant. "I can support my clients much better because I can receive the latest software support and update information. I also receive real financial benefits because I can purchase all software at substantially discounted prices."

Certification can place you one step above your competition for proposals. As mentioned earlier, some government and large corporation contracts now specify that training must be provided by someone certified in the particular software.

Networking and referrals are the lifeblood of the independent training vendor. Referrals to other certified individuals can be done with confidence because you know they have passed the same qualifications you have passed. Certification conferences and electronic forums provide ideal avenues to network with others holding similar certifications. Relationships can develop for the purpose of sharing training ideas, solving problems, and even sharing contracts.

For the independent trainer, there can also be some drawbacks to certifications. Some certifications require extensive knowledge and experience with the product. It may require a great deal of time to gain this experience. For the independent trainer, this is probably unbillable time. Therefore, the costs of certification go far beyond the obvious costs of the direct application fees. You have to consider not only the unbillable hours you spend preparing for the test but also the time lost in marketing and developing future work. The result can be a lot of downtime (time spent with no money to show for it). Other certifications can be so expensive that making the investment is difficult for an independent trainer. Some certifications may require not only testing and application fees, but also the purchase of specific instructor manuals and courseware. You may also be required to attend expensive seminars and conferences. Although it can be very advantageous for an independent trainer to hold several certifications, doing so can be difficult because of the time and moneys involved.

An independent trainer must evaluate whether the value of the certification truly warrants the time and moneys invested.

Certification and the Training Purchaser

What value is certification to the purchaser of training? Certification can provide a measurement of product knowledge. As you have seen, some certifications can also provide a measurement of training skills. This measurement provides a way to ensure the value and quality of the training purchased.

Some software companies guarantee the "certified" or "authorized" training. The purchaser also has not only the reputation of the training provider, but the interest of the software vendor as well.

Certified individuals have usually proven their expertise to an advanced level of knowledge of the product. Some training purchasers have found that hiring certified instructors for *all* levels of training ensures that even introductory courses are taught by people who know not only the basics but also the ins, outs, and shortcuts of the software product. These instructors often provide a more solid foundation of training than trainers who know only the basics.

However, on the downside, because certification requirements usually carry additional monetary costs and time expenditures, training by certified trainers may be higher priced. Some training purchasers have not found certified trainers any better qualified than other trainers.

The Future of Certification

Because the industry changes quickly, the requirements and benefits of training certifications change rapidly, too. Predicting what will happen with certification in the future is like trying to shoot at a moving target. However, we have made some definite observations about computer training over the past year or two.

Companies are downsizing and the training departments are sometimes the first to be cut. As in-house training departments disappear, companies are outsourcing their training more than ever. The type of training is also changing. Gone are the days when it was necessary to have everyone attend *Introduction to Whatever*. Users are at many different knowledge levels and software is so much more powerful. It would take weeks to teach everything about a program. Training is becoming more customized to the end users' needs. If you have attended computer training conferences and workshops, you may have heard terms such as *just-in-time training, just enough training*, and *training at the user's workstation*.

We are seeing computers at all levels of the company's staff. Ten years ago, we were training chiefly the support staff. Now all the managers, executives, and even the mailroom and assembly-line workers are getting computers—and they all need training.

How do these trends affect certification? Is certification more or less valuable? One employer stated that certification has lost its value (see the sidebar, "Quality of Certified Instructors"). Maybe a particular certification in that employer's eyes has lost its value. However, five years ago, training or product certification was largely unknown outside the training network. Today, we are seeing it recognized by end users and training purchasers. We are seeing it as a requirement in some requests for proposals. We are also seeing certification requirements for help-wanted ads in major newspapers. We are noticing a growing interest in developing industry-wide certifications for teaching skills. Often, corporations request certified trainers to train the executive levels on a one-to-one basis.

What place product and training certifications will have five years from now is yet to be seen. However, certification in some form is probably here to stay. Certification and its importance will adjust just as computer training itself has adjusted in this rapidly changing world of technology.

From Here...

If you want to sharpen your training skills to work towards certification, refer to the following chapters:

- Chapter 2, "Becoming a Computer Trainer," lists some of the reasons why you might want to become a trainer in the first place. The chapter continues with explanations of how you can become a *successful* trainer.

- Chapter 3, "Adult Learning: What Do We Know for Sure?," explains how teaching adults differs from teaching children—and how these differences can affect the way you teach.

Chapter 15

The Future of Computer Training

by Elliott Masie

Elliott Masie is president of the MASIE Center, an international think-tank focused on the intersection of learning and technology. He is one of the pioneers in the computer training industry, with over 22 years of experience in assisting corporations and government organizations face the challenge of building workforce skills.

The incredible rate of change in the world of technology creates an even greater rate of change in the field of computer training. Each change to a person's workplace technology results in a direct need to learn more. Think about this rate of change: For every 100 pages of magazine articles about new technology, there are 100 unwritten pages of stories about the struggle of workers to cope with these unending changes to their workplace environment. Every release of a new software package, every upgrade to a suite, every migration to a new form of database access, every expansion of networking capacity, every consideration of a new operating system, and every shift from mainframe to desktop focus yields a need for workers to learn new skills, procedures, and even attitudes.

Some of these workers will be fortunate enough to attend a formal training course at their company. Some will be handed a manual or computer-based-training disk to assist them in learning. Many will use the help desk as a personal—and very expensive—tutor. A large majority will interrupt their daily work tasks (and those of their colleagues in the next cubicle or office) to cope with the changes in an informal, on-the-job learning method. One way or another, the nation's organizations will pay an additional cost for each new piece and version of technology that enters the workplace.

This is the foundation of the computer-training and computer-learning industry and field. Hundreds of thousands of jobs and thousands of businesses, products, and services exist to support the technology-learning needs of our society. These same forces of change are also direct challenges to those jobs, businesses, products, and services.

The past two decades have been the Wonder Bread years for the computer-training industry. The growth of mainframe end-user computing followed by the introduction of the personal computer spawned our industry by creating an immediate need for training and support services. Many of the first players in the computer-training field got there by accident. If, for instance, you had one more week of experience with VisiCalc, the first spreadsheet, than anyone else, you could open the doors of a new training center. If you were able to explain how to send a PROFS e-mail message, you were designated the in-house guru and trainer. Software publishers launched the first Authorized Training Centers as a way of ensuring organizations that actual people were available to teach them to use these new and daunting technologies.

We have come a long way in the past two decades. As technology evolves into an everyday reality in our offices, homes, and even briefcases, computer training becomes a more mature and diverse field.

Good-bye, Mom and Pop

The days of the corner "mom-and-pop computer learning center" are almost numbered. To operate a full-service training classroom, one needs high-end computers with loads of memory, a high-speed network, and instructors knowledgeable about various configurations and combinations of technology. The capital required to maintain these classrooms and to market effectively to major corporations is changing the landscape of the computer-training industry. Each week, I hear of at least two training companies that have merged, been acquired, or joined a national franchise operation. *Expect to see larger players entering the training-and-support business. Watch for The Baby Bells to develop help-desk and support-outsourcing businesses in the next 18 months.*

Outsourcing Rampant

The forces of reengineering and downsizing are driving a large percentage of computer training off the corporate organizational chart. Large-scale and segment-specific outsourcing of computer training is now in vogue. The number of full-time trainers employed by major corporations has shrunk. It is not uncommon to see a computer-training department of only three or four people servicing 10,000 users; primarily, they're involved in the contracting and scheduling of training.

Much of this outsourcing actually occurs right on the property of major organizations. *Corporate classrooms are more likely to have an external trainer at the overhead projector; some classrooms are even being leased to external training centers for total management.*

May I See Your Certification, Please?

The days of self-certification are over. Software publishers, following the strong lead of Novell, have climbed aboard the certification bandwagon. Every major software publisher has created, or is about to launch, a testing and certification program aimed at the technical population of its user community.

Certification of support staff, trainers, developers, programmers, and even end-users is a goal of the software industry formulated to protect the image of its product. If you have a problem with your database or network and can't get good support from your MIS department, you might end up blaming the product. Certification programs aim to develop an envelope of competency and support around each major system and application suite. *Expect to see more tests and greater emphasis on career-track testing (for example, Client-Server Certified Programmer).*

15

Planned Expenditures

This point is based more on hope and need than on a perceived trend. One of my major frustrations is the lack of reality budgeting for computer training. Most companies do not link the acquisition of technology with the undeniable need for increased computer training and support. Immediate needs trigger most training requests. But a *planned* approach to technology-skill investment is infinitely preferable.

Organizations must face the reality that the full cost of each new technology includes the cost of formal and informal computer learning and support. *Planning for learning that is added to the technology migration process will allow for longer-term deals with training vendors and also will encourage more strategic decisions about investing in employee skills.*

I Want It *Now* and I Want It *Here!*

A good percentage of computer training comes at the wrong time. It is either scheduled two months after an employee starts or is on the calendar six weeks before the employee really needs the application. Another large percentage of computer training takes place at the wrong location. Workers away from the home office receive less training than their colleagues back at headquarters. Night-shift workers are rarely on the rolls for computer classes. And mobile and commissioned sales staff are the most frequent no-shows in computer-training programs.

"I want my workers to be able to sit at their desks and learn what they need to do their jobs today," said a manager of 35 banking professionals. "Tomorrow, let them learn what they need to know tomorrow. I can't afford to have my people going to training every time a new package hits the network." She wants her people to learn the new technology but only when they need the information and with as few trips to the classroom as possible. The following sections describe some emerging trends that meet this demand.

Just-in-Time Training

Upgrades will be taught in shorter classes, perhaps only a one-hour live session with a take-away CBT learning disk. One training vendor now has a one-day Microsoft Suite class, where employees self-teach four or five products in six hours. The trainer provides the motivation, context, and overview; the learners do most of the work on their own, back at their desktops.

Integrating Computer Training and Job Training

Most companies still have separate offerings for computer training and job functions. Bank officers go to one training department to learn how to approve loans and then go to the technology-education center to learn how to use Excel or Lotus 1-2-3. Now these two learning tasks are beginning to meld in corporate America. Progressive training departments are combining curricula from the human-resources and technical-training departments to provide single offerings that teach someone how, say, to issue a loan and use the spreadsheet as a work tool. Courseware developers are responding to this trend by designing new technology that allows customers to edit, resequence, and integrate computer courses with internal content.

The Wandering Trainer

Organizations are starting to place trainers in the workplace rather than in front of the classroom. By spending their day working at the desktop with users, trainers can often deliver the critical element of training needed to keep those users productive. One company dispatched its trainers to provide "sneaker-based training," with each trainer spending two days a week in the workplace. In addition to holding impromptu classes, they also were able to tweak the configurations of workers' computers and write a couple of simple but crucial macros to simplify a task. When these wandering trainers returned to the classroom, they often dramatically changed the focus of their classes to match workplace reality.

Scheduled Help-Desk-Based Training

Some applications can be taught by phone through a scheduled training event. When I hooked up our organization to the Internet, I was given a time to call the help desk, along with a set of reading materials. The technician broke from his stream of assistance calls to spend 90 minutes walking me through a complex set of new programs. It was an efficient and cost-effective way to get me up and running. Blend that with computer-based training or a demo, and it becomes a viable alternative to classroom training for certain users and applications.

Just the Disk, Ma'am

15

The thirst is growing for great computer-based training. The growth of CD-ROM technology, the exposure to children's software, and the increased bundling of CBT with applications have preconditioned the marketplace for this category of product. Watch for an explosion of new CBT and learning products in 1996. The open question will be their effectiveness and full acceptance by users. The simple porting of a curriculum from classroom training to disk will not be acceptable. Developers will have to heed the requests of users for the following features in computer-based training:

■ **Freedom of sequence, segment, and style.** Users want to be able to skip the stuff they know or don't want to know; they want to learn without having to answer a test question every screen. They don't want to take the worst parts of a classroom and transfer them to the desktop. They want to make CBT into personal learning, with choice and freedom.

- **Real-work examples.** Users want to work with examples from their own workplace, not from the Acme Company. Developers must allow for easy local customization.

- **Linkage to classroom learning.** Because users will often use CBT before, during, and after attending a class, organizations want to purchase a training process that integrates desktop learning with classroom offerings. The use of in-class CBT for information transfer and remedial assistance allows larger, more cost-effective courses.

Tip

Watch for new players in the business CBT industry. Educational software and entertainment groups have been eyeing the business market as a natural extension for their artists, authors, and marketers.

Over the Net

Distance learning is here! The amazing spread of the Internet is yielding a new medium for delivering learning services. I recently offered a pilot course called "Training Skills for Teaching New Technology" over the Internet. I asked for a few interested folks to help us experiment with delivering content modules to their desktops using Internet-delivered e-mail. A few dozen responses would have been terrific; instead, more than 4,000 people applied! The economics are intriguing because it costs us only a few cents a student to distribute the content modules. Several dozen technology organizations are monitoring this course to adapt the approach to their own continuing-education offerings. As additional tools for network learning are developed and disseminated, *watch for the rise of in-house and externally offered online courses.*

In Your Face

Desktop video teleconferencing is about to hit in a big way. The cost of live, two-way desktop video will drop to less than $1,000 a desktop by the start of 1996. ISDN capacity is booming in most organizations and even in the home. Currently, it is possible for a live instructor at one site to conduct a class for learners at many different sites, with full instructor access to each desktop. Organizations like Picture-Tel, AT&T, and Intel are leading the way with the enabling technology. The computer-training industry will need to adapt quickly to this new channel of information. *Imagine a pay-per-view computer-training course delivered to your desktop through the cable, that allows live communication with instructors during the discussion section. It's coming!*

Scattered Computer-Training Buying

We have watched a shift in the point-of-purchase of training materials and services—from a central office to the business units of organizations. Many corporations enable their business units to buy training from any source, including the internal training department. More people, in more scattered locations, are becoming involved in computer-training decisions and purchases.

Chargeback Confusion

Companies are also struggling to develop models for assessing and recovering the costs of training and support. Thinking of these charges as a form of taxation yields some interesting alternatives. Why, for example, charge for learning but give support for free? Does it make sense to provide an incentive for those business units that depend less on help-desk services?

Employee, Pay Thy Way

Several corporations are exploring the concept of sharing the cost of learning investment with the employee. One beverage company requires that all workers have WordPerfect skills the day they start their employment. They can attend free classes in the learning center, but they must pass the competency test before reporting to work.

This restriction shifts the salary costs of learning to the employee. Other groups are considering employee contributions to CNE certification as a way of emphasizing its impact on workers' future earnings and career potential.

15

Taxes at Work in Learning Labs

The focus on training is generating proposals for tax-dollar support for computer training. Witness the proposed legislation before Congress and in local governments to use community-college training services to attract and support business growth.

Bundled Models for Training Services

Training vendors continue to develop models for pricing classes and services. Watch for all-you-can-learn pricing plans as well as national contracts to provide complete training services at a per-desktop annual cost. The economics of the computer-training business will evolve as the field matures and as learning is recognized as a perpetual portion of the technology-expense budget.

From Here...

Computer training is not a field for the weakhearted or for individuals or businesses that put a premium on stability. In many ways, computer training is a change-adaptation mechanism. We have our jobs, our training centers, and our learning products because technology changes and people adapt accordingly. To survive in the computer-training field—as a corporate learning specialist, a freelance trainer, or the manager of an applications training center—you must try to stay abreast of every change, experiment with every new technology, and adapt, quickly and critically, new models for providing learning to our workforce. Fasten your seat belts; we're in for an exciting ride!

Part V

Resources

Appendix

Index

Forms, Questionnaires, and Surveys

Who Needs Training? Checklist

Before you begin to assess the training needed for a system implementation, you should identify who will require training and some of the group's characteristics. This checklist can help you identify all those who will be affected by the training.

Job titles and classifications

_____ Executives?

_____ Management?

_____ Technical/professional?

_____ Clerical?

_____ Sales?

_____ Systems support?

    _____ Network operations?

    _____ Hardware support?

    _____ Software support?

    _____ Database support?

_____ Application development?

    _____ Project leaders?

    _____ Systems analysts?

    _____ Database analysts?

    _____ Programmers?

For each group needing training, which of these characteristics might affect their training needs?

_____ Age?

_____ Gender?

_____ Education?

_____ Profession?

_____ Union membership?

_____ Years of company service?

_____ Familiarity with computer technology?

_____ Ability to absorb new things?

_____ Reading ability?

_____ Preferred learning methods?

_____ Location?

_____ Availability for training?

_____ Business need for the technology?

For each group needing training, describe their attitudes about the technology change being planned:

- What effect on their worklife will this change make?

- Is this just another innovation, like dozens of others they've absorbed before?

- What disruptions to their worklife will this change cause?

- What other technology changes have they experienced before?

- What are their attitudes about the company, in general?

Pre-Class Assessment Checklist

Please check the following items in which you possess basic skills:

1. Knowledge of keyboard .... ☐

2. Familiarity with DOS .... ☐

3. Familiarity with Windows
(version 3.11 or earlier) .... ☐

4. Familiarity with Windows 95 .... ☐

5. Use of mouse .... ☐

6. Ability to (choice depends on focus of course):
Type a letter .... ☐
Prepare a spreadsheet .... ☐
Create a database .... ☐

7. Familiarity with (*program being taught*) .... ☐

8. Familiarity with other software
(*provide list*) .... ☐

9. Understanding of files and directories .... ☐

10. Familiarity with Windows File Manager .... ☐

Pre-Class Skills Checklist

In preparation for a Beginning Excel class, please rank your skills in the following areas:

1=Very Knowledgeable
2=Comfortable with this Skill
3=Basic to Intermediate Experience
4=Some Exposure to this Skill
5=No Experience in this Area

1. Knowledge of keyboard ____

2. Familiarity with DOS ____

3. Familiarity with Windows
(version 3.11 or earlier) ____

4. Familiarity with Windows 95 ____

5. Use of mouse ____

6. Creation of spreadsheets using Excel ____

7. Editing existing spreadsheets using Excel ____

8. Use of other spreadsheet software ____

9. Understanding of files and directories ____

10. Use of Windows File Manager ____

Please describe types of spreadsheets you plan to create using Excel:

_____

Are there particular skills you hope to learn during this class? If so, please describe: _____

Why are you taking this course? (Job requirement, general interest, particular need?): _____

Pre-Class Supervisor Questionnaire

For use in a meeting with a supervisor before a class in which you will train employees of an organization.

1. What uses will your employees have for the program being taught? (Try to acquire sample documents.) _____

_____

2. What particular skills do you want your employees to acquire?

_____

_____

3. Do you expect your employees to proceed to the next level of training? If so, in what time frame? _____

_____

4. How will you evaluate the skills your employees have learned after they return to their jobs? * _____

_____

5. Are there any particular characteristics about the employees who will be in class that will affect learning? _____

_____

6. What type of computer equipment do your employees have?

_____

_____

7. What versions of the software (Excel and Windows) are employees using? _____

_____

8. Do your employees share files on a network? _____

_____

9. What types of security procedures are in effect for shared files?

_____

_____

* Here's an opportunity for you to offer a post-class evaluative assessment; see Chapter 6, "Post-Class Evaluation."

Beginning of Class Oral Questionnaire

Here's a list of questions you can ask at beginning of class (the assumption is that this is for a beginning Windows spreadsheet class).

1. Describe your previous computer experience.

2. Describe previous spreadsheet experience (both on the computer and on paper).

3. Have you used Windows and a mouse before?

4. (*If yes to #3*) Have you used the File Manager?

5. Why are you here? (Boss, general interest, particular need?)

6. What types of documents and reports will you use this software for?

7. Is there something in particular you want to get out of class?

8. Will you be creating original spreadsheets with this program or will you be editing files already created?

9. Is there a technical resource at your business location?

10. Do you use a network in your office? Do you share printers?

Beginning of Class Written Questionnaire

For use in the classroom setting. Here are some questions you can pass out; ask students to fill in answers and turn the sheets back in to you.

1. Have you used this program before? _____

2. Have you used a similar program before? _____

3. Please list particular skills you hope to learn in class today. _____
   _____

4. Are you familiar with basic Windows skills? _____

5. Have you used a mouse before? _____

Basic After-Class Evaluation Form

Rate the following topics on a scale from 1 to 5, with 5 as the high score:

1. Rate the technical education received   5 4 3 2 1

2. Rate the practical value of the training received   5 4 3 2 1

3. Rate the thoroughness of coverage of the designated topic   5 4 3 2 1

4. Rate the appropriateness of reading material   5 4 3 2 1

5. Rate the exercises performed in class   5 4 3 2 1

6. Rate the allocation of time to subjects   5 4 3 2 1

7. Rate the instructor's knowledge of the subject   5 4 3 2 1

8. Rate the instructor's ability to motivate participants   5 4 3 2 1

9. Rate the instructor's preparedness for the training   5 4 3 2 1

10. Rate the instructor's ability to get ideas across   5 4 3 2 1

11. Rate the instructor's ability to keep the seminar moving   5 4 3 2 1

12. Rate the classroom   5 4 3 2 1

13. Overall evaluation   5 4 3 2 1

After-Class Evaluation Form, Developed by The Future Now

The Future Now Computer Education Center

Thank You

COURSE EVALUATION

Thank you for attending a seminar at The Future Now Computer Education Center. Because your opinion is valuable to us, we ask that you please take a few moments to answer the following questions.

Your responses to these questions are an important part of our efforts to maintain the best computer training in Indiana. Please complete all questions, writing comments where appropriate. Your comments are particularly important to us. We appreciate your responses.

Please circle the appropriate response, where "5" is the highest response, "3" is average, and "1" is the lowest.

1 2 3 4 5   A. The lessons were presented in an effective way that helped me learn.

1 2 3 4 5   B. This class aided my understanding.

1 2 3 4 5   C. I feel more confident using the program I learned in class.

1 2 3 4 5   D. Class content was appropriate to my needs.

1 2 3 4 5   E. The class was generally appropriate to the needs of the group.

1 2 3 4 5   F. Generally, the teacher taught at my level of understanding.

1 2 3 4 5   G. Generally, the teacher taught at the group's level of understanding.

1 2 3 4 5   H. The instructor presented the material in a way that was easy for me to follow.

1 2 3 4 5   I. Questions were thoroughly and clearly answered.

1 2 3 4 5   J. I feel confident that I will be able to apply what I have learned in this class.

1 2 3 4 5   K. I found the written material to be easy to follow and understand.

1 2 3 4 5   L. The instructor was knowledgeable of the program taught.

1 2 3 4 5   M. The instructor was effective at teaching this program.

1 2 3 4 5   N. The facilities were satisfactory.

1 2 3 4 5   O. The equipment was satisfactory.

The Future Now Computer Education Center

Course Evaluation

1 2 3 4 5   P. What is your overall evaluation of this course?

Y   N   Q. Was it your choice to attend this course?

How did you hear about this class?

Thank you for your responses to the previous items. Please provide us specific feedback by writing comments below.

How soon do you think you would be interested in taking the intermediate or advanced class?

If you would like us to send you a monthly class schedule, the instructor will provide you with a card to complete so that we may add you to The Future Now mailing list.

Course   Instructor

Date   Location

Optional information

Name   Company

The Future Now Computer Education Center

Sample Telephone Survey Questionnaire

1. Did the class meet your expectations?

2. Have you had an opportunity to use the program since you attended class?

If Question #2 is answered negatively:

3. Do you expect to be able to use the program soon? (Follow this query with a line of questioning geared toward the user who hasn't yet used the program.)

If Question #2 is answered positively:

4. Have you had an opportunity to use the specific skills taught in class since you attended class?

5. Do you feel you learned enough about these skills in class to apply them to your job?

6. Have you encountered problems with the software since you took the class?

7. Have you noticed any skills you need that you didn't learn in class? (If the answer is *yes,* ask him or her to elaborate.)

8. Do you plan to attend the next level of training in this program?

9. Will you return to this location for further training?

10. What skills did you learn in class that have been most useful to you on your job?

11. What skills have you noticed since class that you wish you had learned in class?

12. Are there functions we covered in class on which you feel we should have spent less time?

13. Can you offer any comments on the competence and presentation skills of the instructor?

Sample Questionnaire for Follow-Up with Supervisors

1. Have you had a chance to discuss the training with your staff?

2. Is it your impression that your staff members are generally pleased with the training?

3. Have your staff members indicated satisfaction with the training they received?

4. Have you had an opportunity to observe the results of your staff's training?

5. Are you personally pleased with the skills demonstrated by your staff members since their training session?

Index

The MASIE Center

The MASIE Center, Inc., is an international thinktank exploring the intersection of learning and technology. The MASIE Center is co-producer (with Que Education & Training) of BriefingWare, the new series for managing technology.

Here is a list of resources from The MASIE Center:

The MASIE Forum, a membership organization for computer training professionals. The Forum Membership includes a monthly interactive telephone conference call, which links leading organizations throughout North America. Forum members include FedEx, Goodyear, John Hancock, and other Fortune 500 companies.

VIDCON Learning, a series of tools and services for distance learning and connected learning. VIDCON provides training in the use of video-conferencing technology for learning.

Learnability Lab, a learning-focused usability lab located at The MASIE Center. The Learnability Lab provides studies in multiple models of learning for new technology products. The Lab provided key studies to Microsoft for the rollout of Windows 95 and Office for Windows 95.

The MASIE Center Network, an online mailing list and Web site for training and technology professionals. Visit us at www.masie.com

Train the Computer: Training Self-Study Kits. The MASIE Center has several kits for teaching the art and science of computer training. These kits include special assistance in preparing for the Certified Technical Trainer exam.

The Computer Training Handbook is the widest-selling textbook in the computer training industry. Available from The MASIE Center for $49 plus shipping.

To receive information on any of the services of The MASIE Center, or to be placed on the mailing list, just call 1-800-98-MASIE or 1-518-587-3522.

THE MASIE CENTER

Elliott Masie, President
The MASIE Center
P.O. Box 397
Saratoga Springs, NY 12866
Telephone: 1-800-98-MASIE or 1-518-587-3522
E-mail: info@masie.com

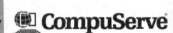